D0590593

The Way of the South

THE MACMILLAN COMPANY
NEW YORK · BOSTON · CHICAGO
DALLAS · ATLANTA · SAN FRANCISCO

MACMILLAN AND CO., LIMITED
LONDON · BOMBAY · CALCUTTA
MADRAS · MELBOURNE

THE MACMILLAN COMPANY
OF CANADA, LIMITED
TORONTO

The Way of the South

TOWARD THE REGIONAL

BALANCE OF AMERICA

By Howard W. Odum

New York · 1947

THE MACMILLAN COMPANY

Contents

v

PART III

TOWARD REGIONAL AND
NATIONAL MATURITY

PART IV

POSTSCRIPT AND PREFACE

PART I

Background and Heritage

CHAPTER I

Nature and Resources

THE STORY of a nation or of a region or of any human society begins with Nature's endowment of resources and their influence upon the culture of the people.

The story continues with emphasis upon the use the people make of the natural resources and the kind of spiritual culture and institutions they develop.

Resources are what the people have to live on and to do with. Sometimes they are what men live for and die for, in terms of native lands they love. Always Nature and resources are the physical backgrounds of the culture of people and the wealth of nations.

Nature's endowment of man consists not only in the abundance of material natural resources, but also in the tell of time, the cycle of seasons, of days and nights, and incidence of cold and heat, sunshine and rain. It consists also in the laws of Nature and of science from which flow invention and technology, and of man himself in Nature.

Because Nature's endowment is translated into resources through man's capacity and will to develop, to conserve, and to use wisely, the chief resources of any society are the people themselves, skilled, trained, and at work in the places where they live and in interchange with other peoples and other places.

It is often said that potential resources are not real until they are used, and that the harnessing of Nature is man's biggest job. It follows that the development, conservation, and wise use of resources can make a wealthy people in a lovely land, but that man's exploitation of Nature or Nature's

3

exploitation of man with the resulting waste of resources can make a poor people in a barren land.

Nature and her endowments, resources and their wealth-giving powers, and the romance of man in Nature were the first measures of the South's golden dreams. Even as the knowledge of Nature is the beginning of wisdom, so the story of this Nature and the cataloguing of her resources is the beginning of the task of understanding what the South is, how it came to be what it is, what its prospects are, and how to go about attaining these ends. To sense the meaning and power of Nature's wealth and of man's fellowship with Nature is not only to magnify the romance of the people but to give concreteness and momentum to their work and progress.

In this vivid portraiture of the South one of the best places to begin is with those riches of Nature and resources that are commonly taken for granted, as a matter of fact. Such resources in abundance are sunshine and rain, temperatures and growing seasons, weather *de luxe* whose benefactions to soil and crops, to happiness and health are such as to make very real the basic resources which constitute the chief wealth of the region.

A week of rainfall, worth literally billions of dollars, is no more spectacular or real than a week of sunshine which contributes immeasurable wealth in crops and industry, in work and play. In order to understand the extraordinary resources of that aspect of weather, one need only compare the lovely lands of the South with desert areas of barren ground, or see what irrigation does to a new domain such as the area watered by the Grand Coulee Reservoir. Or again to see the watered meadows along a thousand creeks and rivers and the mellow sunshine of a thousand, two thousand miles of Atlantic and Gulf coast line with their limitless possibilities for human habitation, recreation, and nurture.

Yet also the picture of Nature and what she does to man

and what man does to Nature is not complete without the challange which Nature offers in her floods and storms, her drouths and blistering suns, and the extraordinary waste in eroded land and the scars of a thousand gullied landscapes. These, too, are a part of Nature.

In the historical picture of southern culture, mountains and rivers, lakes and springs, trees and plants, animals and birds were the first visible measures of resources and situation that made the South what it is. Call the long roll of mountains—a symbol thousand, ranges and peaks rising in rough and ragged splendor, tops and notches, ridges and domes, bald faces and Indian heads—named Appalachia that looks down upon the sea. Big ranges and lesser ridges: the Alleghenies and the Blue Ridge, the Great Smokies, and the foothills. And of the majestic individualists among the towering tops, some were named for men, some named for imagery, and many recorded the epic of Indian names and Nature: Chichwalnercky, Kissimee, Pakataka and Shandoken, Catacton and Massanutton.

What gaps and gorges and hidden ways reflect the epic story of mountain pass and frontier trail! Every gap with its guarding cliffs holds hidden, line on line, chapter and verse of, Nature-history and frontier struggles. And the greatest of these was the famous Cumberland Gap, gateway supreme for the explorers and founders of "old Kaintuck"; epic of Dan'l Boone, biography of a man, biography of an era.

And then a thousand rivers rising in the hills, gaining wild momentum down their mountain gorges, down over the plateaus, down through the plains, down, down, and on until more silently and ship-deep they flow into the Atlantic, or on the other side, across and down in the Father of Waters. Call the long roll: big rivers and little rivers, creeks and branches, brooks and runs, names to conjure with, numbers to startle: the Potomac and the Rappahannock, the York and the James, the Roanoke and the Santee, the Peedee and the

Savannah, the Tennessee and the Cumberland, network of Appalachian eastern tributaries of the inlet-forming, gulf-building Atlantic. And of smaller streams, thousands to water the land in abundance and to fulfill the prophecy of the still waters—brooks and branches, rivulets and valley following creeks: and of middle-sized rivers, another noble catalogue.

And there were waterfalls and cataracts pouring from peak-crack or precipice, on the way down, down, a thousand feet to the valleys below. Sometimes they tumbled their roaring waters down through hidden gorges and canyons, and sometimes, from pent-up waters, like some great dipper, they poured their powerful waters a hundred, two hundred, three hundred, four hundred feet below, to splash and splatter, to spray and scatter, preview to power and scenic beauty that was the South.

At the sources of these streams a hundred thousand springs, bold springs and bubbling; earth pure for thirsty animals or plants; on mountain tops, at the foot of hills, or in meadow lands. Cold clear waters, warm hot springs, sulphur waters, salt lick waters, mineral and heating springs. From one end of Appalachia to another, from mountain crag to shores of sand, lime springs and healing springs, Old Sweet Springs and Sweet Chalybeate, cold springs and warm springs, and five named Sulphur Springs, White, Blue, Green, Red, and Salt. And thousands of incomparable smaller springs became key places for home sites, reflecting frontier pictures of families and their customs, clothes washing and food cooling, so that the story of the water springs of Appalachia runs richly through the fabric of American frontier biography.

Of forests and trees, there were millions of acres in un-counted primeval hardwoods and pines, sprucewoods and cypress, set on stony mountains or deep-rooted in the rich loams of hill and plain and valley, home place of wild life; or for man, Nature's super-parks and playgrounds, or the call of the wilderness; or for commerce in cut cordwood for fuel, for paper pulp or for billions of feet of sawed lumber.

Of individual trees in the midst of great forest areas there was such abundance and variety as to challenge catalogue:

> Pines: Tall and graceful Longleaf and slash of coastal plain,
> Shortleaf and Loblolly of Piedmont,
> Hardy Virginia, pitched and white, pines of mountain ridges.
> White oak and red oak, post oak and water oak,
> Sweet gum and black gum, sourwood and mulberry,
> White spruce and red spruce, river birch and yellow,
> Chestnut and hickory, locust and persimmon,
> Stately golden-flowered tulip poplar, sycamore and ash,
> Hemlock and willow; gnarled, big-bottomed cypress in the swamps.
> Sugar maple and red maple, dogwood and redbud
> And how many hundred species of flowering trees and shrubs?
> Multi-colored azaleas and mountain laurel,
> Riotous blooming rhododendron, thousand-acred gardens of Appalachia.

And there were colors and smells, sound and senses; the sweet smell of cedars and balsam and pine; the golden yellow of tulip poplar with thrasher bird singing in the top; the bright white of dogwoods and the shading tints of crab apple and redbud.

Abundance, too, there was of roots and herbs, of flowering smaller flora of the fields; and of domestic plants: of corn and squash, and pumpkins and melons; of cultivated blackberries and raspberries and blueberries, fruits of the soil in immeasurable abundance.

Of the wild fruits of Nature's orchards and gardens there was abundance: crab apple and persimmon, chestnuts and

chinquapins, million-billioned acorn oaks; successions of gol-
den-leaved, autumn beaming hickory trees; hazels and
beeches, black walnuts and locusts, wild plums and haws.
And from the White Mountains of Northern Appalachia to
the lower reaches of the Blue Ridges, blueberries north,
huckleberries south; and everywhere after their kind and season blackberries and raspberries, dewberries and strawberries,
gooseberries and buckberries; and for the birds edible seeds
and grasses, uncounted.

Of the riot and beauty of flowering things, there abounded
not only the mountain laurel, the deep-flamed and pink-
blooming azaleas, and the multi-colored giant flowering rhododendron of lilac-purple, rare pink, and white; but a host
of smaller flowering plants of primeval vintage and color,
catalogue for botanists and plant breeders and Nature-lovers.

> Of the families of the Lily and the Heath and the Mint,
> Of the crawfoot and the poppy and the iris,
> Of the figwort and the madder and the lobelia,
> Of the pink and the rose and the dogwood,
> Of the gentian and the geranium and the bluebell,
> Of the amaryllis and the honeysuckle and the orchids
>   and the meadow beauty,
> Of the milkweed and the morning-glory and the violet,
> And the purslane, the pitcher plant, and the composite.

And, again, of the lilies: the yellow pond, the meadow,
the red, and the sweet-scented white water. And a hundred
and one distinctive individuals: anemone and arbutus, aster
and azalea, barberry and bee balm, black-eyed Susan and
bluebell, bluets and buttercups, clovers and columbine,
daisies and dandelions, foxglove and foamflower, goldenrod
and geranium . . . But why try to name them?

And there were grasses for birds and animals, green grass
meadow by running stream, haven for wild life and for Indian
village; for settlers' paradise and twin-partner with trees for

ecologists' biomes and optimum regions. Primeval grass was builder of Nature's stable economy. It was new preview of new frontiers. "It's been here for centuries. It'll stay for more centuries. . . . It nev'r dwindles. It stands and grows forever. When you and me are rotted to dust, when all these damned cities are sunk to ashes and rust, this grass will still grow, finer than ever."

> Native grasses on the mountains.
> Native grasses in the valleys.
> New hay grasses of blue grass and rye, of orchard and oat.
> The wonder grasses of Lespedeza, Common and Tennessee, Korean and Kobe.
> And of clovers: Sweet White and Burr, Crimson and Red, Alsike and Ladino.
> And a million meadowlands of oats and barley, of wheat and rye.

This great Nature of forests and mountains, of rivers and plains, of fruits and flowers and grazing grasses, was abundantly inhabited by another magnificent nature world of wild life, whose billions of swift-running beasts and flying fowls constituted the first basic primitive wealth of the nation. It was so for Indian people; it was so for colonial settlers. Not only was there a fine ecological balance between the animal world and Nature's feeding grounds and haunts before man, but in this southern scene, animal and bird were of the finest and most consistent thread running through the whole fabric of man in Nature. Complete for its area, there is enough in numbers and kinds for all purposes. Of mammals:

> There was the order of the flesh-eating mammals and their picturesque suborders.
> There were orders of whales and porpoises for the future commerce on the Atlantic.
> There were orders of moles and shrews, and orders of bats.

There were orders of gnawing animals, and there were
hoofed runners and flesh eaters.

There were orders of toothless animals and orders of
duffers.

And there were pouched mammals and ever-present
rabbits and fur-bearing beasts.

Of birds, never such abundance in kind and numbers, such
that they clouded the sky in their flying and swarmed in the
trees and on the lakes. Nature's abundant offering for needy
animals and hungry men was never more lavish. The wild
pigeons—millions darkening the sky, breaking the limbs of
trees at roosting time, swarm on swarm uncountable—in a few
short years had vanished completely from the face of the
earth. Call the roll of other birds:

The order of the beautiful perchers and the singers;
The orders of the woodpeckers and cuckoos;
The orders of the cooing pigeons and doves;
The orders of the upland game birds, newly conserved
and developed by man;
The orders of the shore birds, orders of crane and rail,
and coots;
The orders of the heron and storks and ibises;
The orders of the ducks and geese and web-footed
birds;
The orders of the tube-nosed swimmers, the long-
winged swimmers and the weak-winged diving
birds;
And the orders of the birds of prey, the owl and the
hawk, the eagle.

But how name them and describe them? A great world of
Nature, substance and brilliance, they were again the perfect
complement to the magnificence of all Nature.

Of colors galore: *Orange and red*—the tanagers and the
cardinal, the crossbill and the red-breasted grosbeak, the
painted bunting and the purple finch, the redstart and

the orioles, the red head patches of woodpeckers and ruby throat of the hummingbird.

Of blue birds, omen of beauty and fortune: the indigo bunting and the blue grosbeak, the cerulean warbler, and the blue jay, and the "bluebird" itself, harbinger of spring.

Of the *golden yellow birds:* the Maryland yellowthroat and the yellow warbler, the hooded and the Kentucky warbler, and other warblers galore—palm and Cape May, Nashville and bluewing, Canadian and yellow-throated, parula and black-throated green, magnolia and myrtle; and always the yellow-breasted chat of the elusive and hidden ways, and the meadow larks by the millions; the blackbirds and the goldfinches.

Of the *brown birds:* the wrens and the cuckoos, and the thrashers and the thrushes, the robins and the creepers, the waxwing and the towhee, the bobwhite quail and the doves, the fox sparrow and the vesper, and native sparrows of many and useful varieties—chipping and field, pinewoods and Savannah, grasshopper and seaside.

And of the *black and white birds,* again abundance: the chickadee and the junco, the warblers, blackpoll and black-and-white, the white-throated sparrow, and the white-crowned sparrow, the nuthatches and the woodpeckers, the blackbirds and the grackles.

Here was organic Nature's extraordinary contribution to the richness of lore and language. Color, color, names and symbols of cultures were everywhere abundant in the primitive life rapport between Indian and Nature. Here as later in the American epic, Nature was America; it was true of man in Nature; it was true of Nature and God in history. No more could it be separated from America's foundations than it could from Walt Whitman's dream.

The wild gander leads his flock through the cool night, . . .
The brood of the turkey-hen and she with her half-spread
  wings, . . .

Where the panther walks to and fro on a limb overhead, where
the buck turns furiously at the hunter,
Where the rattlesnake suns his flabby length on a rock, where the
otter is feeding on fish,
Where the alligator in his tough pimples sleeps by the bayou,
Where the black bear is searching for roots or honey, where the
beaver pats the mud with his paddle-shaped tail; . . .
Where the quail is whistling betwixt the woods and the wheat-
lot, . . .
Where the mocking-bird sounds his delicious gurgles, cackles,
screams, weeps, . . .
Where band-neck'd partridges roost in a ring on the ground with
their heads out, . . .

Yet, again, mountains and forests, rivers and lakes, beasts
and birds, were not all of Nature's endowment of potential
resources. So were the Gulf and the Atlantic, and the bays and
inlets, multiplying the coastal miles a hundredfold. From
the Atlantic and from the Gulf came America's first white
settlers to contest the freedom of the fields and forests of a
new world; from the Atlantic saw the Indians first the great
white-bird ships bearing strange newcomers to rugged shores
to fight it out in the new world, and to set up new ideals, new
ways of doing things, new ruthless mastery over the continent.

From the sea, too, came the first avenues of the new commerce. There was shipping to be done to the old countries;
and if shipping, then the need of ships; and if the need of
ships, then of shipbuilding; and if shipbuilding, the growing
of a great industry and skills. And if ships and products, then
sailings; and if sailings, then absence occupations and menfolk away from home; and if menfolk absent, then womenfolk at work in mastery and skills, in management and might;
and if womenfolk dominant, then the beginnings of the new
epic of woman in the new world.

And from the sea came the new fishing: fishing for livelihood, fishing modeled after the old-world fishing industry.

And not only in the sea, but in the rivers and brooks, lakes and ponds, again, abounded the orders of the fishes and the amphibia:

> The orders of the spiny-finned fishes, the bass, bream
>   and perch, and the order of the pikes,
> Orders of the trout and the salmon,
> The suckers and the minnows, the catfishes and the
>   flatfishes, the gars and the eels,
> Orders of the frogs, and salamanders, orders of the
>   lizards and the turtles, and the alligators.

And in the smaller streams and the lakes, such abundance of fish that it was often told that little equipment was needed for a full catch—trout and bream, bass and pickerel and pike, Nature's added enrichment of the continent through the living waters, later to be replenished and multiplied by man's devices.

Yet, once again, these were not all of Nature's endowment of resources. For land itself was of great richness and variety such that one hundred, two hundred, three hundred and more subregional classifications of the great American soil could be made by the experts in the days to come. So potent did the land become that it was considered by many to be the chiefest of all wealth and the most important of all resources. And in the South land became the symbol of plantation wealth and the symbol and reality of western resources.

> The rich lands of valley and plateau,
> The little river bottoms of fertile soil,
> The lands of black belt and cotton,
> The sand hills and coastal plains rich in undiscovered
>   wealth,
> The flat lands of woods and poorer soil,
> The tropical lands for fruits and gardens,
> The marsh lands of millions of acres,
> And unmeasured marginal lands to be tested and tried.

Yet under the earth for the deeper diggings of the new-comers were still more of Nature's reserves of power, sources of the new age of machines and technology. Comparable in abundance and variety to the flora and fauna, to climate and soil, were these vast stores of Nature's wealth of the ages. Two-score major families in the mineral kingdom, more than twenty-score individual representatives:

> Aluminum and arsenic, barium and beryllium, bismuth and boron,
> Calcium and carbon, cobalt and cerium, columbium and copper,
> Gold and iron, lead and lithium, mercury and magnesium,
> Phosphorus and potassium, silicon and silver, sodium and sulphur,
> Titanium and tungsten, uranium and vanadium, zinc and zirconium.

This superabundance of endowment of Nature's wealth came soon to be the "answer to prayer," the first fruits of the American Dream, the optimum setting for the development of vitality in peoples and cultures, for abundance in economy. There were the concrete realities of specific things, of land and trees, of things that grow, of living Nature in countless thousands of units.

Of land and crops, there was that rare concurrence of the optimum quartet of *temperature, moisture, surface,* and *soil* that occurs in few places on this earth. There were rare abundance and variety of sunshine and winds and of growing seasons, with also such variety and complexity and such Nature-stimulating and Nature-testing qualities as to challenge initiative and inventiveness, courage and integrity of all purpose. There were, too, in the extreme range and variety of life zones and climate, of soil and topography, of resources and reserves, intangible and unmeasured combinations which made the promised land one which would afford opportunities for richness in culture, in leisure, and ways of living.

There were, therefore, those other composites, not measured merely by units and catalogues of items, reflected in the grandeur of Nature as such, in the powerful conditioning influences of a magnificent geography, symbolic of the meeting of man and Nature, of the spiritual and the physical, of aspiration and reality.

And as always, the folk beauty of the hills, the folk wisdom of the people, the ruthless aspirations of man in Nature. Struggle and conflict, mastery and survival were powerful recurring motifs in the great American epic, drama in the grand manner. Reflected alike in the aspirations of the simple folk from mountain frontier or the artist's crescendo or poem powerfully recording some cosmic onomatopoeia, this was American Nature in the beginning: "Thar betwixt the loneliness of the broad seas and the fearsomeness of Indians and forests, a many a brave man an' woman perished."

Of the successions of men who survived, struggle and striving, found surcease: " 'Pears like all yore cares and discontents they roll away, a-leavin' you calm an' contentedlike. . . . When all the colored flowers they are a-bloomin', gold an' scarlet an' purple among the green, the air it's mighty sweet, also, with smell of berries a-ripenin' in the sun. . . . An' a-listenin' to the little noises of the small wood creatures. . . ."

Always the time quality and the footfall of God by the river's edge or on mountaintop or in the deep, dank piny woods; and always the succession of seasons and the cycle of suns and the age-old incidence of concurrence and diversity, of conflict and harmony; and always the mystery of what is not known and is to be discovered; and the immeasurable quantitative reserves of Nature's endowment to man, her habitat for his unending pilgrimage, toward the promised land.

In the South the folk were Nature-folk longer than in the rest of the nation. The mountains and rivers, the hunting and fishing, the weather working on man to give him the Nature character—all these were elemental factors. And men partook of the hard way of Nature. Sometimes they were prophets of doom, sometimes of the rainbow's end. Sometimes they loved the bark of dog or the low of cow more than the bloom of flower or the crop of corn. Sometimes they loved the sunset and mountaintop and sometimes they brooded in isolation.

Sometimes they loved the rippling, dreamily drifting river and sometimes they cursed its muddy-watered floods. Sometimes they loved the whispering and murmuring of pine trees, and sometimes they cut and burned them to death.

Storm clouds, high winds, cold frosts, wet grounds vied with hot sun, parching winds, baked grounds, and burning drouth to mix the moods of the folk.

There were rippling fields of oats, waving fields of wheat, tasseling tops of corn, white-fleeced cotton fields; and there were horses and mules, cows and calves, hogs and chickens, hounds and cats, wild life and wild woods. There were winter and summer, day and night, breakfast and dinner and supper. And the days went on with sickness and health and children a-borning and dying. The days were full, and the folk were not so much interested in civilization as they were in the crude folk culture and in living in the way of Nature. And sometimes, too, the people drifted so far along with Nature that there was more lore of folk than science of Nature.

CHAPTER II

The Frontier and Migrations

THE MAGNIFICENCE of Nature and the abundance of resources with which the South was endowed included a great deal more than the mere catalogue of material things. One supreme measure was in terms of situation consisting of a vast frontier peopled by a magnificent Nature folk, the American Indian. Both frontier and Indian were to be conquered and were to exert a powerful influence upon the ways of the South, and of all America, as in the future this frontier was inhabited by the migrations of white men, founding fathers of the new society.

Inseparable from frontier and Nature was ever the fleeting red man, himself a sort of personification of Nature, sometimes slipping through the trees on hidden paths, or silently skimming along stream routes; sometimes boldly becoming a part of the landscape, as if he ran down from Appalachia to the sea to be first welcomer to strangers; sometimes terrible, sometimes indescribably pathetic; sometimes as simple and beautiful as Nature folk; but always an unforgettable picture.

As the early frontier settlements advanced farther upstream and into the interior, Indian man and Nature were inseparable forces to be conquered. If the American picture has inevitably been portrayed as the epic of pioneer in the mastery of frontier, the red man was always the inevitable accompaniment, inseparably associated with the frontier. It was so in the coastal plains; it was so in the plateaus and highlands and the mountain ranges of the Appalachians; it was so back through Cumberland Gap and "old Kaintuck" and in the Ohio country. If the frontier was Nature, Nature was part red man,

17

aboriginal, and frontier was of Nature and Red Man, twin hosts and enemies to all newcomers.

The Indian heritage was of the essence of Nature, not only because the American Indians, a million strong, were part and parcel of the continent to be conquered and taken, but also because the Indian culture was native and natural; because Indian tribes and families and languages reflected an extraordinary consistency in cultural natural-geographic clusterings into regions; and because, of all cultures and peoples, the American Indians have approximated the personification of Nature and earth: voice of the wilderness and of rivers, lover of trees and colors, of animal partnership in a universe which existed for the glory of natural struggle and survival or for death and the long sleep of Nature.

Here again was Nature's magnificent endowment and Nature's primitive example: as gentle or as ruthless as Nature, stolid as a tree, fierce as a wildcat; in crisis immobile as the stone or quick-running as the deer; alike changeable and unyielding as the inevitable seasons. Brave and good enough to scalp his enemy, whether red man or white, surviving even as Nature does. Nature and the Great Spirit, in partnership, were the eternal arbiters and measures of precept and practice continuously adjusted to wind and weather, sun and moon, seasons of winter and spring, of summer and autumn; to the four winds of the four corners of the earth; to land and water, mountains and plains, hunting and wandering, fishing and farming, food and shelter, fighting and war.

Yet, these Americans were Nature-men, drawing their sustenance, their living, and their entertainment from Nature and her resources, in another powerful way. The first new-world American economy, even as the chief pursuit of the first Americans, was developed from the single occupation of hunting. They hunted for food. They hunted for raiment. Tools and shelter, ornaments and weapons were of the sinews of the hunt.

This hunting economy was not only symbolic of great

natural resources. It was that and much more. For the chief occupation of the settlers through many moons was hunting, to which they added fishing and subsequently agriculture. In the hunting pattern of the frontiersman, transmitted down the centuries to us, were thrill and sportsmanship, combat and skill. Not only subsistence and zest of frontier occupation were found in the hunting economy, but for both Indian and whites it long set the stage for the first great American industry, the million-dollar fur trade.

Still more of America's destiny and character were to be welded in the white heat of a hunting economy. For men who hunted went out to kill. They gave no quarter. The law was that of "tooth and claw," and men went out to kill. It was a great game of death, virtue being measured by success. So came America, both Indian and white, setting a price on the scalps of men; the hunting of men in ruthless death search became for many generations the game of all frontier America. And far into the growth of the great American people Indians were shot down, and counted as savages to be slaughtered.

This hunting economy, of course, went still further in setting the character of frontier America. For just as competition for game and hunting grounds set the incidence of Indian warfare and the slaughter-patterns, so the ever thinning game reserves and the ever encroaching white settlers—hunters, to the Indian—kept the whites and Indians in constant fighting; and the realization that the white man was taking his hunting grounds away from him led to many of the desperate and final massacres of Appalachian whites. Here was, again, economic struggle which might well have set the pattern of later ruthless exploitation of Nature and of slaves.

Definitive of the southern heritage and prophetic of the years to come, this influence of frontier America and the red man set the incidence of much of America's future and provided measuring points in the history of civilization on and up through the twentieth century. It conditioned the incidence of exploitation not only of red man, but also of Negro and immigrant. It set in motion the ever-ruthless trend toward the extinction of the American Indian. It gave the religious coloring of political and economic institutions, and it provided a complex cultural background for the coming mighty struggle over the rights of common man and the conflict of races.

Yet this earlier frontier influence was not all that was important. In the later influence of the frontier and the open country were to be found many of the forces which conditioned not only the culture of the South but that of the nation as well. For there was a striking parallel between the early influence upon the nation of Washington, Jefferson, Madison, and other statesmen of the aristocratic South and the influence of such frontier leaders as Andrew Jackson, James K. Polk, and Andrew Johnson—all leaders in the new frontier approaches to American democracy. For in these leaders there was foreshadowed much of the politics of personalities and much of the tropism of the people toward political expression that characterized the later South in many of its major political episodes.

The products, however, were not so organic or far-reaching as the total cultural effects of the frontier on the enduring character of both the Southeast and the Southwest. For just as the early plantation South had laid the foundation for a regional culture of aristocracy, race, and caste, so the opening of the new Southwest, stemming out from North Carolina through what was to be Tennessee, set the stage for a sturdy folk democracy that was to influence that part of the South and extend northwestward through "old Kaintuck" and across "Ol' Man River," north and later south, and beyond into Texas and Oklahoma. In both great southern levels of early Americanism the open country, the expanding frontier, and an agrarian life set the patterns of the institutions.

Still more specifically, the frontier fixed the character of the southern folk as they reflected the American ideals of work, individual love of freedom, religious faith, the fighting spirit, the philosophy of neighborliness and mutual help. The South was nurtured in the frontier world perhaps no more than the West of America; but, more than the rest of the nation, it retains in its fabric of folk culture threads of the frontier struggle and reflects the costs that went into building a frontier society.

All the epic prelude to our frontier society is rich in myth, in biography of pioneers and stories of feats which appear incredible to persons who do not know that extraordinary epoch of man and Nature in the early life of the nation. First and always, Nature was forever setting the pattern and the pace; creating stamina and endurance; providing for powerful folkways and mores; laying the groundwork for American literature and institutions. This was America; this was the South, the voice of the wilderness, the voice of the frontier, of the pioneer, and of the grandmothers of America asking, "Do you remember?" "Have you forgot?"

Do you remember the long trails, blazed by the frontier men, always and ever supported by frontier women?

Do you remember the crossing of rivers, the piloting of caravans, accident and hazard?

Do you remember the death chant of squaws, the screaming whoop of dying-fighting Indian chiefs, the silent endurance of Indian youth?

Do you remember the blizzard and the storm, the disease and the famine, the fighting and the feuds?

Do you remember the scream of wildcat, the moan of wind in lonely wilderness when frontier mother tried to live through the borning of a new America?

Do you remember the arduous work of felling forests and building cabins? roughhewn tools and blacksmiths' inventions? bullet molding and tool sharpening? the divers skills and never-ceasing industry?

Do you remember the thrill and the gratitude, the romance and satisfaction when first the roof and the mud-chinked walls and chimney vouchsafed warm comfort and shelter from wind and weather, from animal and savage?

Do you remember the victory shouts of discovery of new lands or waters and the glory of blue-sky weather of spring when it was new? Do you remember the beauty and the grandeur of mountain vistas a-blooming, and of the promised lands of river valleys?

Do you remember when the rattlesnakes struck and the felled trees took their toll, and croup and pneumonia came with quick vengeance, and when frontier mother stooped, lagged, faded, and died with such hurt heart as only those can know who have paid the price?

Do you remember first things in the American drama, tragedy in the grand manner, "sadness and pathos lost in victory"? Do you remember the epic stride of Man with purpose in the cosmic setting of Nature's world?

One does not have to accept all the premises of Frederick Jackson Turner's theory of the role of the frontier in American life to appraise the very large influence of the frontier in determining the character of early American culture. Turner assumes that the American frontier has conditioned American culture, and therefore that the study of the frontier is necessary to the understanding of American culture. The Turner assertion is that "American social development has been continually beginning over again on the frontier. This perennial rebirth, this fluidity of American life, this expansion westward with its new opportunities, its continuous touch with the simplicity of primitive society, furnish the forces dominating American character." And again: "The existence of an area of free land, its continuous recession, and the advance of American settlement westward, explain American development."

The first western frontier was really South, representing the approaches to the Appalachians prior to the breaking over to the real West. There were movements from eastern New York and Pennsylvania toward the western parts of these states, and subsequently the great southwest trek to the State of Franklin and towards western North Carolina and Tennessee, followed by the next westward movement which represented the exploration of Kentucky through the Rabun Gap and similar overflow behind the Appalachians.

A next western frontier represented movements into Ohio and preliminary approach to a next great westward movement, which might be termed the great Northwest, moving up toward the Great Lakes and to the Mississippi River.

Still another series of frontiers reflected the westward movement toward Alabama, Louisiana, Mississippi, and technically then the Louisiana Purchase area, and later came the great exploration of the Mormons and others across the Mississippi and the more or less isolated continuation of the westward movement.

Then came the great Oregon Trail and the California gold rush, followed by a rebound from the Far West and a revival of the westward movement to the Northwest into the northern Great Plains. Following these, then, were the great southwestern movements of the Plains, including Texas, New Mexico, and Oklahoma.

In many ways, the whole settlement of the South—first the Southeast, then the Southwest—was symbolic of this continuous frontier flow west and south, such that the story of the settlement of the South was first of all a story of America. Eventually it came to be a sort of specialized America with a continuing frontier fringe, either in physical settlement or in cultural expansion. The South had always been a frontier, rich in struggle and conflict, romance and adventuring, victory and tragedy. The twentieth century saw it still a frontier

country, even though it had been "first" in the development
of America.

On the shores of the river James there had been some of the
earliest American settlers, and from them was descended
much of the "royal" blood of Virginia. Here was the "general
assembly" covenanting a year earlier than even the Mayflower Compact of 1620. Later settlements and counter inva-
sions from the north added numbers and variety for many
generations. On and on they came; farther on they moved. At
one time within a period of five years in the early nineteenth
century more than two hundred families from New York alone
settled in a single Virginia county. Even so, others were moving farther south. And earlier in the nineteenth century than
this an overplanting of cotton and the slump in the market
in Virginia started migration south to North Carolina and its
eastern borders, to Tennessee and its western range, to Mississippi and its rich deltas, to Louisiana and on "from Virginia
to Alabama, from Missouri to Texas, every whence every
whither, people took ship or flatboat, or set forth in carry-alls
or covered wagons, with tinkling cattle and trudging slaves,
if they had them." Overproduction and bad management,
hardship and misfortune, Indian conflict, and neighborhood
and state quarrels, sometimes sheer restlessness, all contributed to shifting and reshifting of peoples, always seeking a
promised land flowing with milk and honey. Some farther
west, some back across Mississippi into Alabama and Georgia,
into the new Cherokee and Creek lands. And still others ventured farther back and up into Ohio and Indiana, always willing to undergo pioneering hardships in order to find new land
and abundance, and early starting the South's contribution
to the stocks and settlement of frontiers farther west.

There were "Friends" and German sectarians, crowded out
of Pennsylvania and Maryland, moving down to the Piedmont
of Virginia and the Carolinas to meet the other streams from
Delaware. There were Moravians and Mennonites and Pres-

byterians to mix with Quakers, Anglicans, Methodists, and Baptists. Thence these spread in all directions south and then across the Cumberland Gap with its varied romance and adventure as represented by the blazing of trails by George Rogers Clark, Daniel Boone, and hosts of hunters looking for the new promised land. "So rich a soil we had never saw before, Covered with Clover in full Bloom. The woods alive abounding in wild Game, turkeys so numerous that it might be said there appeared but one flock Universally Scattered in the woods . . . it appeared that Nature in the profusion of her Bounties had spread a feast for all that lives, both for the Animal and Rational World . . ."

Then there were other migrations to the lower South differing from the earlier ones in Virginia and Kentucky, where people were impelled from their first settlements by lack of land or hard times. Here were new caravans of people merely desiring to get on in the world. From the vantage point of New Jersey, Rhode Island, and other northeastern states, the lower South looked like a land in which great wealth might be developed. Then the slave owners of Kentucky and Virginia and the would-be slave owners of Indiana and Illinois, or of the East, looked longingly to broad acres and white-columned houses deep in the lower South where adventure and wealth were theirs for the possessing. And some moved on into new states, being bereft of loved ones in an old state or disappointed by the turns of fortune.

There were many pictures of sub-settlements and migrations within the various states. In Mississippi and Louisiana, besides many others, from New Orleans to Natchez there were early Tories migrating from South Carolina and Georgia westward, to be joined by similar folks from northern states. These, well fortified with rich alluvial lands of the river bottoms, were met by other groups and settlers coming by boats from Virginia, Kentucky, Tennessee, and from northern states. Or again by still others coming from Georgia and the Carolinas to merge in a regional group expanding somewhat to the east until stopped perhaps by still another group which represented the overflow of those who had failed, or were too restless to succeed, in the sand hills or seacoast range of the more easterly southern states.

There were other streams of settlers—Welsh, Quakers, Scotch-Irish—moving, one branch from Pennsylvania westward, then south through the Shenandoah Valley into the Carolinas to be joined by similar groups who had landed in Charleston and had extended their wanderings wherever adventure led. These pioneers, "hardy, proud, land-hungry," had in them the making not only of the traditional southerners but of the sundry borderland southerners who extended themselves north, south, east, and west. From these came not only Indian fighters and continuous pioneers but a later brood of southern leaders like Calhoun, Quitman, Prentiss, Yancey, Davis, new southerners in the vanguard of that great tragic region of the United States.

To these, and many more like them, were added others, French, Spanish, German, Santo Domingans, Italians, Minorcans, Choctaws, Cherokees, Greeks, and Seminoles, and the host of Negro slaves from many sources whose stocks multiplied and mixed with many strains. The one-third of a million slaves who had been imported had multiplied until by 1850 there were three million, most of whom were in these southern states. Thus, these mixtures were calculated to make the South anything but a provincial and pure-blooded section of the nation. And always the stragglers, the failures, the gamblers, the heavy-handed highwaymen moved hither and yon, from Piedmont to Texas, from Richmond to Natchez. What stories, beyond the skill of pen, what pictures transcending living portraiture! Sam Houston, Daniel Boone, rough-riding youth, covered wagons, trail blazers!

Or, there was plenty of romance in the earliest settling of South Carolina from early Charles Town to Charleston, expanding with the varied folks from England, Scotland, Wales, Ireland, Germany, Switzerland, France, the West Indies, and then from New England and New York and other parts of the United States. Here was regional culture from which an old-time city-state might develop, with its own full-fledged government, commerce, shipping, social life. Thus came the glory that was and remains Charleston. Even just across the Georgia border and the way places, were people quite different, speaking different accents, having different manners. Here again new pictures from the founding of Georgia's "eighteenth century embryo of the nineteenth century humanitarianism." Here was a peculiar project symbolic of a philanthropy, seeking to serve God by enabling prisoners to start a new life in the new country and to serve Mammon by using the new experiment as a buffer against Florida Spaniards. And here were hardships, troubles, quarrels, limitations, tragedies, resulting in one man in every ten being soon lost to the new colony. And ever the new cycle—rich lands, rice crops, cotton, indigo, slaves, liquor, and new people coming from many sources, eager to start again, joined by New England families, a veritable mixture of all that was America in the forming. A Nathanael Greene, New England Quaker, favorite of Georgia, subsidized by the state, and later Mrs. Greene becoming a model of Georgia hospitality for many years to come.

And Florida, land of flowers, potentially a great national playground, land of Spanish adventure, of British ambition, featuring plantations founded with Greeks, Italians, and Minorcans. And the other mixed groups were prophetic of a later day. Hardship, poverty, failure of the soil to yield rich promise, rebellion, and wilderness beset by Seminoles were impeding its development. Even so late as the 1820's the population was less than that of many of Florida's small cities in the early twentieth century would be. And, again, some of the people were restless and shiftless enough to portend later unprogressive elements of a great state. Then under Spanish and foreign jurisdiction again, with outlaws smuggling fugitive slaves, and foreign barriers to commerce. Then a state of the Union, wagon trains from the Carolinas and Georgia, lumber folk, traders, adventurers. Then new eras and a romantic Florida and a mad nation pouring its thousands into a trek such as only the gold rush had ever rivaled. And the verdict that the Lord surely loves Florida—behold the sunshine and its glory—and the Lord loveth whom He chasteneth, with storm and panic and fruit fly.

Then on to Alabama with the pressure of Indian concessions, the southwestern drive for rich lands and warm climate. Then on to Louisiana, full of contrasts and strange admixtures. Products of French Revolution and French masters from Haiti, migrants through Cuba, others from Virginia or Carolina bringing their families and slaves. These and the other settlers already described were militant pioneers and followers of dominant leaders with all manner of colonists, good and bad, transported, supplemented by shiploads of slaves, until a region judged uninhabitable sprang suddenly into the metropolis of New Orleans—region of glamour and romance and sad beauty, rivaling any other part of the nation. Here again was American experience with its national spirit, all manner of men, first French, then Spanish, then French again, attempted British, then American. Here was witnessed alike the passing of New France, the last phase of Spanish power, and the irresistible and engulfing wave of American advance. Here, it had been pointed out, "more strikingly and with more contrasts perhaps than elsewhere America has played out that drama of the impact of a polished civilization upon a wilderness environment that is so large a part of American History."

And still farther on to the Texas empire, bigger in area than a dozen lesser states and with experiences vivid enough for them all. Romance and hardships, pioneering and adventure, variety and range such as to provide stories and history for all manner of chroniclers. Under more flags than Florida . . . French under the adventurous La Salle . . . Spanish direct from Mexico . . . Mexican away from Spanish rule . . . American against Mexicans setting up a republic . . . Then the republic into the Union—out again in secession into the Confederate States—and back in the Union. Such a state and such a portraiture of the making of civilization! And on to Oklahoma, which could neither be included in the South, nor be left out; where "anything might happen and almost everything has"—"where only the truth was unbelievable."

The influence of the frontier was, of course, of many sorts. In general there were two fundamental conditioned results of the frontier forces: one on the character of the culture and institutions of the people, and one on the character of the people themselves, particularly the psychology of the individual and the folk. These make up the culture and behavior of a people and may be used as measures of any early civilization. This is true of early American culture and its continuing traits, whether it be the folk culture of the mountain folk or of the plain dwellers, or whether it applies to the product which was Walt Whitman, Nature and Frontier Man personified; and the same would be true of the powerful folk cultures of the great open spaces of Russia, or of the product which was Tolstoy, unharassed spirit of Nature and the frontier.

The general influence of the frontier upon American culture has been appraised by Turner and others. Illustrations are numerous, from the realistic study of the various frontiers of America, or from the study of literature and the history of the various regions of America. When we come to apply this measure to the southern regions, it must be very clear that the task is almost synonymous with the cataloguing of many of the main traits of southern culture. For here was a regional culture which featured strong individualism, great religious influences, strong sense of honor and personality, strong allegiance to the family and morals, quick tempers and emotional reactions, impatience with organization and formal law and control, love of freedom and the open spaces, and not too much emphasis upon finished standards of art, education, work. There were the frontier patterns of all earlier America as reflected in the homogeneity of native white, northern European stocks, Protestant churchgoing, Sabbath-observing, patriarchal folk, abounding in the spirit of honor, fighting politics, liquor-drinking and little love of the law.

So, too, the rural influence still constitutes a powerful factor in the individual lives and behavior of the southern people. Morning, noon, and night, spring, summer, and, winter, the language of the weather becomes the language of the people. The farmer loses, wins, breaks even in his contests with rain and drouth, storm and flood, cold and heat. A sizable storm may destroy years of achievement. A year of drouth penalizes with high financial loss and personal suffering. Blizzards and floods, weevils, and worms, disease and hazard multiply their toll until the farmer's gamble becomes a part of his daily life.

Yet he and his family are hardened by the experience, tested by a thousand vicissitudes of nature and strengthened by years of mastery over hardship. There is love of the land and Nature, sturdy allegiance to the open country, freedom and independence and the raising of children to replenish the nation's people.

It has often been said that the "open spaces in America are symbol of our myth," and that every people must, of course, have its myths. There was the early symbol of Daniel Boone's type of frontiersman, who was reputed to "move on" whenever a new neighbor settled close enough for him to hear his dogs bark. All of this reflects the certain product of Nature and the frontier on the people and constitutes an important psychological factor in the development of the regional folk.

All of this is reflected in the behavior not only of the individual but of the whole folk culture; for, of such persons

as are not now rural, most have a recent heritage of country
life and deal with country folk in their business and professions. Out of this grows a sturdy democracy in which the
people admit no classes of aristocracy of blood or of cities
and wealth.

For the frontier has been powerful not only in its earlier
character-forming influence upon the region, but in the
conflict between frontier folkways and the technological,
psychological foundations of modern society, basic to the
understanding of much that characterizes pathological behavior. Dr. Franz Alexander in his *Our Age of Unreason*
thought that Frederick Jackson Turner's writings "explained
the most common conflict of the American neurotic, the
thwarted ambition among people trained to admire individual
achievements, as their ancestors had done in the days of the
Open Frontier, yet situated in a standardized industrial civilization which imposed uneventful routine and offered no real
security in return." One need not agree with this conclusion to
sense, however, the essential importance of the way of the
frontier in the total way of the South.

CHAPTER III

The Plantation South and the Negro

THE MAIN CURRENTS of the regional development of the South
found the bold springs of their origin in Nature's resources
and were abundantly replenished by the frontier culture of
early America. The main stream of this southern frontier culture was constantly growing wider and deeper because of the
many tributaries of migration flowing into it in many places
and from many sources.

Yet there was another major stream first flowing parallel
and then merging with the main currents of southern culture
and economy whose origin was also conditioned by the South's
natural conditions and resources. This was the "Old South"
of the plantation economy and the Negro, first as slave and
then as the chief factor that created a folk culture which made
the South different from the rest of the nation, in so far as it
was different.

The Nature factors which set the incidence for the "Old
South" consisted primarily in climate and land. The picture
was somewhat oversimplified by Ulrich Phillips, who began
his story of *Life and Labor in the Old South* by insisting that
the weather was the chief agency which made the South different. "It fostered the plantation system," he said, "which
brought the importation of Negroes, which not only gave rise
to chattel slavery but created a lasting race problem. This led
to controversy and regional rivalry for power, which produced
apprehensive reactions and culminated in a stroke for independence. Thus we have the house that Jack built, otherwise known for some years as 'The Confederate States of
America.'"

Yet the land and the growing of cotton, related in what came to be known as the "cotton economy," were also inseparably related to the utilization and waste of the South's resources. For the continuous quest for more and more rich land to grow more and more cotton—first through the plantation system of slaves and master, and later through the farm tenant system—impoverished a region while making it rich: wasting land and men, and impoverishing one folk culture while enriching another.

It came to pass, therefore, that the cotton economy which bought the South into one crop system—a cash crop system in which tobacco later played a part—led it into that colonial economy from which it has not yet freed itself. At the same time the region was weakened in its human and cultural resources, and was neglecting its technological resources in science, invention, organization, so far as to fall behind the rest of the nation before the Civil War and especially after it. The later exploitation of a defeated region led to many levels of economic discrimination, such as freight rates, rates of interest, and the long catalogue of deficiencies which flow naturally from the dominance of other regions in centralized wealth and power.

Most histories of the southern states have been devoted to the planter aristocracy and to the later conflicts of war and reconstruction. It is true that the historical interest in the South was centered around the Old South, which, of course, conditioned the upper and lower brackets of white and Negro culture. While this was only a part of the total southern culture, it is important to note here the historical verdict that there *was* an ideal of the older planter aristocracy which sought to produce the gentleman in the framework of a Greek democracy, or to transplant an English aristocracy to American soil. This ideal was to be set against the New England money economy of industrial and urban society, as being superior to it. Something of the story of the planter aristocracy is told in our later chapters on the Old South, its "glory that was" and its "grandeur that was not."

Yet the southern aristocracy was only a part of the total picture. There was the ever increasing upper middle class, to which belonged not only the great farmer group but merchants, commercial farmers, professional folk. Among the important neglected factors in the interpretation of the agrarian South is the large number of upper middle-class, non-slave-owning white folk who constituted the backbone of reconstruction and recovery. Their contributions were definitive in the regional culture. It was upon their sturdy character and persistent work that the New South was largely built. They illustrated the Sumner theory that "the share which the upper strata [the large middle group] of the masses have in determining the policy of the masses is therefore often decisive of public welfare." This group stands out in contrast to the "planter class," to which so much attention has been given, and which numbered for the southeastern states fewer than two hundred thousand compared with as many as a million and a half farm folk corresponding to the upper farmer class in the earlier East and Middle West. This group, however, restricted by Negro and tenant on the one hand, and by artificial patterns on the other, has not been normally articulate. Yet, in all the averages and distributions of deficiencies and lags, it still constitutes the norm around which judgments should be made and plans developed.

Just as the South has been portrayed in earlier popular literature as the romantic Old South, so, strangely enough, in later years it has been portrayed even more vividly in terms of its lower levels of folk-culture—the culture of what have been called "poor whites." It is less important at this point to describe this level than to show how it was developed. Mildred Mell has pointed out how, "as the tidewater sections became the old, established regions characterized by the plantation system, the early homogeneity of the population gave way to classes more or less well defined except on their edges where they faded into each other. These classes were the planters, the yeoman farmers or small-holders, and the poor whites at the bottom of the economic ladder."

It was different in the North, where commerce, manufactures, and transportation "played increasingly important roles giving opportunity through a wage system to those with no resources of their own, while in agriculture the landless man could be the 'hired man' working for wages with no lowering of status and biding his time until he could start out for himself. But agriculture based on slave labor as the dominant pattern of life in the South marked to all intents and purposes the limit of opportunity, this limitation becoming intensified by the characteristic features of the utilization of land."

It is pointed out further that in a region peculiarly subject to erosion because of its physiographic aspects, and to soil exhaustion because of the development of a one-crop system using slave labor, the planters constantly shifted to new lands, leaving in their wake "old fields" promising little or nothing to those who expended labor upon them. Thus in the plantation areas farmers on a small scale had scarcely a chance for a good living, because sooner or later the planters brought such economic pressure to bear that they got possession of most of the good land, leaving the less desirable and worn-out land to a few of the small holders and the poor whites. "The majority of the yeoman farmers found it more advantageous to establish themselves outside the areas of the large plantations; but some who owned a few slaves managed to hold on to good land alongside the planters, while others who worked their own crops cultivated the inferior lands which planters found it uneconomic to cultivate with slave labor. On the worn-out lands, the poor whites 'squatted,' eking out an existence which was uncertain at best, but no worse than what was possible for them on the sand hills and pine-barrens where there was land which they could hold because no one else had ever wanted it."

Strangely enough, however, the Negro himself, both through his influence upon the plantation South and through his later increase into a third of the population of a biracial culture, exerted an even more profound influence upon the life and labor of the whole South.

As if the South up to this point did not already have enough of the elements that go into the architecture of all cultures, there were yet to be added the powerful factors of race and caste, which were to make the region different from all other regions of the nation. Alongside, therefore, the two great streams of southern development already under way, there was to be a third—the three at flood tide converging into a powerful current of mixed waters to make the symbolic muddy river of southern culture. For paralleling the plantation aristocracy was the ever widening and swift-moving stream of slavery, growing larger from the springs of population increase and the tributaries of economic and sectional conflict. And in the uttermost parts of the South was the other widening stream of migration of white groups with varied ethnic heritages to mix and mingle with the other two.

For the source of this new stream we return to the powerful role of Nature in the development of the South; namely, the influence of weather upon crops, the place of cotton among southern crops and consequently the role played by Negro slavery in the cotton crop and its economy and culture. For in the coming of the Negro into the picture there were introduced at once not only the factors of race but a double basis of caste—one of blood, and one of sex. In the first place, the plantation aristocracy had already evolved into such class and caste that the distinctions between this at its highest level and the white South at its lowest level formed an almost unbridgeable chasm so far as intermarriage was concerned.

That caste culture had had an inevitable weakening influence upon the upper brackets of the white South and had left a heritage of embitterment to the rest of the white South. Then, later, the heart of the South's biracial dilemma was to be found in the essential race-sex caste nature of the Negro problem, which rendered the dilemma insusceptible to the usual modes of adjustment. The understanding of these factors is essential to any appraisal of the way of the South as it matured in later years.

In any biography of the South there must be, then, separate stories of no fewer than four classes. Yet one story it was, too, the composite of which makes up the powerful folk culture of the total South. These classes were the plantation aristocracy and the Negro slave folk on the one hand, and the middle-class whites and the "poor whites" on the other. How these levels of life with their multiple and complex elements constituted the way of the folk will appear as the life and culture of the South are portrayed in their total cultural aspects. For the present it is important to examine these new factors of race and caste as they begin to make the southern regions distinctive from other regions in the nation.

First of all, the South inherited race conflicts, race prejudice, and race exploitation, such as had been well-nigh universal among men through the ages wherever race relations were involved. And, second, the South was to have its own special race experience through slavery and reconstruction and through the later stages of a biracial culture seeking satisfactory adjustments. Here universal prejudices were augmented by the tragedy of war, the bitterness associated with the destruction of the South's old civilization, the cultural complexes stored up from the reconstruction period and gathering momentum through the years of conflict and outside criticism.

With reference to the general heritage, it must be clear that the South did not stand alone in its race conflict and exploitation. Witness the story of mankind throughout the world and especially in the new global problems of the world-war eras. Somewhere high up in the catalogue of human tragedies must be listed the great phenomenon of race conflict and the exploitation of minority peoples with the long train of resulting structures and processes, cumulative conditioning and conflict, product of the religious, political, and general cultural evolution of societal relations. In this vast inventory are a multitude of exhibits: racial attitudes and conflicts; myths and patterns of racial superiority and inferiority; confiscation, annihilation, exploitation, appropriation of person and property; economic, political, and religious discrimination, and cultural exhaustion; prejudice, intolerance, distrust, emotional complexes, false conclusions of both science and sentiment, dominating folk-ways and mores made to coincide with whatever coercive state-ways were wanted.

There were other evolutionary and cumulative elements in the South's complex background. One was the assumption that race was a purely biological phenomenon, and that races, being different in this respect, were naturally superior or inferior. This has been a well-nigh universal credo. Another element was the assumption that, because race conflict always had been a major cultural phenomenon, it always would be. Indeed, in the historical theories of society, race has often been posited as the definitive element in social evolution. Here indeed, it was assumed, was a major phase of the natural law of survival. Inheriting these general assumptions, the South had rationalized its theories as being realistic on the one hand, and scripturally justified on the other. It was natural that the assumption that the Negro was an inferior race subject to the logical processes of exploitation and domination would constitute the main credo in the southern philosophy. Thus, the South was a fine example of transmitted culture, following in the wake of all these human heritages and intensifying them through its own concentrated folk-ways of racial purity and dominance.

There were still other important factors in the evolutionary heritage. One was the American will to exterminate or exploit the American Indian. This American pattern, first grounded in the religious intensity of the New England forefathers to convert or to kill, was reflected in the tragic Custer's last stand, now generally considered to have been criminally unnecessary. There could be no doubt that this American heritage set the stage for the later tragedies of race conflict throughout the nation. Here, again, the South was following in full force that heritage long promulgated through American history and education. And later the folkways of survival, where Negroes outnumbered the whites, naturally developed into the philosophy of keeping the Negro in his place or destroying individuals who tried to rise above the standard norms.

Economic factors were involved in the total struggle for societal as well as biological survival. Under the premises of what had actually been the racial backgrounds and the historical development there was an honest base for questioning whether a completely changed culture-economy could survive under the American frontier and later economic framework. Many theorists held that the problem was primarily one of economic competition. And certainly the problem of integrating all the people, equally and alike, into the same opportunities and a unified system was of such complexity as to overtax the people's energies and resources and leave them forever faced with moral dilemmas.

Thus, the unfolding picture of the South afforded a standard example of a complex culture, symbolic of how all cultures grow. The South was essentially a culture of the folk, close to nature and close to the land. And conflict was close to nature. The power of nature and its nurture, in river valleys and mountain places, in the piny woods and cut-over lands, in all the episodes of cold and heat, storm, rain, drouth, had created a folk culture of distinctive quality. But, more specifically, the culture of the South was the culture of this folk also conditioned in its historical setting through the influence of slavery, the Civil War, and the reconstruction period. It easily followed, therefore, that the South had become so conditioned to race as class and caste that it reflected the racial situation as supreme over all others, a symbol of cultural survival and an issue of life and death. When to this had been added the well-nigh irresistible force of a people who had made their *folkways* of race heritage coincide with their *stateways* of race segregation, the southern scene was flowering into powerful maturity.

Thus the organic situation as reflected in the southern United States of America was one in which the race problem came, after the war and reconstruction, to symbolize the old slogan of what men live and die for; namely, "for God, for home, and for country." That is, in the separation of the northern churches and the southern churches, the issue of race became one of supreme religious importance. When the Kingdom of Heaven was to be a kingdom of race, the issue came to be one "for God." In the philosophy of race purity, white supremacy, protection of womanhood, it became a question of the home. In the loyalties of the South and of the different states to the beloved "Southland," set over against the North, it came to be "for country."

Now, manifestly, people grounded in the loyalties of these three noble motivations and having had no opportunity or experiences through which to sense any other attitude cannot be "bad" people simply because they work on these motivations. On the contrary, they are "good" people as measured by the values of their institutions. But more powerful than their moral moorings is the fact that such psychological conditionings are more difficult to change than are many of the traits and environments that are called "physical." The question is not one of what might be right or wrong, or what might be different under different cultural heritage, but one of what the realities are.

If we try to recapture the processes through which the Old South and then the New South came to their relative maturity of culture and hence of their folkways, mores, institutions, and behavior, the story of the Negro in the South becomes, from the moment of his coming to complicate the picture, the most decisive factor in the architecture of southern culture. First, here was the coming of a new people, representative of a black race, in bondage and sold for a price, primitive and "heathen" and on no account assumed to be the equal of the whites. Introduced by northern traders and trafficked from abroad, the Negro was held in the same esteem by North and South and by representatives of other nations who traded in slaves. For did not the captains of the slave ships get their sailing orders from the Lord, hand touching the Bible that "The pay's good pay, but it's the Lord's work too—"

> Captain Ball was a Yankee slaver
> Blow, blow, blow the man down!
> He traded in niggers and loved his Saviour
> Give me some time to blow the man down.

And then more slaves came, and more economic and moral debating, North and South. And finally the decision was made. Negroes and slaves were to continue South and not North. As more and more came and multiplied they became the key resources for the plantation economy and set the incidence for aristocracy against the common people, the philosophy of slave labor, and the South's attitude toward work and all the rest of the long train of results.

There was also the noble society of the Negro slaves themselves with their loyalty and manners and the affection which they had for the whites alongside the great esteem in which they were held by the whites. There were the "uncles" and "aunties," the "black mammies" and the patriarchs among the older Negroes. And always the multitudes of little Negroes called to this day indescribably rich and attractive in their personalities, challenging education and society to do them justice. And the South grew and prospered and flowered into its own great "civilization," the story of which has been told often enough.

Then the conflict between North and South and the sectionalism called "America's Tragedy." And then the War and reconstruction and fighting and exploitation of brothers, stranger than fiction. Carpetbaggers and scalawags, philanthropists and reformers, politicians and adventurers swelled the stream of fear and hate and misunderstanding and multiplied the points of renewed conflict and hate. For a while the North and the Negro ruled. Then the power of the folkways, with all their institutions—the home, the school, the church, the farm and factory, the community and the state— as well as the hidden ways of Ku Klux and vigilantes, was stronger than the power of the stateways. And all the king's horses and all the king's men could not avail to conquer unconquerable folk.

And so it was that the end of an era was not the end of the southern epoch. The nation was to learn that that which was destroyed and buried would rise again in all those aspects in which the Negro was involved. Yet some things there were that could be buried. Some things were forever gone.

> Bury the bygone South.
> Bury the minstrel with the honey-mouth,
> Bury the broadsword virtues of the clan,
> Bury the unmachined, the planters' pride,
> The courtesy and the bitter arrogance,
> The pistol-hearted horsemen who could ride
> Like jolly centaurs under the hot stars.
> Bury the whip, bury the branding-bars,
> Bury the unjust thing
> That some tamed into mercy, being wise,
> But could not starve the tiger from its eyes
> Or make it feed where beasts of mercy feed.
> Bury the fiddle-music and the dance,

The sick magnolias of the false romance
And all the chivalry that went to seed
Before its ripening.
And with these things, bury the purple dream
Of the America we have not been,
The tropic empire, seeking the warm sea,
The last foray of aristocracy
Based not on dollars or initiative
Or any blood for what that blood was worth
But on a certain code, a manner of birth,
A certain manner of knowing how to live,
The pastoral rebellion of the earth
Against machines, against the Age of Steam,
The Hamiltonian extremes against the Franklin mean,
The genius of the land
Against the metal hand,
The great, slave-driven bark,
Full-oared upon the dark,
With gilded figurehead,
With fetters for the crew
And spices for the few,
The passion that is dead,
The pomp we never knew,
Bury this, too.

Yet bury they could not the racial heritage with all its complexes and problems. For the way of the South was the way of race, and the way of the folk, and the way of history, and the way of culture, and the way of Nature. In the flowering of the southern culture, in the wake of the Negro's culture and in the aftermath of tragedy there was something that the South's emotions valued higher than life, reminiscent of why they fought. What was it?

It wasn't slavery,
That stale red-herring of Yankee knavery
Nor even states' rights, at least not solely,
But something so dim that it must be holy.
A voice, a fragrance, a taste of wine,

A face half-seen in old candleshine,
A yellow river, a blowing dust,
Something beyond you that you must trust,
Something so shrouded it must be great,
The dead men building the living state
From 'simmon-seed on a sandy bottom,
The woman South in her rivers laving
That body whiter than new-blown cotton
And savage and sweet as wild-orange blossom,
The dark hair streams on the barbarous bosom,
If there ever has been a land worth saving—
In Dixie land, I'll take my stand,
And live and die for Dixie! . . .

There was then the span of southern culture following re-construction and beginning an era of the New South just before the turn of the century. There were eager leaders North and South committed to better understanding, to better opportunities for the South, to better cooperation beween the North and the South. There were Negro leaders and white leaders striving to do the best that could be done.

Yet on the question of the Negro there was always misunderstanding. The rest of the nation never understood the South, and the rest of the nation never ceased to enforce its moral principles; and the South never ceased to resist and resent. Yet there was progress, morale, and hope for enduring relationships, and for solutions that would grow out of the day's work. The story of the South here is the story of a great epoch in which the "good South" was trying to do the best that could be done. The demagogic South was still keeping the race issue afire, and to the great mass of folk it was still the same issue of race equality which could never be in the annals of southern culture.

So came the South to the Second World War and the revivification of the whole problem through a crisis, the greatest since the days before the Civil War and the days within its duration and since. Then there was the new crisis of the 1940's, which brings boldly to focus again the racial conditioning of the white South, as well as the national nature of the problem. The story of this crisis is the story of the South matured to its highest point up to now. It is the story of the South and the nation. And within the South it is the story of two great regional folk cultures caught up in the midst of transition between the powerful heritage of the past and the mighty pull of the future.

For here was the white South, a great people often doing little things and a good people often doing bad things. And here was the Negro South, caught as always between the upper and nether millstones of conflicting forces and also paying the price of extraordinary transition from level to level of cultural achievement and needing plenty of sympathy and guidance. And here was the white South inexorably conditioned in cultural complexes, suffering terribly and needing sympathy and help as few peoples ever needed it in the annals of man. And, even more important, the two, white South and black South, were part and parcel of a great national culture whose dynamics, scarcely less than the two regional cultures, needed the sense of time and wisdom, of organic regional perspective, and of the essence of cosmopolitan, global culture.

And the story, like the reality itself, must be told in the language of the folk, not overmindful of the sensitiveness of those who get too far away from the people. The story is of the crude stuff of which realism is made, and needs the hand of a double Walt Whitman, one whose sense of nature and organic unity can portray crudeness, diversity, and conflict in terms of esteem and affection, and one who senses the democracy of the folk and the spirit of America.

For abundant evidence in the catalogue of rumors, tensions, conflicts, and trends justified the conclusion that the South and the Negro, in the early 1940's, faced their greatest crisis

since the days of the reconstruction, and that many of the
same symbols of conflict and tragedy that were manifest in
the 1840's were evident again a hundred years later.

And so the current of Negro dilemma flows on in a new
flood tide, reinforced by many events, chiefest of which was
the incidence of war with its attendant demands and opportunities and its philosophy of global democracy. These had
all been logical and inevitable products of the time, reflecting
the cumulative power and sweep of a logical long-time evolutionary process. While an adequate cataloguing and understanding of the mass of war episodes and influences
constituted a first step, it was the portraiture of the reaction
of the South and the explanation of the folk psychology involved that were essential, first, to understanding the situation and, second, to directing next steps. And by the same
token the folk psychology of the rest of the nation and of the
Negro was part and parcel of the total picture.

A major element in the crisis was found in the South's vivid
reaction to the total situation. More specifically was the role
of reaction to outside criticism and war efforts to force her
hand in making radical change of policies. Over against the
outside verdict of denunciation, the South was thinking all
along that it had made great progress toward better race relations; that it had attained a good deal of unity; and that perhaps it was finally on its way toward such interracial cooperation as would lead to the best possible adjustment.

There was, for instance, great pride in the Negro leaders
and educators of distinction whose fellowship and participation in regional development were so highly valued. There
were common gatherings and conferences between leaders
of both races. There were meetings between the white and
Negro college youth. Many things were being done, as a
matter of fact, in racial fellowship which a short time ago
would not have been considered. There was less and less vio-

lence and more and more inclination to increase the Negro's participation in all matters economic and cultural.

Furthermore, there were increases in appropriations for Negro education, often as much as 50 to 100 per cent. Teachers' salaries were more and more being equalized and special efforts were being made to develop Negro institutions of higher learning and to give the Negro increasingly great opportunities in professional equipment. There had been such great strides in the reduction of lynching and mob action that already the hope was being expressed that a new era was in the making.

Then suddenly, as it appeared to the South, there was a flood of criticism, denunciation, demand. Measures of coercion were proposed which seemed to assume that the South was doing something new and quite bad in its whole pattern of biracial culture. It was as if there came the assumption that the South was initiating backward policies in which it boldly challenged the rest of the world in new reaches of injustice and discrimination. Instead, therefore, in the light of a normal and logical period of development, of being credited with substantial measures of progress, the South found itself in wartimes reflecting, relatively, retrogression in comparison with what was demanded and in comparison with the commitments of the American people to global democracy. And the South, hoping to achieve some measure of united patriotism, felt that the war crisis was no time to split the nation again and to foment bitterness and violence.

Once again, it was as if the rest of the nation, in particular the publicists, the intelligentsia, and the youth of other regions, had suddenly discovered the structure of the South's biracial culture. They kept saying, "What is this new thing the South is doing to the Negro? What are we going to do about the South's treatment of the Negro?" Yet, it is not surprising that the new generation of the nation, largely ignorant of the earlier backgrounds of national development, should know little or nothing of the tragedies of the South. There grew up quickly, therefore, a remarkable concern to save the South, to free the South, to take the occasion of war to purify American democracy. It was one of the most dramatic episodes in the long history of America's idealism.

What the South had done was, of course, nothing new. It was an old story except that the South was of the impression that it had actually made many concessions and had grown in stature through certain logical, advancing stages of development. The South was assuming, as it always had, a continuation of the economy and culture of a biracial caste culture and therefore appraised its progress as new gains. Who ever thought the South would abandon segregation anyhow? Hadn't the issue been settled over and over again? Was there not a powerful heritage of trial and error to make this sure? Had not every community or group of communities in the old days lived in the shadow of fear and in the relative disgrace of some racial tragedy? Was this to be done over again?

Yet because of the war and the revitalizing of America's ideology of democracy and freedom in global war, and because of the new discovery of the South by the nation and consequently a new level of irresponsible agitation, even with the progress that the South had made, its culture economy reflected to its critics glaring inequalities that appeared to be neither right nor necessary. And even though there would be no inclination on the part of many southerners to deny the great distance between what the South was doing and what needed to be done, nevertheless the psychology of the sudden impact of criticism and accusation, when the South had thought it was going forward, was the key to the speed and intensity of reaction. The South, too, needed sympathy and understanding, the people thought, instead of denunciation and misunderstanding.

And here the South was following its standard folkways of resentment of outside criticism and Federal coercion. Southerners were back again in united defense against outside aggression. "If outsiders," they began to react again, "would let us alone, we would work out our problem." "Mrs. Roosevelt and the New Deal," they would say, "are trying to make us discard the pattern of segregation." From the governors to the common man the refrain was that the southern people were quite capable of running their own government and would continue to do so. In the light of American experience, this was, of course, nothing new. Yet the South might very well have replied: "Well, of course, the rest of the nation is still trying to make the South over. Who said they were not? What of it? From their viewpoint, why wouldn't they? That, too, is an old story, and we will not let it get us excited again." But that was not the way of the South, and so here again was basic soil for the multiplied rumors and rifts of a threatening crisis.

And then the Negro portion of the biracial culture was proceeding to assume attitudes and to initiate action in accordance with this new and radical freedom, whereas the white part of the South was not only acquiescing but finding a new unity in resisting, to the end that they went to extremes reminiscent of the old days of reconstruction. They did things and talked and listened to rumors that to the outsider could not be interpreted in terms of any logical and reasonable explanation. And because the rest of the nation did not understand, and because its verdict was primarily a "group" judgment, it advocated partial and unrealistic solutions, often advocating action without estimating the costs that might follow.

One of the first tasks, therefore, essential to the understanding of the situation and preliminary to the cataloguing and interpretation of what happened was to sense the realistic, living credo of the South with reference to the Negro and its relation to what might be called a symbolic credo of the rest of the nation. The understanding of a folk psychology, which was committed to the defense of this credo at any cost, by the same token, was a first essential.

For, against this well-nigh universal southern credo came assumptions and demands that appeared to the South to be about as near the complete opposite as it would be possible to find. In substance, here was a sudden demand for the South, long conditioned in the Negro complex and southern loyalties, bottomed in the long heritage of race prejudice and cultural evolution, to change its whole structure of race relations overnight. And, equally vivid, from the outside regions was reflected what seemed to be an unreasonableness of the South in not being willing to conform to the larger American credo of democracy and the American dream of equality.

Now the bare statement of an organic credo, which would startle even most southerners, appeared crude and harsh. So here again it was important to repeat and repeat the question: Was it true that the South believed these things about the Negro? Or, if not, now that it was put down in black and white as the composite feeling and folkways of the South, what part of it was *not* true? Of course, no southerner ever wrote such a credo for himself, and no one ever heard a southerner parading his credo as such. Yet, tested and checked in private life, in religious attitudes, in politics and law, and in the defense mechanisms of the region, in the great body of common folk, was this the South's credo, and was it the heart of the whole drama?

Without an understanding of the South's organic feelings and beliefs it was not possible to explain such violent reactions to episodes and experiences which appeared to outsiders as mere commonplace behavior. Keeping in mind the variations of a composite credo and ratio of different groups of southerners who might dissent, and also the possible comparison with what people in the other regions held, it seemed important to ask again and again whether the white South would face the issue of its beliefs.

Here, again, as always, there were paradox and contrast. While one group of leaders would protest the unfairness to the South of the presentation of such a credo, another large group would seem to say: "Sure, of course, that's what we believe. Why mention it? Everybody knows the Negro is just a Negro." Yet it was in many ways a startling credo that seemed to be the heart of the crisis. It seemed possible to count a score of units in the total and to ask again, Was it true that the South believed—

That the Negro was a Negro and always would be that and nothing more; that, being a Negro, and different from the white man, he therefore could not be expected ever to measure up to the white man's standards of character and achievement;

That, not being capable of full achievement, and being of an inferior race, he should logically be kept in an inferior place, which was "his place"?

It followed that this was a white man's country, and that therefore the white man would dominate it about as he chose. Laws and resolutions only made matters worse.

Political equality and equal educational opportunities, if given to the Negro, would lead to social equality and the mixture of races, which was contrary to all the major premises of the southern way of life. Furthermore, political and social equality would lead to the domination of the white South by the Negroes and their northern supporters. Discrimination and segregation, therefore, were necessary to keep the Negro in his place and protect the interests and integrity of the whites.

It was assumed that the Negro, when kept within his rightful sphere, should not be treated unkindly or unjustly; that he should be given fair trials and protected by law; and that he should be paid a living wage (since, however, his standards of living were lower, he could live on less than a white man could). It was assumed that, if given too much pay, the Negro would waste the money and get out of bounds to his own harm as well as to the detriment of the South; that he was by nature inclined to criminal behavior, partly because of his animal nature and partly because of his irresponsibility and immorality. Moreover, the Negro was better off in the South where he was "understood," and where his best friends were.

It was assumed that, while as a race the Negro was inferior and generally untrustworthy, as an individual he was often honest, loyal, lovable, capable, and even talented and distinguished (yet this was the exception); that his music, his carefree, patient disposition, his homely philosophy added interest and color and richness to the culture of the South; that recognition should be given to the Negro for having made outstanding progress in many fields since being freed from slavery (yet the Negro in general was not capable of taking great responsibility or of assuming leadership); that no self-respecting southerner would work under Negro supervision.

It was assumed that, if the New Dealers, northerners, and reformers would let the South and the Negro alone, peaceful adjustments of the race problem could be made; that those who were inviting the Negro to discontent and trying to force his participation in industry and politics on an equal basis were fomenting race riots which would hurt both whites and Negroes, and the total nation in the long run; and that, finally, this was not a debatable issue.

There were, of course, various self-evident facts with reference to such a credo. In the first place, there were some variations from the norm as indicated in this credo. Yet, for all practical purposes this made little difference, since it was the mode of southern attitudes and folkways which gave rise to points of tension, conflict, and the like. This credo was presented, not because there was anything new in it, but rather in order to high-light and make more vivid the folkways of the South concerning the Negro. Such bold and bald statements of a credo were so vivid that it was perhaps surprising to southerners, and, therefore, might go a long way toward explaining why the other regions of the nation have rediscovered a level of their own national life with which they were not acquainted, or which they had forgot. The credo was in such complete contradistinction to the urgings and demands that were being made on the South in the name of war and freedom and Americanism that the resulting tension and conflict were easily explainable. It had to be repeated often that the understanding of the realistic folkways of the South was necessary also to explain the reaction of so many people from other regions to what seemed to them arbitrary and unreasonable, and entirely unfair attitudes and procedures in the South with reference to the simplest, most common, everyday, reasonable expectations of the Negro for life, liberty, and the pursuit of happiness.

These are but samplings from the powerful conditioning factors of race and caste that made the South what it was. From this point on the Negro and his part in the regional culture is the recurring motif most commonly characterizing the story of the culture which was the South. Here was extraordinary drama, tragedy of the Greek, tragedy of the Roman, comedy for Aristophanes, comedy for Plautus, but always and ever the eternal drama of the black man in a white world. And here were foundations for all that behavior complex of frustration and aggression, of adjustment to a quick-changing world that was to contribute powerfully to the disturbed personality in the modern world. The South would have its double portion. The Negro colored every phase of southern life; he colored every impression which outside observers had of the South. Not only was the South impotent to achieve untrammeled objectives in industry, agriculture, education, democracy because of the complex of Negro-white relationship, but the North would not let the South pursue its course fully in any aspect of life until it first would give satisfaction that the Negro would not be segregated. This could not be done under the existing regional imbalance of culture and economy.

In the total regional equality of America there could be no equitable equilibrium and balance between the white and the Negro until there was a redistribution of the Negro people throughout all regions of the nation to the end that he might be reintegrated into the national melting pot. This was manifestly an unrealistic prospect. The South could not and would not give the Negro equal opportunity. The North could not and would not, after all of its years of trial and exhortation, do what it insisted the South must do. Neither the South nor the nation was willing to reexamine the fundamental premises upon which conflict and frustration were based.

As always, the Negro was caught up in the midst of all the pressure that stemmed from the sudden attempt to integrate all races and ethnic groups alike into a common culture. This, again, was the way of America, but it subtracted not one whit from the essential difficulty of the southern scene. With religion, race, and caste in the South it became the most powerful of all the folkways and mores which characterized the region. In the South the folkways of white supremacy, made to coincide with the stateways of state legislation, were more powerful than race or the total stateways of the Federal government. And until new techniways of readjustment could arise to transcend the folkways of tradition, the South with its folk not only would be different from the rest of the nation, but would be proud of the difference.

CHAPTER IV

The People, and the Way of the Folk

IT IS MORE than a truism to recall that the supreme wealth of a region or nation, after all, is to be found in the people and their work; and that the way of any culture is the way of the folk. The people, representing the universal human resources of a society, constitute the physical basis of human culture, even as natural resources and the earth itself constitute the physical tabernacle in which all cultures build their material structures. By the same token, just as the amount and kind of material wealth are determined by the range and quality of natural resources, so the quality of a culture is determined by the number and kind of people and the nature of their life and labor. It must be clear, therefore, that a region rich in natural resources, in which science, skill, technology, organization— in other words, technological resources—have been utilized to translate natural wealth into capital wealth, would have a material abundance adequate for supporting a rich culture. Such a product, however, assumes a virile population, well trained, and so socially minded and educated as to utilize the wealth which comes from its abundance of resources in the development of its institutions and thereby in the enrichment of the human resources themselves.

The people are, however, basic in another sense in which the "folk" is the universal constant in a world of variables. This means simply that the people, as they develop in each region and create its culture, are the ever-flowing and limit- less source from which arise new cultures in the wake of de- caying civilizations. By the same token, the folk is as inde- structible as are Nature's powerful processes and cycles of succession. In the folk-wisdom of many cultures are sayings about people, symbolic of their organic role in human society. "Vox populi, vox Dei," like Fiske's "Through Nature to God," represents a scientific verdict as well as a popular translation, "The voice of the people is the voice of God." "Of, for, and by the people" was not merely a spoken shibboleth, but reflects also the new realism of the people in the universality and timelessness of their search for mastery in a quick-changing world. "Nothing matters but the people" is not only a poet's powerful piece of writing but a functional verdict of the scientist as well. So, too, the common exhortations to keep close to the people and close to nature are symbolic of the folkways of survival.

All of this is particularly important in attempting to understand the way of the South; for not only are the southern people multiplying and replenishing the nation's population, but in their folk-quality on its many levels is found the key to the whole southern scene. In the South there is in round numbers nearly a third of the people of the nation; and the rate of reproduction is much higher than in the rest of the country. In the Southeast with more than thirty million people and the Southwest with nearly half as many, there is realism and romance not only in the kind and numbers, but in the changing status of the people as they move hither and yon within the regions and out of them.

For, when all these southern people shall have been counted and classified, there will still remain the dynamics of a migratory society in which many of the folk are constantly moving hither and yon, within a state, among the states, out of the region. Millions of others, however, do not move along—some "homebodies" close to the soil, some belonging to communities for generations, some leaders and builders of communities and fortunes, yet changing powerfully from generation to generation. Some are of the "best people," remnants of the earlier culture, and others are of the vanguard of the

new builders of tomorrow. Some are of those who waste
away, and whose children reflect a situation that is very un-
American; namely, they have less prospect than their parents
had. All these people are of great variety of folk and of economic status, high, low, and middle groups, making for the
most part what we have called middle folk and common man
and pictured in a later chapter.

Of those who move hither and yon, a multitude still seek
always some promised land; their restlessness is symbol still
of a continuing frontier folk. There was the lamented Ben
Robertson writing of his Carolina kinfolks as restless folk
who could abide awhile by the cotton fields and hill ridges.
Sometimes, he would say, "we can forget time in our country
and be contented, and then the old restlessness will stir
again, like a wind rising, and we have to travel. We are all
like that. High winds and lonesome sounds disturb us, something within makes us go. We must ride to town or visit among
the kinfolks or strike out for Texas. We must see what is going on, see what other folks' crops look like, cross into new
country. . . . We have rambled long distances in our time,
for the road that passes our house leads all the way to California, and we have never been able to resist it—traveling
on that road has been a vice and a virtue with us. . . . My
kinfolks, I think, were born to ramble. It is a troubling quality
in a people who are religious and serious and who have been
drilled from their youth to accept duty, to work hard, to settle
down. . . . Daniel Boone belonged among our kinfolks, and
Aunt Mollie Boone, who is buried in our burying ground, told
a sister-in-law of hers who told her grandfather who told my
Great-Aunt Narcissa that Mrs. Daniel Boone said Daniel was
a mighty poor provider . . ."
Of those who have moved from the South since the turn of
the century, there were more than four million: sometimes, as
in the 1920's, wave on wave to set a high level of migration;
and sometimes merely as streamlets trickling into every known

place and circumstance of the nation's far-flung regions. There were those who became distinguished in the Northeast or Far West or in the Middle States. There were those who helped make the Pacific Northwest or the lower reaches of Illinois and Indiana. There were literary folk and workers, publishers and secretaries whose work added to the urban metropolitan East. Washington, D.C., sometimes assuming the characterization of a southern city, is alive with the ways of the South.

A million, two million Negro folk, have moved on into the ever growing urban centers of the nation and into varied walks of life and occupations that have created a new record of expanding Negro-national participation in American life. Some have achieved genuine distinction; from Texas to Los Angeles, from Florida to Washington, from Alabama to Detroit, from Georgia to New York and back. A million Negro common men, migrants and workers, have made the fabric of the American population a new and variegated one. Another million white workers have moved on up and into the industrial centers, creating new names for southerners and revivifying old traits of alleged southern character. Wherever they have gone, the southern way has gone with them. Southern they came, southern they remained—these southern people, from Cincinnati all the way to Detroit, from Baltimore all the way to Denver and in the way places in the cities that mark the upper water level railroad lines and in the cities between Chicago and Philadelphia on the lower rim.

But not all of the moving folk traveled so far. A million here and a million there moved from countryside to town and city within the borders of their own states or region. A hundred counties in a single state lost rural people in a single decade, so many that the rural Southeast and Southwest had the highest rate of urban growth in the nation in all the recent decades. There were multitudes of farm tenants who moved often, sometimes every year, sometimes near, sometimes far, seeking to find a satisfying home. They seldom did. White cotton-mill workers moved hither and yon, seeking to better themselves and to find something that would satisfy. They seldom did.

Negro folk who had always belonged to the land moved to the city in such tides as to change the whole farm fabric of Negro labor. Sometimes they moved on from city to city in the South and still kept on going: from Georgia and South Carolina to North Carolina, and then on to Washington, to Baltimore, to Wilmington, to Philadelphia, to New York; or from Alabama and Mississippi up to Memphis, to Louisville, to Cincinnati, to Indianapolis, to Chicago, and the Twin Cities. From Texas to Los Angeles and up the Far West. These were southern people trying *not* to be southern, even though many returned for one reason or another in the depression days. But when they came back, whether for visit or for longer sojourn, they did not reflect the way of the South as white folks did wherever they went.

Here, again, the way of the South as affecting the way of the nation is powerfully illustrated in the story of southern folk throughout all the regions. This is true not only in so far as the South has contributed to the other regions, but also because of its potentiality to keep on pouring its new reserves into the depleted urban industrial centers. Vance points out that, while the great urban industrial areas of the Northeast and the middle states still lead in population, the Southeast and the Southwest are gaining on them. There was the spectacle of the Southeast during the decade 1910 to 1920, in the face of all its migration, gaining nearly three million people —or nearly 16 per cent of the total increase for the nation; and the more extraordinary spectacle of the Southeast gaining the same number of people in 1930 to 1940—but this time the gain was nearly a third of the whole nation's growth.

Yet this seeming contradiction is in character with most of the other contradictory situations and trends in the South. For one thing, it means that the South, retaining the rural character of early America, is nevertheless moving gradually into the boasted maturity of the nation as it becomes more and more predominantly urban. It still remains rural, although increasing its urban population more rapidly than all others, since it started from a predominantly rural base. In the same way the South contributes a greater proportion of its public moneys to education; yet because its wealth is relatively small the amount contributed is absolutely small. Or again the South as preeminently religious still follows the earlier American pattern, so that again it differs from America by holding on to the chief trait of early American culture.

These illustrations are especially important for an understanding of the continuing contradictions in the status and occupation of the southern people. Some of the contrasts may be oversimplified by further illustration.

For instance, so the verdict runs, the South has too many people, yet not enough folk on its economy to give adequacy to its culture.

The farms have too many people, yet not enough farmers and farm youth devoted to the highest type of agriculture.

The South as a whole, it is often stated, has five million too many people, yet the exportation of its folk has constantly kept it poor.

The South should develop its resources and its occupational opportunities to the end that it may use wisely for its wealth nearly all of its people; yet manifestly the nation needs its surplus and the South needs to have its surplus wisely distributed.

The North and West need the South's workers, yet they affirm that workers from the South are far from satisfactory and are often scarcely welcome.

The South's superabundance of human resources is often characterized by the economists and the biologists as one of its greatest liabilities, because of the too many and the not too good!

The nation complains of the poorly educated and trained

workers who come from the South, yet is unwilling to equalize funds for their more nearly equal opportunity.

And so on and on, the characterizations multiply and lead to questions to be asked and answered: What will the South do with all its people—have them migrate, or build an economy to keep them and so to enrich the regional and national culture? If they migrate, where will they go? If they do not move, what will they do at home? Of those who migrate, should the migratory be Negroes? And will there be a national policy to the end that Negroes may be well distributed where they can be well educated and then adequately employed and given equal opportunity? What proportion of Negroes should profit from such a planned population policy, and achieve a better balanced culture as between the two races throughout the nation? Or, once again, will many of the youth of the South at the highest level of education and training continue to assume that their greatest opportunity will naturally be outside the South?

The story of what these southern people do and who they are is reflected in the powerful folk culture of the South, strangely unified in its complex fabric of many weavings. For the South is many Souths, yet, even in its major empires of Southwest and Southeast, one South. And the way of the South has been and is the way of the folk, symbolic of what the people feel, think, and do as they are conditioned by their cultural heritage and the land which Nature has given them. That is, they reflect more of the culture and ways of the folk than they do of the civilization and tempo of organization and technology. The reason for this is that the southern folk culture is deeply bottomed in the realities of Nature and the frontier struggle, in the heritage of multiple migrant people, in the rise and fall of an upper-folk aristocracy, and in a later powerful race and regional conflict. This is an elemental reality definitive of most of the South's culture and economy. The folk society of the South is well-nigh all-inclusive and is reflected on many levels of time and class and in the organic nature of the folk-regional society as definitive of how all societies are formed and grow up.

The elementary sources of this powerful folk society are reflected in a fourfold heritage. There was the growing up of the earlier frontier folk in their struggles with Nature and the Indian alongside the earlier folk culture which was of the vintage of Virginia and the planter aristocracy. Then for a time nearly all of the South consisted of the rural folk with their rugged individualism and their struggle with land and climate, with victory or defeat, of harvest time in their blood. And there were the remnants of frontier folk symbolic of mountain culture or flatwood frustration or swamp and bayou levels of living in the out-of-the-way places throughout the Deep South. And finally there was the powerful folk society of the Negroes themselves as both apart from and a part of the dominant white folk.

The first fruits of this heritage were easily discernible in four levels of folk culture which clearly accounted for the institutions and behavior of all the southern people in their considerable diversity, yet in such essential unity as to be characterized as the South. More accurately the southern folk society was a variegated fabric made from a fourfold pattern: the upper levels of the plantation aristocracy; the upper levels of the middle white South; the lower levels of the disadvantaged whites; and the Negro folk society itself reflecting three levels.

One of the three levels of the Negro folk society was that of the slave level distinguished in any story of universal culture and exerting a powerful influence upon the institutions and behavior of the white South. Another was the white-Negro folk society after freedom, a dual culture that distinguished the South from the rest of the country and symbolized folkways for which men were willing to die. The third was the new Negro folk society separate from and within the state society of the white South. This, again, was a magnificent example of folk culture in the making and showing remarkable vigor and power of survival, because it was of the essence of the folk.

It must be clear, therefore, that the biography of the South is essentially the story of the folk, who must still be defined in sundry ways to portray them not only as the chief actors in the drama, but as even more than this; namely, the very essence of the life-giving qualities of society. The full meaning of the folk, as well as the most common misunderstanding of the nature and survival power of the folk society, must be vividly made clear in any adequate "life of the South." For whereas the common connotation of the folk in the South has been that of the white mountain or flatwood people who retain the remnants of the earlier societal unwritten culture or of the folklore and folksongs of the southern Negroes, among the most powerful folk cultures were those of the aristocratic planter class and the conflicting ideologies of the upper brackets of the white South where always democracy and earned privileges have been the folk motif.

How clear-cut and vivid were the folk conflicts was brilliantly pictured in many places by the lamented Ben Robertson, war casualty of the clipper tragedy at Casablanca in 1943. There was, for instance, the traditional conflict between folk of Charleston and those of the Carolina hills and valleys, sometimes symbolized by the earlier and later episodes of an eloquent John C. Calhoun. In his *Red Hills and Cotton*, this interpreter of the folk insisted that all his kinfolks and their kin "did not live in magnolia groves with tall white columns to hold up the front porches. We did not care for magnolias—they were swampy; and as for the white columns, we considered them pretentious. We did not call our farms plantations in the Upcountry, and we did not call ourselves old Southern planters—we were old Southern farmers. We understand in our country why Walt Whitman liked to sing the names of American rivers, why for apparently no reason at all he listed them one after another. We know what swept Thomas Wolfe when he wrote of the golden Catawba, of the Swannanoa, of the Little Tennessee—it was lightning from his heart . . ."

Symbols of the folk power might be multiplied to show how timeless and resistless are the processes and products of the folk society everywhere, and how specially they are typified in the southern culture on its main levels. Yet again there is a strange thing on this earth, that men forget the realities as soon as they remove themselves afar off in the separateness of machines or wealth, or politics, or intellectualism or blood aristocracy. The urbanite laughs with great gusto at the patriarch of the Wyoming hills who affirms, "New York is all right, but it is so damn far away from any place." Yet that is exactly the essence of his feeling for values. Or the sophisticated urban intellectual looks mighty small and insignificant to the folk of the countryside when he scoffs at the funeral tributes they pay to the beloved dead among them, or when he belittles their religion, their folk music and art, or their substantial enjoyment of the earth things of life.

These are supreme symbols of a reality that lies at the heart of the conservation, development, and planning of the new eras of our culture. And because they are so elementally powerful and necessary, and because they are not understood by most and are forgotten by many, it is of the utmost importance to reexamine and recapture the meaning and role of the folk in both the understanding and the directing of society. In the study of the South many of the elements of the folk culture may be observed and portrayed. It is through their understanding that the South at its best and the nation at its best will synchronize into the more perfect union of intercultural understanding.

More vivid in the understanding of the South, as in that of any society, is the more popular and intimate characterization of the folk; for in the voice of the folk we find not only the aspirations and the arrangements of the people, the universal constant in a world of variables, but the essence of folk loyalty and patriotism to homelands and culture—the struggle and power to seek balance and equilibrium between human living and physical environment, between resources and culture which give distinctive control, character, and survival to each nation. And in the folk is found the very essence of the human spirit and dauntless struggle as symbolized by the individual: the inner supreme worth of the spirit, his love of life, his love itself, in all its powerful romance and realism; his right to work and live for his loved ones, for freedom, for the expression of his inner self which is found in music and art, which is in the search for individualism, for work and play, for self-respect and expression. And for all that, too, the sometimes pitiful trial and error, ignorance and listlessness, crudeness and selfishness, still reflect the folk in their eternal struggle for freedom. The folk live and always will live as irresistible as Nature herself, that knows no defeat, no turning back.

How these definitive concepts of the folk help to understand the South, and how they may be further tested in the analysis of the southern culture, may be illustrated in many ways. One is in the practical distinction between the culture of the rural folk and the civilization of the urban center. That is, some of the institutions and behavior of the southern people do stand in contrast to other levels of intellectual, industrial, technological, and urban civilizations. Whatever else the South may be, it is not essentially and primarily intellectual. And although the census figures register its accelerating trend toward cities, it is as yet still primarily rural. And it still fights the technology of industry and organized labor, of planning and centralization of power.

Another way in which the power of the folk may be illustrated is in the southern folkways of the Negro as definitive of the South's chief dilemma, for the heart of the southern credo was manifest in the central theme—"the Negro is a Negro, and nothing more." It was difficult for many southern leaders to agree that this was the central theme of the southern folkways of race, yet the measure of this appraisal appeared everywhere to be abundant; and because this, together with the power of caste, was at the bottom of the southern culture complex and explained so easily what had happened, it was of the utmost importance that southerners face the plain assumption that they did not appraise the Negro as the same sort of human being as they themselves were. This was no revival of the old southern scriptural argument that the Negro was created to be the hewer of wood and drawer of water— which had long been relegated to a past level of cultural and religious heritage. This central theme, through the tensions of the early 1940's, made articulate something more realistic, that appeared to be organic in the structure and function of the southern culture. If it was true, what evidence was available to indicate that it was true? and, if not, what evidence could be cited?

The catalogue of exhibits is as comprehensive as the name and nature of all the southern folk-culture of race. We may cite one or two. Perhaps the first exhibit submitted, to indicate the fact that the Negro was not human in the same way as the whites, was the almost universal refrain: "The Negro thinks he can act like white folks. Well, he can't do it down here." "These niggers coming back South try to do like white folks, but it don't take us long to put them in their place." "A smart nigger knows better than to try to act like white folks." And here was a common refrain offered by religious youth, defending their appeals for better treatment of the Negro: "I know the Negro is just a Negro and must be kept in his place; but he is just as dear in the sight of God as a white person." Which means that he is entirely different from the white man.

The South professed to be the most Christian and religious of all the regions. In professed Christianity the "fatherhood of God" and the "brotherhood of man" had been basic planks in the total religious platform; preaching at home, missionary .work abroad. "But the Negro, that is different. You don't understand. He is the Negro. No, we can't worship with him, work with him, vote with him, associate with him. Don't you understand? It just isn't done. It just can't be done." Why was southern conduct, then, so contrary to all preaching and principles which, without a peradventure of doubt, were sincere? Why didn't the tenets of fellowship and Christian religion hold here? The only answer was that the Negro did not come within the framework of human brotherhood.

These and other folkways of race must everywhere be appraised as definitive traits of the folk-regional culture of the South which give it distinctive quality, making clear the essential difficulties of national integration. It is first of all, then, a problem of culture, the distinguishing trait of mankind.

Now the sheer reality and power of this situation, in its conditioning of the South and the resulting action, had little to do with what might be right or wrong or what might be in the future or might have been under other circumstances. The facts were as they were, and the deeper and more "organic" the cultural conditioning, the more impossible it was to ignore it as a part of the scientific and humanistic picture. It seemed clear that any student of cultural anthropology or of race or religion might have known that such a culture complex was the product of the long-time process together with the sanctioning of the folkways, to which there were added the stateways and institutions.

Always there were the folkways of politics in the solid South and of religion, the most powerful folkways in the world. And there were the folkways of manners and customs, of food and drink, of clothing and apparel, of housing, and the other traits common to universal culture. For the way of the folk, finally, then is the way of culture. "The past that Southerners are forever talking about is not a dead past—it is a chapter from the legend that our kinfolks have told us, it is a living past for a reason."

In the South there is not only the fundamentalism of the faith once delivered to the fathers in matters of religion but the folk loyalty to the land and the wisdom of the mothers. It is not only in the anchorage of the Tennessee Valley folk to the land and to their traditions. It is as if everywhere the grandmothers were speaking to their grandchildren:

> You tell me that I must forget;
> But I say unto you, you must remember,
> Remember and remember, and what of old you do not
>   know
> Learn and learn and learn, that you may remember,
> For is it not all there for the telling and the learning and
>   the remembering?
> And how can one understand if he does not know and
>   remember?
> As it was told to me by my mother,
> And to her mother and her mother's mother from long
>   ago,
> And to all the mothers of America and to their children
>   and their children's children.
> Those who came seasick and heart-weary to Plymouth,
> Those who came down the valleys whence trailed the
>   forbears of Abraham Lincoln and Jefferson Davis,
> Those who were born and grew up from the blood of
>   the Virginians and the Carolinians,
> Those who were English and Scotch and Irish,
> Those who were Dutch and Welsh and Swedes,
> Those who were Germans and those who were Jews,
> Those who were black mammy-mothers, slave-weary,
>   forgotten women of the new freedom.
> And before them, squaw-women mothers, with the
>   death chant on their lips returning in primitive
>   majesty to their own mother earth.

Learn and remember, for in this story as it has been
    truly told—
If it can be learned and remembered,
If there is insight and wisdom and understanding—
There can be new knowledge of man in Nature,
And men can know what this South is and what is the
    meaning of this much-used and misused word
    "Americanism."
And men may learn the answers to many of the ques-
    tions that perturb a troubled world.

CHAPTER V

The Way of Culture and History

IT MUST be clear by now that this vigorous and lusty South that was growing up in the way of Nature and the frontier, of race and the folk, could be understood only through a knowledge of the way of all culture as it develops from the earlier folk stages on through various maturing levels until it flowers in civilization. For this thing we call culture is the heart of human society and is the sum total of all the processes and products of a given people and their society at any given time and region in which they grow up and expand into wider areas and more complex relationships. Culture does not grow up overnight, neither is it changed in the twinkling of an eye.

What personality is to the individual, culture is to society. As the supreme character of human society, culture not only is what men die for, but is the product of all that for which they have lived and died, constituting also, therefore, the rich heritage of the past. Culture, moreover, is of and by all the groups, wherever found, whether dominating or not, so that the total culture of a people is interwoven into a fabric made up of variegated threads of folk culture that have been neglected in the attempt to document and to describe society of the past.

This is particularly true of the South. For both the historian and the popular writer have been accustomed to making the culture of the South coincide with the limited romantic Old South and its plantation economy which was dominant in the halls of the nation and in international relations. Yet that was only a part of the culture of the South, even on its philosophy and policy-making level, for the Jeffersonian emphasis upon the individual's personality and rights was quite consistent with the Jacksonian rugged democracy of the frontier. But, more than this, culture in the South, as everywhere, is the rich process of total living and experience even more than the formally recorded product of history and politics. The intensity and quality of culture, like a man's character and personality, dominate life and behavior and make up the very essence and drama of living society. Culture may very well be the Santayana "public experience . . . the stars, the seasons, the swarm of animals, the spectacle of birth and death, of cities and wars . . . the facts before every man's eyes." Many of these, the documentary historian cannot see. Nor does he always get the Carl Sandburg sensing that

> The people is every man, everybody,
> Everybody is you and me and all others.
> What everybody says is what we all say.

And applied further, what everybody feels is what we all feel, and what everybody does is what we all do. What we all do reflects the individual and group behavior which is culture.

Culture is of the mass behavior, yet also of the individual. It is of the individual, yet also, and more, of the institutions which come nearer than anything else reflecting the total culture and measuring the orderliness of a society. Culture is more than civilization. Total culture comprehends but is different from civilization, which represents specialization in the upper brackets of certain types of achievement. And especially the folk society, which is culture, is different from the totalitarian state society, which is civilization.

All of this is of the greatest importance in the understanding of the South, its varied folk societies, its institutional character and personality, and its traditional modes of behavior; for, within the fourfold pattern of southern folk culture there had grown up strong institutions, deeply bottomed in the culture of the old aristocratic South, the old frontier South, and the

later South of the upper and lower brackets of white folk
strongly conditioned by the black South of cultural tradition
and of postwar change.

In order to sense the essential importance of all this, it is
only necessary to recapture the power of Nature and the folk
in the conditioned culture of the South, to look briefly at the
analysis of southern culture and institutions in their background heritage, and to trace the stream of American history
with its southern foundations and permeating influence in all
the other regions. And always there is the ever present reality
that the biography of the South is first of all an American
story, for, as Lewis Mumford puts it, "American culture had
its roots in the folk and emanated from their fresh experiences
in a new land." And these folk, contributing to "our rich cultural compost" included Indians, Negroes, Moravians, Puritans, Shakers, farmers, merchants, miners, lumbermen,
cowboys, capital, labor, North, South, East, West, and all the
places between.

Within all these diversified groups there are, however, certain elemental factors and processes in which all cultures are
alike bottomed, and through which all societies can be basi-
cally explained. These elements include behavior on the levels
of race, sex, religion, war work, rural life, and art; they include
diet, dress, houses, play, humor, ceremony. When we have
ascertained the relationships between them and culture, and
when we have sensed the nature, range, and power of the
folkways and mores which grow inevitably out of this experience, we have gone a long way toward understanding any
early society.

When, therefore, this experience has ripened into matured
institutions, we have the explanation of the enduring nature of
culture. The main institutions which grow out of the maturing
mores and morals of society cluster around the family, religion,
education, government, work, and personal association, which
in their modern maturity take form in the home, the school,

the church, the state, industry, the community. These give stability and order to a culture with increasingly the state expanding more and more in its services and its covenants to the people.

Now, in order to sense the culture of the South as dominant in still other powerful ways, it is only necessary to apply the sanctions of these institutions to problems and to note the application of the folkways of race, of religion, of sex, of work, living habits, and ideals. Respect for the culture of a people is not based necessarily upon values or esteem so much as upon the knowledge of how it has grown, and of how the people esteem it. So, too, the powerful control of the folk culture is cited, not to indicate that it cannot be changed, but to illustrate the organic and time quality of culture itself. Contrariwise, however, in the newer demands for social planning are found the basis for change through what we may call the *techniways,* which, as ways of meeting needs and surviving in the modern technological order, transcend the older folkways and the mores. Yet the essential facts here are that any planning which is to be enduring must provide for balancing nature and culture, resources and the people, in such harmonious adjustment as will insure survival as well as achievement. It is precisely in the understanding of culture traits that the best ways of balancing the people and their culture with resources and technology may be found.

We have already illustrated the power of the *folkways of race;* yet a more specific example of how the major institutions function may well be needed to illuminate the essential cultural problem involved. There was, for instance, the case of a southern youth on a visit to the nation's capital on a field trip sponsored by the high-school course in civics. This particular youth was head of his class, captain of the football team, high up in Hi-Y and Sunday-school work and was rated as the top citizen of his class. Yet he found himself in the hands of "the Law," arrested by Washington police on a charge so flagrant and easily proved that there could be no doubt of his guilt. The boy had attacked a Negro for what appeared to him to be undue association with white women and for the violation of segregation rules as well as the whole system of mores he had inherited. Furthermore, every institution—the school, the church, the home—the community, the laws of the state, and the practice of industry had not only sanctioned but taught and enforced segregation. Here then was conflict of cultures which alone could explain why that which was "good" was "bad" and that which was "bad" was "good."

The sociological importance of race and ethnic groups is not in the fact that the people in America are of varying physical make-up, but in the fact that each folk-group represents a different set of folkways and customs. Wherever different racial stocks come together in society, economic, political, and social strife results. This is the process of cultural development and of the folk society. Where race is involved the cultural traits are more deeply entrenched and more powerful. The new concept of race held by the sociologists, psychologists, and anthropologists removes much of the false belief in mental and physical inequalities inherent in certain racial stocks. The assumption that there are no inherent race differences, and therefore no superior or inferior races, should aid in the formation of a new and valid theory and make possible successful plans for ameliorating many of the problems of conflict.

The southern culture was also *strong in the institutional power of the family*. The family was supreme, with some of its frontier heritage of patriarchal power still surviving and reflected in various forms of paternalism in matters of race and industry. The sanctity of the man-woman relationship in marriage and the frontier pattern of "justice" were reflected in the jury verdicts of acquittal for homicide on the basis of the

invasion of the home. The pattern was even much more powerfully enforced in any case where Negro men and white
women were involved. The caste system here was inexorable,
and the very mention of change was a matter for death. Yet
the plantation slave-master relationship had so relaxed the
sex and family relationship between white men and Negro
women that the pattern of intermixture lasted long after the
end of slavery, although its sanction was soon relegated to
the past.

In the culture of the South, the role of woman was distinctive. Something of this will appear in our later picture of the
Old South. Yet, once again, the story of southern women is,
first of all, a part of the American story and must be told in the
perspective of the total picture. This is true both for the
purpose of understanding the heritage of the South and for
that of noting its distinctive culture in this area in contradistinction to much of the rest of the nation. In this way only
can the many contradictions of the southern culture be explained. There was, for instance, the South with its chivalric
attitude toward women and leisure having the largest ratio
of women working in the fields and, with its classical concept
of cultural education, establishing the first colleges for industrial and practical training of women.

As a matter of fact, in the story of women in America, we
again find an admirable example of the normal development
of a new society on the frontier of a new environment. Professor Ernest R. Groves has pointed out that the Old World patterns of the patriarchal family were broken in the struggle to
colonize the Atlantic coastal areas, but that, with the first
promise of a more stable and fixed society and an accumulated
margin of comfort, the people returned to the older cultural
standards and fashions which they had known in their native
European cultural groups. With the return of the old, however, there were new conceptions as to the role of woman in
society, conceptions that had been formed out of the efforts

for survival and adaptation to a peculiar regional environment and out of the gradual changing of folk attitudes.

In colonial days the role of the woman in New England was in strong contrast to that of the woman of the plantation South. In both cultural groups, woman had little function other than that of family propagation, household duties, and social embellishment. The intellectual freedom of women was determined largely by the economic and social classes in which they found themselves. Tradition has it that in the southern aristocracy women were cherished social ornaments; yet we know of the ceaseless round of household and plantation duties of the "mistress," the large families to be cared for, and the superficial definition of gentility which demanded that the woman be accomplished in the arts and literature. In New England the wives and the daughters of the wealthier merchants and of the professional classes enjoyed greater freedom of activity and expression, although they were limited by puritanical ideas of conduct.

The Civil War brought the woman's movement to its full impetus outside the South. Women nurses and doctors became acceptable, and greater numbers of women were welcomed into industry and the field of education. In 1890, smaller women's suffrage associations were united to form a national organization. Whereas there was a union in the East for the attainment of suffrage rights, as early as 1869 Wyoming had granted its women the vote. The West also led the way in the educational field. Oberlin College, admitting women in 1833, set the pattern for coeducation, a pattern soon adopted by Antioch College, the University of Iowa, and Chicago University.

Yet this had relatively little effect in the South. There, the tradition of the plantation and the gentleman held that woman's place was in the home and church and the field of the social graces, and the tradition of the common folk provided for woman's part in rural life and in the patriarchal, paternalistic type of family. The campaign for the new Woman Suffrage Amendment following the First World War found many of the southern states adamant against it, and the cultural tradition led what appeared to be a majority of the women to oppose or be indifferent to it. There was clearly a southern culture in which woman in ideals, literature, and concept was placed on the highest possible pedestal, symbolic of romance at its best. There was, by the same token, on the same level the culture which refused woman the minimum of rights and privileges under the banner of democratic, equal opportunity. This is not to appraise the culture as good or bad, but to explain it.

By the transfer of the tradition to the ideology of the common folks, only Negro women were to do domestic work; and there grew up the southern domestic economy in which white women assumed an inherited right to servants, paid at nominal rates, and thankful for the privilege of serving the white folks. All of this is of the greatest importance in understanding the race conflicts that were to arise in later years. For the historical and cultural backgrounds gave rise to powerful folkways in both races reflecting a part of the caste-sex conflict: the long, long inner conflict between Negro women and white women, and the revolt of the Negro woman against being placed at the bottom of the ladder of southern personalities. For here again was another gross contradiction. The southern white woman was at the top of all chivalric patterns; Negro woman was at the bottom. This again is explained by the southern folkways that the Negro was just a Negro.

So important was this conditioning of the southern culture that its understanding is necessary to the interpretation of much of the individual and community behavior of white women in all the brackets of southern culture. And here, too, are to be explained many of the standards of work, of housekeeping, of wages, and hours as well as the southern women's relative lack of interest in community problems or artistic and literary activities. Here, in the whole cyclorama of southern culture was to be found much of "the grandeur that was not," as well as "the glory that was." The standards of behavior here, and the contradictions in morals, were to permeate the whole body-culture including the area of religion, where the fatherhood of God and the brotherhood of man reflected no realism where the Negro was concerned.

Again, in southern culture *the role of religion* has been large; yet this was true of all early America and especially of New England, which set the standards of much of American culture in the upper brackets of literature and worship. It is a strange thing that so many Americans have forgot the powerful influence of religion and the folkways of observance which have grown up around it. In the biography of man, both the individual and the group, religion appears early. It would be difficult to understand human society without knowing the role of religion in its development. It may well be true, therefore, that next to the culture itself religion affords as nearly a universal approach to the cataloguing of the elements of society as almost any other societal phenomenon or trait. Certainly, religion appears to be universal among all peoples. Religion has conditioned nearly all aspects of social development. It has conditioned the cultural patterns of early peoples, and it has fixed the fundamental mores and behavior of the moderns. Moreover, it has generally been assumed that the most powerful of all the folkways and mores have been those based upon religious sanction. Yet, even as the gods of the different nations have all been distinctively native to the cultures of the peoples, so religion and religions, the cultural force and later institutional church, have been not only the constant molders of behavior but the creators and interpreters of varying cultures.

The way of religion in the South was for the most part the way of all the nation in its earlier days. America was founded on the religious note. All earlier documents and even letters began with the symbolic salutation, "In the name of God, amen"; all laws, constitutions, and covenants were made in the name of God. Strong Puritan New England culture grew up from religious foundations; early American institutions of learning were based on religion; federal constitution, state constitutions, important documents of state, inaugural addresses of the Presidents, and procedures in the swearing in of officers, all reflect the religious basis upon which American culture was founded. Standard oaths in many of the states are still taken with the Bible as a tangible witness, while some state universities still present a copy of the Bible to their graduates. In fact, religion is an index of American cultural life today even as it was in the earlier colonial and statehood days of the people. The most powerful of all folkways and mores, Christianity has played a far-reaching and effectual role throughout the growth and development of our national institutions.

Desire for escape from religious persecution, and dreams of a group life more nearly realizing Old World Christian or Protestant ideals, seem to have been foremost in the hearts and minds of the earlier settlers of Virginia, Pennsylvania, Maryland, Massachusettes, and Rhode Island. As New England Puritan, Pilgrim, Quaker, or nonconformist, the migrant folk translated their religious beliefs into concepts for their social patterns. When the years saw full settlement along the Atlantic seaboard, religion again became one of the primary forces in extending the new civilization across the Appalachians into the great West. In the vast middle western region the Mormons, fleeing from oppression and intolerance and in search of Zion, led the way across the plains. The Millerites, the Zoarites, and the Amanans also played their parts in opening up the frontier areas beyond the Mississippi. Most importantly, wherever the fundamentalism of the East came into contact with the fresh spirit of the frontier, new life was engendered into belief, and freedom from artificiality was welcomed. The role of religion in the settlement of the nation and in the fostering of educational institutions, art, and literature of the various periods has been fairly generally recognized; but few people have comprehended the psychic structure with which religion in the past and in the present day has supported all institutional growth.

Another universal trait of early culture was its *ruralism*. The South has been and is still largely rural, either in reality or in symbol and heritage. So was all America in the earlier cultural foundations. This is of great importance in the understanding of the nation. A part of the picture has been given in the story of the South's frontier heritage. The case for rural life as an elementary factor in cultural development has a threefold basis. First, it is well-nigh a universal matrix of all societies. Secondly, it reflects the physical environment of all societies. It is essentially the natural society, both in genesis and development and in closeness to nature. In the third place, it represents the bottoming of society in the primary occupations, from which man started his long occupational adventure.

We cannot, therefore, understand society, either of the past or of the present, without interpreting the role of rural life in the whole societal process and history of the human race. Sometimes, the understanding is important because of the contrast between the earlier rural and natural and the later urban and technical. Sometimes it is important to understand the basic, elemental factors that are inherent in rural life, in order to note their absence from later societies. And, by the same token, the societal problems of adjustment in the transition from the rural to the urban constitute important fields of inquiry.

If in the modern world again the dominant societal process often seems to be one of urbanization, what is the relation of the rural society to the total culture? The trend seems to be towards a megalopolitan culture, a super-city, a world of concentration of people and behavior. On the other hand, if the beginnings of all cultures were rural, is this rural element—which was probably a natural stage in the evolution of society—an essential element, or is it merely a stage of development? Or, again, if urbanization is synonymous with decay in socie-, ties, and if urbanization is not prolific in population, is the rural therefore an elemental, basic, and natural prerequisite for survival?

In some ways we may think of rural life as the synonym of the natural human society in that the physical basis of rural life, in its earth and plant and animal life, constitutes the geographic environment of all societies. Even the great cities are enmeshed within great rural hinterlands. And, in the evolutionary process, being close to nature, working with nature, mastering the physical environment have always gone hand in hand with the development of cultures, whether in economic, religious, or other aspects.

This rural symbol of life has been epitomized in a thousand ways, but perhaps in none more than in the glorification of the land as the chief reality of life and location. Yet in the southern heritage the story of the land is again one of contradiction. There was the very abundance of lands that set the incidence for the building of plantations and estates and for the pioneering on ever new frontiers, West and South. Yet the greater cultural tradition of the South has been one of exploitation of the land and its resources. Great pine forests which in later years would have reflected astronomical values in dollars and cents were sold for fifty cents an acre and wasted beyond the measure of the needs of the region. And the erosion of soil has been so great that the South has become symbolic of wasted lands. And, finally, the exploitation of the land with the one-crop system of cotton and tobacco did more than anything else to fix the nature of the South's culture and economy.

Another elemental fact in the development of culture is the *basic process of work*, from which develop not only types of industry and agriculture but, in later levels, types of invention, technology, and art, and subsequently the social aspects of organized labor and capital. In the southern United States there are powerful contradictions and great variations from the rest of the nation that can be understood only by relating them to the total cultural fabric. Yet the southern culture rests upon both the universal heritage and the national frontier folkways and cultural development, from which then the South has deviated in certain important ways. In particular, there were two major developments which conditioned the South's economy and standards of work. One was the effect of the Negro upon the attitudes and standards of work, and the other was the paternalistic pattern of industry and antagonism to organized labor. Both were clearly the product of the two main southern currents; namely, the plantation economy and individualism, which was characteristic of all early America.

Now the South inherited and built heavily upon the doctrine of work. If a man would not work, neither should he eat. This was a fundamental doctrine of the southern folk, such that the shiftless people who came to be called poor whites were the very symbol of that which ought not to be; and idleness and shiftlessness were everywhere the opposite of what was admonished. Yet the South came to have the lowest standard of work, the least industrious of all people, and this lack of industry and thrift extended in the period after the Civil War all the way up to the remnants of the planter class.

In the culture of the planter aristocracy it was bad form to do what Negroes should do, and Negroes were trained and classified through division of labor to do well everything in the field of manual labor. The families of the white upper brackets were not trained or habituated to work, and never overcame that handicap even in the days of necessity, although there were millions of individual cases immediately after the war to illustrate a noble application to work.

This pattern of having the Negro do the essential work set the standard and attitude for the whites in all other brackets to some extent, although again thousands of notable exceptions prove the rule. The extent to which this was all true may be seen from the further historical records of planter and slave and poorer whites. For the present it is enough to record what it has done in conditioning the South even up to now and especially in characterizing the South and its culture to the folk of other regions.

The other major field in which the southern culture is affected by work is the prevailing mode or attitude usually described as paternalistic. This, too, is usually attributed to the plantation pattern, later transferred to the field of industry, in which leaders built the cotton-mill villages, equipped them with what they believed was needed, assumed the personal relationship to labor, and by the same token felt that there was no need for organization of labor. This attitude, however, was also the product of the way in which mills were built and labor recruited. That is, the movement to build cotton mills in order to give employment to rural and village folk in the South was, in a way, patriotic and religious, and workers were thought fortunate to be recipients of such benefaction. Here was developed a new class whose work was considered to be below the level of the farmer or the middle-class townsman. There was another elemental factor in the outside agitation by labor leaders, which then fell into the southern folk-ways against northern criticism or coercion. In all these instances the facts are the same; namely, they constitute a logical and powerful background of southern culture in this area.

Much of this and its measuring indices of the South could be illustrated by the formula of the noted regionalist and planner, Patrick Geddes, in which place-folk-work was offered as a basic combination for all needs. That is, the folk working in its own region would determine the nature of its culture; or the kind of work a folk did for and to the place where it lived would determine the character of its culture. Such a formula might well be utilized to characterize southern culture in nearly all of its main aspects.

If again in our search for the understanding of society we seek some universal measure or trait which will help us to trace the development of society from its earlier folk culture through to the later stages of civilization, we may turn to that which we call "art." By "art" we understand not only the application of skill, training, and procedure to certain of the aesthetic fields—such as the making of pottery, the painting of pictures, the writing of poetry, the development of music, the singing of songs, the rhythm of dancing—but the whole range of artifacts, which represent trial and error, training, skill, and experiment toward specialized ends, which have reflected the history of culture from primitive time up to now.

Among the universal elements of the folk art are the love of beauty and the primal folk music which "tells us the deepest truths of human life" and becomes "the one perfect medium for this dream of humanity." It applies to the individual and the mass and is the nearest of all universal appeals to the folk soul. So, too, the elemental folk dances and folk drama, handicrafts and pottery, and play and games in which power is manifest in both the passion for creative expression and social usage. Yet there is the other great attribute of art, including aesthetics and music, in which it is universally accorded the highest achievement of civilization. The city, wealth and leisure, intellectualism and science, all are partly defined in terms of their capacity to encourage and produce art at its highest level. Art and civilization have always been synonymous.

In the biography of the South a large portion must be devoted to the folk art, *and not so much to the art of civiliza-*

tion. In the story of the South as it has developed through the years, we shall therefore devote a chapter in Part II to folk song and music. The reason for the lag in the South between folk art and formal art is as self-evident from the story of the southern culture as are the other traits already enumerated.

Enough has been said to indicate the powerful role of the cultural heritage in the behavior of the people, and in particular to show how the way of the South is essentially the way of culture. Many other aspects might be cited, such as the role of *war* in culture, the great body of general folkways of the South in matters of *dress, housing, food, recreation, worship,* and the many variations due to regional differences and to conflict with other regional cultures. One other, however, will perhaps be more than adequate for a final illustration of certain distinctiveness of the southern culture.

This illustration also is bottomed in certain *demonstrable traits of culture in contrast to civilization.* It has often been said that the South was less civilized than the North and East of the nation. Such a characterization is important both for understanding the South and for measuring its potentialities. The truth is that civilization is a very specialized product or stage of culture fabricated from five basic elements; namely, *urbanism, industrialism and technology, intellectualism and scientific humanism, centralization of power, and the totalitarian state*—the last of which is a flowering of the one before it. On this assumption the folk culture of the South is often quite distinctive from the civilization of the metropolitan-industrial-urban regions. And whatever the southern culture has been, it has not been so essentially "intellectual" as it has been "folk," and its general folk culture traits have been more marked than its science and technology.

Finally, it remains to emphasize the importance of *historical records* and of factual accuracy in the portrayal of southern culture. It is not a part of this story of the way of the South to feature documented history. Yet we must insist on the checking of what was true in each period and area of cultural development.

In the biography of a region the more intimate observations and explanation of the folk culture help us, in the words of Carl Sandburg, to sense "the feel and atmosphere, the layout and the lingo of the region, of breeds of men, of customs and slogans, in a manner and air not given in regular history." Yet, to sense the stream flow of events, we need not only the cultural approach to history, but also and finally the historian's account of what has gone into the making of each regional culture and, by the same token, of the total national culture. Even though, in the past, much of our history may have been deficient in the first-hand knowledge of people and regions, more recent history, often vividly and brilliantly written, with adequate, scholarly documentation, not only beckons to those who would know more but provides the authentic formal picture of the folk culture backgrounds so essential to understanding.

The life of the South has been rich in experiences and episodes about which have centered strong emotions and differences of opinion. Yet about the main facts of its birth and its growing up there can be no doubt, for history has recorded the dates and many of the circumstances, so that, like the universal cultural evolution of the region, its history constitutes the essential reality which makes the way of the South the way of history. It might have been different under different circumstances. The South might have chosen to make it different. The nation, living its history over again, even as the South, would never introduce slavery. Yet that which is written is written, and the way of the South is the way of history. That which was done was done, and cannot now be changed; and the understanding of what was done is essential to the understanding of the South and the nation. There is needed, moreover, knowledge not only of whether this or that event happened; whether these or other facts were true in the total historical record.

Most of the history of the South is no more or less logical than the history of the rest of the nation; it has simply been revivified and interpreted in such partial and partisan manner as to make it appear a thing apart. The truth is that the way of the South has been the way of America, and that southern history has constituted an integral part of American history. Thus, the way of the South, as the way of culture, has also been the way of history and the way of America. The story of the distinctive character of the American South becomes then the main feature of later development, rather than its historical and cultural backgrounds. Yet knowledge of the earlier story of the South is essential to understanding the later South, even as was Bradford's story of early America, about which it was said that "not many Americans will gaze upon it without a little trembling of the lips and a little gathering of mists in the eyes, as they think of the story of suffering, of sorrow, of peril, of exile, of death, and of lofty triumph."

PART II

Through the Succession of Years

CHAPTER VI

The Old South Fades into the New

So CAME the South to early twentieth century America. So grew the southern states that their composition and tradition were peculiarly national, yet symbolic of both the American traits of resemblances and differences in the same region. The South of the new era was essentially a new testing ground for America. It was of the past, but more essentially of the present and future. But it was first of all an American region. For the South of the early twentieth century was still many Souths made up of varying groups.

There were remnants and representations of the aristocratic and plantation South.

There were the great majority of southerners, composed of middle folk and common man.

There were remnants of the old failures and stragglers and of the extreme fringe of poor whites in everyday places of every state.

There were flatwood and sand-hill folk, middle state and eastern coast group.

Sojourners in the piny woods.

Sturdy stock of yet varying types in mountain and Piedmont.

Hosts of mill-village folks and white tenant farmers.

Negroes from farm and Black Belt, tenants and laborers.

The general Negro common man in town and country, worker and farm owner.

The more educated and cultured Negro in professional life, or wherever he could find his way.

Indians in Alabama, Arkansas, Florida, Georgia, Kentucky, Louisiana, Mississippi, North Carolina, Oklahoma.

91

Urban and rural contrasts, agricultural, industrial, and
commercial groupings.

Northerners and westerners come South, part remnants
and issue from reconstruction days, part leaders and
progressives developing southern resources, contributing to southern progress and leadership.

Southern states abounding in classes and groups.

Yet in their lives, vicissitudes, and environmental settings
were also visible the social elements commonly found in the
architecture of other cultures, whether in the earlier frontiers
of America, in the development of western civilization in
general, or in concrete examples of special regional cultures.
There were present to a remarkable degree the elementary
forces whose blending creates new cultures and challenges
human vitality, tested in a social crucible white-hot with the
stirrings of physical power, emotional conflict, and intellectual
striving. There was a heritage, on the one side, of maturity,
experience, prestige, glory, and aristocracy; and, on the other,
of primitive folk-stock and fresh blood, roughhewn pillars
and strong foundation fabric for some noble superstructure.
There were youth and strength and temper. There were
ability, temperament, and genius. There were trial and error,
successes and failures; and again failures and successes. There
were time and unforeseen resistless incidence. There were
social conflict and revolution, fire and sword, death and exile.
There were old and new epochs witnessing the rise and fall
of new leaders and followers. And there was the flowing
stream of social processes, now suddenly shallow and sluggish, now bursting forth in full volume and power.

So came the generations of southern Americans whose
changing cultures provided the most dramatic episodes in
American history and comprehended every known element
in the architecture of modern civilization. For here were
peculiarly reflected collective pictures descriptive of American reality, rich in power, range, and contrast, shaped and

proportioned by strong backgrounds whose unfolding episodes quivered of life. Here were epic and romantic materials
of history and literature alongside measurable elements for
the scientific study of human society. Here were illuminating materials for the better understanding of American life
through the study of regional situations and folk society. Their
consistency was often in their contradictions, their unity in
their diversity, like some masterpiece of orchestral harmony.
Or, like some unfolding evolution of social culture or some
masterpiece of narrative, charm and power were revealed
only through dramatic unfolding, episode upon episode, year
upon year. Here was a civilization slowly gathering together
its processes and patterns until the magnitude of the whole
had been fashioned, and yet whose power and brilliance were
cumulative, residing unescapably in separate units, but also,
and more, in the high potentiality of the final unity.

So came an American Epoch that was the South. An era had
ended. An era had begun. Old golden pages of history, shining parchment records of culture, then yellow and faded,
scorched and seared with years of embattled conflict, and
epic struggle . . . Gallant figures on black horses and white
. . . and crude, simple folk, sore with the footfall of time,
passing across an epoch which was to be destroyed by physical
and cultural conflagration and to rise up again in another
American Epoch strangely different and vivid and powerful.
Cultures in the making, social processes at work, portraiture
descriptive of how civilizations grow. All the South's yester-
days, with their brilliant episodes and with their sordid pictures receding, giving way to the South's tomorrows, through
a sweeping American development reminiscent of universal
culture.

Both the old and the new culture abounded in sharp contrasts and logical paradoxes. There were many Souths, yet *the*
South. It was preeminently national in backgrounds, yet provincial in its processes. There were remnants of European cul-

ture framed in intolerant Americanism. There were romance, beauty, glamour, gayety, comedy, gentleness, and there were sordidness, ugliness, dullness, sorrow, tragedy, cruelty. There were wealth, culture, education, generosity, chivalry, manners, courage, nobility, and there were poverty, crudeness, ignorance, narrowness, brutality, cowardice, depravity. The South was American and un-American, righteous and wicked, Christian and barbaric. It was a South getting better, a South getting worse. It was strong and it was weak, it was white and it was black, it was rich and it was poor. There were great white mansions on hilltops among the trees, and there were unpainted houses perched on pillars along hillside gullies or lowland marches. From high estate came low attainment, and from the dark places came flashing gleams of noble personality. There were strong men and women vibrant with the spontaneity of living, and there were pale, tired folk, full of the dullness of life. There were crusaders resplendent with some perpetual equivalent of war, and there were lovers of peace in the market place. There were freshness and vivacity as of a rippling green-white rivulet, and there were depth and hidden power as of gleaming dark water beneath an arched bridge. There were sluggish streams, slimy as of accumulated filth and there were bitter bayous as of poisoned waters. And there were streams of limitless power flowing down through the hills and valleys, of impotency and waste.

The first third of the twentieth century revealed pictures of this paradoxical, rapidly developing, eager, and puzzled South taking stock of itself and its role in the changing nation. Here were regions comprising a third of the nation's area and people, yet reflecting a far smaller ratio of participation in many aspects of the national life, with some indication of a still decreasing ratio. There was a background of the original South, which had begun as the most American part of the nation. It had long been the dominant power, and it had contributed major portions of early political and social culture.

There was another background of war and reconstruction and broken chain, and still another of reconciliation and the New South with its phenomenal recovery. This same South had now grown big with almost unlimited resources, yet was face to face with the consciousness of a growing provincialism in its culture somewhat out of proportion to its proper regional distinctiveness. And the new literary and scientific realism had made the South restless with the presumption that the rest of the world might be leaving the South behind, and that the measure of its economic and social waste might be greater than the measure of its resources and their utilization.

And the rest of the nation was also taking stock of the South and its role in the changing nation. In many ways the North was generous and sympathetic, eager to please the South and help weave its fabric into the larger epoch; but it often failed to understand the social and cultural backgrounds or the magnitude of the problem. On the one hand, there was a revival of interest in the Old South and its culture; and, on the other, there was a revival of the old bitter criticism and denunciations. There was a keen interest in the newer vigorous and realistic contributions of the South to the nation's stock of creative effort and experience, and there was protest against its backwardness. Romantic pictures of the Old South were much in demand; realistic pictures and interpretations of the New South brought enthusiastic recognition; but still the South was "different" and apart. In both North and South, and in Europe, the old pictures, silhouetted against the new, were sought, partly because of new literary and artistic currents, and partly because of vigorous inquiring into a modern culture being fabricated in the crucibles of science, humanism, and religion. Nevertheless the white light of national criticism was focused chiefly upon certain southern patterns of race, of religion, of industry, and of politics. The South was again missionary territory, backward province, and lawless section. There were, therefore, pictures of the South not only in

intellectual and emotional tension because of its own problems of culture and development, but troubled because of the
sweep of its outside critics and saviors and some widening
distances between "the South" and "the North." Why, asked
the South, couldn't the North join hands in working out the
southern-national economy without losing its patience and
insisting on reforming the South overnight? And why, urged
the North, couldn't the South stop losing its temper and cease
to be the "sensitive South"? Was the whole drama of misunderstanding and emotions to be enacted again? But the
South with all its efforts and earnestness did not or would not
know itself. And it was hurt, impatient, and bitter against
those who came from without to coerce or to reform, mani-
festing little of its traditional chivalry and hospitality toward
them. And pictures from the North reflected even less knowledge of the South, and little more patience and sense of humor.
The North seemed unable to view the peculiarities of the
South as it did those of the rest of the country or of Europe.
The South felt that, no matter what normal limitations and
errors it reflected, the verdict was always the same—they were
"southern" manifestations. And it was too often using up its
energies in protest rather than in development of its powers.
If only the South would see itself and laugh! and work! If
only it would add to pride humility, to humility humor, to
humor zeal, to zeal knowledge! If only it would *look at* its
problems instead of *feeling about* them! If, too, the North
would see itself and laugh, and laugh with the South! Or if
it would only study the building of cultures and understand
how civilizations grow! And if only it would add to criticism
fellowship, to fellowship sympathy, to sympathy knowledge!
If the North and South would only learn something from the
pictures of the past!

So came the challenge to critics, North and South, in
America and Europe, who saw the South capable of contributing powerfully to the greater American epoch of the twentieth
century. Whatever contributions the South had made, what-

ever forms and patterns had evolved in the past, had grown out of realities, now springing from soil rich in romance and large undertaking, or from poverty and hardships, now sinking back into the sources from which they came. These sources remained in perpetuity and awaited the full development of a well balanced civilization. To the pictures of the Old South and the New South, therefore, must be added still other pictures of a South of the New American Epoch yet to be built. And whatever the distances backward or forward, the measures of resurrection or resurgence or of new trail-blazing were to be found in the vigor of the commonplace, in the power of new biological and cultural combinations, in the social potentiality of these generations of southerners, and in the happy blending of these elements with the other essential elements of the nation and of the times.

In characteristic pictures of the nation there were many factors of the new technique which gave promise of bridging much of this distance of time and cultures. And yet there were unmistakable signs of widening distances. It was one of the most interesting of the cultural phenomena in America and one of its most important problems. Here again paradox and exception appeared to prove the rule. The very fact that the North and the South were being brought closer together and becoming more intimately acquainted with each other gave rise both to better understanding and to misunderstandings. Old conditions in the South, even those greatly improved, when viewed for the first time by thousands of citizens from other parts of the nation, were considered by them as new and acclaimed as objectionable. Criticism thus threw the South back anew on its old defense attitudes.

Again, interstate commerce and communication, the extension of industry and the development of many uniform standards of economic and social life throughout the nation made it impossible for the South longer to remain in isolation, a region unto itself. It had to go forward with the rest of the

world, or continue as a region of markedly arrested development. The movement of industry South and the migration of
Negroes North were factors which challenged new readjust-
ments. The influx of thousands of tourists to the South and
the investment by northerners in southern properties constituted another factor. Increased philanthropy in the North,
more leisure time, larger endowments for research and social
exploration, a growing social consciousness, together with the
improved facilities for travel and the conflict-episodes in
labor, race, and religion, brought the South into a new spot-
light. And the South was inviting cooperative forces from
without to join it in working out its new social economy.

The South, much of it, was also getting acquainted with
much of the North which it had never known. Southerners
were going North; northern students were coming South.
Adventurers of many kinds found the slogan, "Go South,
young man," tempting. It was virgin territory for reform and
adventure in a nation seeking new adventures. Both South
and North often judged issues on the basis of exceptional
evidence. Some of the intelligentsia of the North were inclined to appraise all phenomena of other regions in terms
of their own restless and all-too-standardized criteria, while
the South was equally militant in proclaiming its own standards as supreme and without fault. On the other hand, the
South's rapid progress in all phases of life, its close relationship with the rest of the country, and its increasing participation in all aspects of American life brought it face to face with
the fact that it was competing at last, not merely with southern
situations but with national as well, and that its standards
must forever henceforth be those of the rest of the world.

And so, in the midst of its successes and its failures, the
South was still a little boastful about its progress and a little
sensitive about its shortcomings. The picture was one of a
South which experienced great difficulty in attacking its
problems and its work without the ever present consciousness that they were southern. And the rest of the nation

seemed incapable of judging anything in the South aside from its southern aspects. If a thing was done in the South, whether good or bad, it was southern rather than national— a book, a school, an industry, a strike, a mob. And if southern it was *prima facie* below standard, with no distinction made between the temporary products of a regional culture and a permanent capacity for achievement under different environ-ment. And, paradox again, there was a certain subconscious feeling throughout the nation that somewhere, somehow in the southern order there were backgrounds and possibilities for superior culture and ways of living; and a certain good will, a certain yearning for the South, and, paradox again, a certain tinge of jealousy and fear of what southern culture might bring with it.

What neither the nation nor the South seemed to compre-hend in a practical way was the simple fact that the key to the whole situation was found in the fact that it was all a normal problem of social culture, essentially an American problem, and secondarily a southern problem. The South was different, and it should be different. But it was the normal difference of an important region of a great nation, and should not continue to develop a sectional difference as of one sec-tion over against another. It was the southern region, but a region within the nation. It was the South, but it was the American South of the United States. What the South did and how it developed were therefore important to the South, but far more important to the nation.

There were possible contrasting pictures of the future. The South could develop a peculiar civilization bounded by the mechanical geographical lines of the old political Confeder-acy; or it could develop a powerful regional culture growing out of normal geographical and cultural conditions which transcended mere state boundaries, and gain strength from its normal regional advantages, merged into the national pic-ture. Thus southern culture or southern portraiture, like that of the Middle West or the mountain region or the Pacific coast, would have its setting in the national picture. Viewed from this vantage point, the nation would cooperate with the South in the new architecture of its civilization without losing its patience and temper, and the South would correspondingly rise above its former sensitiveness and handicaps into a national and cosmic destiny rather than a primarily provincial society. As such the South would cease holding the untenable position of wanting to be let alone. It had tried this, and it had failed; there was little doubt of that. It was ready for the new order. It would henceforth remain regionally conscious, but it would cease to be sectionally conscious and resentful of "outside interference." It would face national and world competition with high courage and intelligent action.

The southern problem was, therefore, essentially that of any modern society challenged to find its way forward through effective adaptation to new difficulties, new problems, new environments. The picture was one of the gradually unfolding process required of any civilization, with perhaps two exceptions. The first was that the South had the task of bringing "a new world to birth out of the dark confusions of an old world that had crumbled." The second was that the immediate problems of the South were a little more difficult than those of other regions. That it was an unusually hard job the South had to do, was nowhere denied. There was nowhere merely an academic picture. There were realities to be faced. There were the usual cultural situations to face. There were normal economic factors involved. There were the current problems of meeting the accelerated processes of social change. And there were some additional and extraordinary cultural, bi-racial, and economic elements which made the problem of the new equilibrium one for strong leadership, unusual courage, skillful adaptation, powerful reserve, as well as common sense and intelligent cooperation from the rest of the nation.

Yet the old pictures of the South had revealed high potentiality in all of these. The bravery of the South in war and after had been brilliant and basic, so much so that later episodes reflecting fear appeared as temporary moods. The South had shown great recuperative powers, persistence, and reserve, such that later tendencies to "lie down on the job" and "quit" appeared to be utterly foreign to the southern character. And the South had proved to be a great seed bed of population for the nation, such that its reserve power had long been contributing important factors to the making of the national culture. Moreover, with all of its weaker episodes and waste, the South of the 1940's was a better South than it had ever been and appeared to be nearer the threshold of its possible national destiny than ever before. Careful analysis of its status and resources justified the conclusion that not a single one of its major deficiencies and limitations had been due to other than temporary, superficial, and remedial causes. It seemed plausible, therefore, to interpret the southern picture as one revealing unusual opportunity for scientific study and for very effective social guidance in the future. Nevertheless, the picture of the future, if it was to be a satisfactory one in the total national picture, must reveal considerable contrast to that of the past and that of the present.

This contrast between the new pictures of the South and the current ones would not be reflected, it was repeated again and again, in terms of capacity or intelligence, except in so far as it revealed the South's improvement in the *use* of its abilities and in intelligent *action*. The differences were rather those of enlarged social experience and training, more skill in all its activities, the will to pay a greater price in hard work and patience for its desired attainments, and a new facility in conceiving its situations and problems as generic and national rather than southern.

The projected picture of the South realizing its possibilities in the new American Epoch was therefore a colorful picture of an achieving region rather than a pale print of the sensitive South. It was a South thinking less highly of the past than of the future; a South seeking to do all things *well* rather than merely a few things *big;* a South which appraised work more highly than talk, truth above dogma, integrity above acclaim. It was a South unafraid; not afraid of Sinaic thunders echoed by false prophets; not afraid to do its own thinking nor to create in pioneer fields; not afraid of the truth, and the freedom which truth reveals; not afraid of the past, the present, or the future. It was a South devout with *religio poetae*, with the humility of the scientist and seeking to conserve its fighting energies through eminence in social science and literary achievement rather than in wasteful conflict. It was a South set to the task of conserving and developing its limitless resources in materials and men and to stopping its vast leakage from economic and social waste. It was a South seeking to extend the bounds of its work to the whole range of human endeavor; to measure its efforts only by the highest standards of excellence; and to appraise its contributions in terms of broader national and international application and of permanent values. It was a South able and willing to work out its economic, social, and political problems by scientific methods and persistent efforts. It was, in fine, an American South of continuing and new achievements, transforming its deficits of social waste to a balance of social gain, and becoming representative of the best that America could produce.

Whether such a picture of the South was to be realistic or utopian was to be explored further through an inventory of the elements of regional reality and their combination with similar elements in other regions, the nation, and the new global culture. These elements would include a full catalogue of resources, the folk, the culture conflicts inherited, the natural and technological wealth available, the states themselves, and their regional integration into the national whole. All these again are reflected through the years of the South's regrowing after the war of brothers and its desolation.

CHAPTER VII

The Grandfathers to Grandchildren

THERE WAS a man in the mid-channel, "since-the-war" South whose name was John. He was known locally, wherever he was known at all, as Uncle John because of his benign character and to distinguish him from other Johns of the same clan. As bearing the national heritage, he was also named for George Washington, patriotic father of them all. Neither this man nor his father before him owned slaves; yet he and his brothers fought through the War Between the States, with indifferent fortunes, for the independence of a Confederacy whose cornerstone was slavery. All were wounded; some survived, to return to broken homes and wasted lands. So returned also some of the slave-owning neighbors to rebuild their fortunes. Uncle John was among those who survived, and his life, therefore, reflected a sample American scene, featuring a stalwart southerner, the span of whose seventy-eight years encompassed the beginnings of two American epochs as reflected in changing eras of the southern United States of America. This southerner was of heroic stature, with bushy, gray hair, of the forceful yet happy-faced type. A plain man who could neither read nor write, with more than his allotted threescore years and ten, he revealed a remarkable survival and reflected a realistic type, midstream between an unbelievably sordid and bitter reconstruction period of the South and the new epoch of the first third of the twentieth century.

A late afternoon was gold and lavender with sunset and an atmosphere such as only an approaching twilight in the South could produce. Green trees, fragrant breezes, floating clouds, the twilight song of birds, spring flowers and up-sprouting new crops in the fields were part and parcel with the pungent smell of new-plowed loam and burning brush. Uncle John unhitched his mule from the plow after the day's work, fastened the rings of the trace chains to the top of the hames, and mounted the big, black, good-natured work-steed. The sweat of the man and the sweat of the mule were measures of the day's work. Briskly they started from the field. The big mule had a way of fox-trotting homeward, and the big man had a way of singing favorite hymns, of which there were many. Now, without consciousness of matching his song to his mood, he sang forcefully as usual, even though with something of restraint and wavering in his voice:

> "I saw a way-worn traveler,
> In tattered garments clad,
> A-struggling up the mountain;
> It seemed that he was sad:
> His back was laden heavy,
> His strength was almost gone,
> Yet he shouted as he journeyed,
> 'Deliverance will come.'
> Then palms of victory,
> Crowns of glory;
> Palms of victory,
> I shall wear. . . ."

Sunset and song were natural and pleasant substitutions for troublesome evening regrets or memories of recent hard, bitter times, or the earlier losses of war and reconstruction. These were always kept in the background so far as possible. Yet there was always somewhere the ache of the past and the fear of the future. Nevertheless, like the past, the future was very far away, a matter of simple faith and some far-off tomorrow. The present was lost in self-expression and in the hopes of his children and his children's children.

Back home, around the house and in the orchard, on this evening and others to come, straggling honeybees would be sampling old-fashioned flowers and orchard blooms in season

—apple blossoms in profusion, pink-blooming peach trees matching sunset tints, white plum flowers like the floating fringe of the clouds. Mingling with the last notes of the mockingbird, were the good-night *jo-clack* chatter of the guineas, the impatient squealing of pigs, and the cluck of the mother hen who often would, but could not, gather under her wings the growing brood of feathering chicks. And over against these were an unpainted house and barn, drab contrasts to the brilliance of a southern evening in the spring. A southern farm scene revealing life and nature irrepressible, powerful, natural, heedless of place or time, South or North or past or future.

Reaching home, this sturdy individual fed his stock, milked the cow, not delegating this to the womenfolks as was the custom, attended to the odds and ends around the barn, stepped over across the road to a daughter-widow's yard, cut up a generous supply of stovewood, carried in fresh water, came back home and set himself, like Paul Bunyan's loggers, to the joyous task of a big supper. For his eating, as everything he did, was no halfway measure.

Then quickly he changed to his Sunday clothes, or partly changed, hitched his mule to the buggy, and, with the companion of his years, journeyed apace to prayer meeting, where he prayed eloquently for all humanity and his neighbors, but particularly for his children and his children's children. The eloquence of his prayers was surpassed only by the power and roll of his bass singing. In church, always from the amen corner, echoing far and wide, the bass of his own inimitable and lawless tempo. Elsewhere, at home or in field, always a powerful raising of tunes and vibrant harmony. The measure of his voice was a measure of his personality.

Leaving the house of prayer, he started homeward again, only to run into a gang of rowdy youngsters, half drunk, on horseback, and profaning the atmosphere around the House of God. He strode up to these and ordered them to "clear out." In reply to their profane inquiry as to what business it was of his, he seized the bit of the leader's horse, kicked him in the belly, told them all to be off at once or he would thrash the last one of them. Knowing him as they did, they moved on. He always advised his neighbors and his grandchildren strongly against fighting. "But," said he, "if you *do* have to fight, give the fellow a good licking and ask the Lord to forgive you." Here as elsewhere,

> What you have to do, do with your might,
> Things done by halves are never done right.

Yet the big old man in his later years was never called upon to fight his battles by physical combat. There was something about him which seemed to make him immune. On one of his regular Saturday afternoon visits to the county seat he was attracted by a disturbance on a side street. Glancing that way, he saw a white man knock a Negro down. The Negro got up, and tremblingly said, "Boss, I didn't do that." Wherefore the white man called him a liar and knocked him down again. The Negro got up for the second time and said nothing. Wherefore the white man, calling him an insolent son-of-a-gun, knocked him down again. This was too much for Uncle John. He was no apologist for the Negro, yet he strode up to the man, and seizing him by the front of his shirt, shook him much after the manner in which his noted mink dog, Lope, would shake a mink. That was all, and that settled it.

On another occasion he came upon a group of neighbors digging a well. A Negro helper was deep down, evidently overcome by gas. The men were puzzled and panicky. No one wanted to go down to rescue the Negro helper—he was, after all, just a Negro. Not so, Uncle John. With an explosive snort, he had taken off his shirt and breeches, and ordered them to let him down. He was none too soon. He brought the Negro up, spent fifteen minutes rubbing him to life, like some great massaging machine, and left. Somehow folks didn't want to fight that sort of man.

Back home on this night after the prayer meeting, he talked

very briefly with his wife, a few years his senior, mother of twelve children, a matriarch remarkable as ruler and servant of the big old man and his children. She it was who, during the war, with an old neighbor and a broken team of horses, drove seventy miles to camp to visit him when he was wounded, and take him back home with her. Throughout the long return trip she sat flat on the floor of the wagon body and held his knee in her hand, lest it receive the least jolt that would start the wound a-bleeding to the death, as the doctors had told her it would. The big old man never forgot this heroic devotion. He himself had dared things, once to rescue a comrade, once jumping up on the ramparts to taunt a cursing, challenging Yankee enemy, and once in a gallant and hopeless charge. And always, whether in work or worship, or contest, he was intemperate with his strength, heedless of harm. But these were different from the long, quiet, heroic, matter-of-fact devotion of his wife.

Now it was bedtime, and they knelt in family prayer. Again, he prayed eloquently for his neighbors and all humanity, but especially for his children and his children's children. Presently, in primitive fashion, he was in bed; and in the twinkling of an eye he was sleeping loudly the sleep of the just, restless only for the shifting of his tired body.

On the morrow, up and about before the light, feeding his stock, patting the black mule, which he appraised as the best kept in the whole country; back for breakfast ready with candlelight, and off to the field again at sunrise to the accompaniment of mockingbird and morning breeze. There was a sort of fellowship between him and the big black mule. The step of the mule was longer and slower in the morning, and the song of the man was steadier and more vigorous:

> "Through many dangers, toils and snares
> I have already come;
> 'Tis grace has brought me safe thus far,
> And grace will lead me home."

To the field and plow, with a cheerful greeting to the neighbors and helpers, and another day's work began. Helping unload the sacks of guano, he reminded the boys of how in early youth, before he was wounded, he could shoulder a two-hundred-pound-sack of guano, and jump up and crack his heels twice before hitting the ground. He regretted casually that there were no more log-rollings and house-raisings where men could pit strength against strength as in the olden days. Then to his own work, following the plow, in tune with the smell of the fresh-turned soil, a certain simple rapport with all life and nature; and again his *gee* and *haw* voice was a measure of the man, with, nevertheless, now and then a mechanical easing off of his pent-up self in more songs of relief as the morning wore on:

> "Oh, sometimes how long seems the day,
> And sometimes how weary my feet;
> But toiling in life's dusty way,
> The Rock's blessed shadow how sweet.
> Oh, then to the Rock let me fly,
> To the Rock that is higher than I.
> Oh, then to the Rock let me fly,
> To the Rock that is higher than I."

Sunday was a day of difference—"Welcome, sweet day of rest." It was a rest day at least for the big black mule, who was sometimes allowed to rest while the folks walked to church. As for Uncle John, it was the brightest of the seven days. Sleeping a little later, reminiscent of "everlasting rest," clean clothes, shaving, if not indeed already Saturday night, trimming of the long mustache. Grandchildren of any age coming in, ready for preaching, and always Sunday dinner in abundance, home-produced: chicken pie and dumplings, fried chicken and gravy, hot biscuits, string beans and corn-bread, pies and cakes, that the "old lady" had prepared for on Saturday and the womenfolks had cooked together on Sunday. Kinsfolk were in to spend the day, children and grandchildren, brothers and sisters, and the picture was in great contrast to the earlier days after the war, when wheat bread was rarity of rarities, and coffee was made from parched corn with "long sweetening"—meaning molasses—instead of sugar.

> Here afford us, Lord, a taste
> Of our everlasting feast.

And after dinner, the men to walk over the fields, appraise the crops, hope for prospects. The women to wash the dishes, nurse the babies, tilt their chairs back on the porch, and talk and talk and talk. And dispersing with many goodbyes, to go home again. Evening, worshipful moods, and early to bed.

> How sweet a Sabbath thus to spend
> In hope of one that ne'er shall end.

For Uncle John was forever having his face set to some Haven of the future. Yes, the past was very far away. To him a thousand years, when it was past, was as yesterday, but also a thousand years to come, in the promise of his children and his children's children, was as a watch in the night—to be lived through in some blind, powerful, biological, and cultural faith carrying with it the unmeasured and unseen power of the race.

One of his neighbors with whom he often talked across the hedgerow between the farms was a proud old Confederate officer who had owned several hundred acres of land and twenty-five slaves. He could swear as fervidly as Uncle John could pray. Yet in a philosophical sort of way he liked the religion of Uncle John. It was good for other folks. And he liked Uncle John. The old officer often recalled the bitterness of the war and reconstruction. He had been wounded twice, once losing a leg. His three sons had been killed; and the postwar hardships were severe. Of his daughters, three were married to the stalwart, attractive, albeit less educated, sons of Uncle John, and a fourth daughter had later, as a second wife, taken the place of her sister who had died. With the intermarriage of these two families much of the older feeling of superiority and·inferiority had been lost in the common struggle, and a reasonably wholesome fellowship had developed in the rapidly growing, eager, and ambitious families.

This old Confederate officer, former slave owner, still owned many of his original acres and rode a favorite bay horse, Selim, in making his way about over the farm. He was also tax receiver for the county and, like Uncle John, was well known and liked. He was mildly reconstructed, yet he had suffered more by contrast than Uncle John, who had always been poor. In bitter moments, he recalled the passage of Sherman and his men; how they had stripped his house and place of all manner of supplies and goods, silver, watches, wearing apparel, money, breaking into trunks and bureaus, destroying fences and houses, cutting down fruit trees, offending the womenfolks, and appropriating all possible resources in what seemed to be a most insolent and riotous manner. The early growing crops reminded him of how the soldiers had turned their horses and mules into his orchard and garden and fields, destroying everything, and in the meantime killing poultry, slaughtering young hogs and cooking them in his own kitchen to be served up before the homefolks in the officers' tents. And he never ceased reviling them for the theft of another favorite horse and the stampeding of all his mules and cattle.

Uncle John, as always, wanted to forget. This, he would remind him, was all in the past. He seemed thankful that the recent boom of guns in Atlanta, celebrating the second election of Cleveland, although reminder of war and defeat, was really symbolic of a new day for the South. Anyway, it was easier to forget and do the day's work. Folks had to work or go under in this terrific struggle from the 1870's to the turn of the new century. On this same general principle, Uncle

John was not much for attending Confederate reunions. Partly he had his own reasons; partly it was easier not to go.

The old Major, broad of forehead, with large eager eyes peering out from a black-whiskered face, after such a discussion was inclined to explode "All right, all right," and gallop on over to where were working the black folks who both esteemed and feared him. They were the children of the old slaves, most of whom, after the war, had come back like the white folks to start over again. Always these black folks—now neighbors, too—followed eagerly the fortunes of "their" white children until time and numbers and changing scenes separated them all far and wide. There was Tom-Jim especially, who assumed perpetual guardianship of all the grandchildren of the old Major, and one of whose own grandchildren was to achieve distinction in the musical world. Some of the black children of the black children of the old slaves were destined to achieve strange lives, some in travel and attainments, some in the tragedies of race conflict. Some of the grandchildren of the slaves would outdistance some of the grandchildren of Uncle John and the old Major. There were to be descendants of the old slaves and of the old officer destined to distinguish themselves in interracial amity; and there were other descendants of the slaves destined to die through mob action of the descendants of Uncle John and the old Major. These, too, were representative of a formative South whose portrait was soon to be reset in the national picture.

On the other side of the small farm was a neighbor of a different sort, a tenant farmer working to buy his place. The family included the father, mother, and two small boys, hardworking folk, seeking to develop all possible prospects of a better day. The wife and mother was one of the few graduates of a women's college in the community. Like many another woman in the South and many a man, she had lost her artist's soul in the fabric of reality. Coming back from college, she had married a young man, poor and unlettered; they had settled on the little farm and started, like thousands of others throughout the South, to achieve destiny through industry and the promise of their children. The man almost worshiped the woman and coveted for her companionship of those more erudite than himself. And she, faithful and devoted, notable for her housewifery, looked far beyond any horizon the present day could reveal. Through these and other children that were to follow she was to reap abundantly where she had sown.

Across the river were other neighbors of a still different sort. Shiftless, hard-drinking and fighting, they constituted a neighborhood fringe for which Uncle John prayed, and at which the old Major swore. Neither availed much; while they in turn continued to multiply and be more shiftless, a clan of mixed folk, some scalawags and their children, some carpetbaggers and their remnants, some just common folks, leftovers blindly kicking against the pricks. They, too, were full of promise of a new leadership and a new following, which were to be a part of the new mixed South to come—and to come quickly.

Farther east and south on Uncle John's side of the river were other neighbors, remnants of the old plantations, aristocracy and near-aristocracy, mixed with poorer folk, relatives and acquaintances both of the old Major and of Uncle John. Here were former owners of many acres and many slaves, now broken remnants of distinguished families on run-down places, in decaying mansions. These felt more exclusive and looked with more condescension upon Uncle John and his folks than did the old Major. Here were elderly unmarried ladies, old men, vociferous philosophers, and occasionally strange marrying and giving in marriage among classes such as had not happened often in the Old South. Some glory there was left; some tragedy; some humor; and much of the mixed picture of the recovering South and of Nature's inviolable processes.

Then across the width of counties toward the west and north began the fringe of mountain folk, which extended far and wide within the borders of three states. The nearest neighbors here were found in a settlement of predominantly mountain folk, strong, independent, loyal, and virtuous. Sometimes feudists and fighters, mixed with weaklings and strong, into which had married sojourners from the North, missionary folk or upstanding remnants of the carpetbagger regime. There were northern churches and no churches at all; missionary schools and no schools at all. Covered apple wagons in the fall brought some of the people down from the hill country, and they always met with cordial reception from Uncle John, who was in sympathy and character with their sort.

Still farther to the east and south and west, whence had gone representatives of all the neighbors, were the stirrings of cities, of industry, and of new wealth. Here were founders of new fortunes and builders of cities. And here were stirrings of all that conflict between white and black, Populists and Democrats, Methodists and Baptists, Protestant and Catholic, city and country, which was to enter into the new fabric of the South of the twentieth century. And, strange as it may seem, over apace from these cities and towns, where near-by cotton mills were springing up, grandchildren of Uncle John and the old Major and of their neighbors had migrated to work in the mills, following the wake of poverty and sickness and restlessness. Here were forming new classes, made up of farm folk and mountain folk, town and city remnants and a few from the "foreign" states, heralding a new industrial revolution in the South. Such towns and mills were wonder places to Uncle John and his neighbors, providing markets for produce as well as outlet for large families. It was a new era, the full nature and import of which could not yet be foreseen at the beginning of the second third of the twentieth century.

These men, John Washington Southern and Major Thomas Leaven, then, with their children and their neighbors and their neighbors' children, were not only reminiscent of the biography of the first epochs of the American South, but symbolic of its organic extension into the future American scene. Of their own children there were a score. Their children's children, numbered unto the third and fourth generations, building rapidly upon the foundations of hard-working parents, were to extend their influence into all the states of the Union and unto some other parts of the world. They would sail the wide seas. They would travel far, and their work would comprehend many vocations and professions. They would marry widely into a great variety of families: rich, poor; old, new; southern, northern; English, German, French. The families into which they married would multiply and be fruitful. There was one family of fourteen vigorous children, all surviving to maturity except the oldest, who went to war a little before he was sixteen in order to be in his own father's regiment. Wounded in the same battle with his father, he was placed by his side in the crude hospital tent, and died in great agony in spite of all that the wounded father could do. There was another family of twelve, another of ten, and others of lesser measure. One daughter of Uncle John, reputed to be the most beautiful girl in the whole region, died at thirty-three, and left eight children. Another fell in the grim struggle before twoscore years had passed, and of her issue six were living and three dead. And the others lived and multiplied and were strangely reminiscent, on the one hand, of the large families of the common people, and, on the other, of those distinguished Virginia gentlemen, one of whom gave the world twenty-three children through four wives, and another eighteen, and another seventeen, with the score of nine living to eight dead within a span of less than forty years.

Of the heritage of these families and their relations there was great variety, from the poorer people, through the wide range of middle folk, all the way to descendants from the first blood of the land. In the backgrounds of their own families and their children and their children's children was all that was reputed to be American of American. There were Scotch and Scotch-Irish pioneers, later to be migrants from the Carolinas to the deep South and back again; Scotch Covenanters and English of those old families from Maryland; Virginia, and the Carolinas moving south and west and north and back again; and German and French stalwarts from the upper lands of the old continent. Thus the lives of these men were to penetrate, as they already reflected, the whole of the southern region of the United States through which had come much that was most dramatic in American history, and which was soon to enter upon another great American epoch. The whole range of physical environment, geographic distribution, economic condition, and cultural status was perhaps no more vivid than the contrast between the Uncle John, for instance, who at the end of the war trudged on foot the last long mile of the dusty road from Gastonia to take up anew a broken life in the South, and his descendants who later were to return from various parts of America to a Carolina steeped in industrial development and social conflict.

This southern epoch comprehended long distances in time and space. There were long reaches into the powerful biological and cultural urge of destiny. It was a long way from first pioneer days of hardship and struggle to the glory of the ante-bellum South. It was a long way back again from the glory that was the old South to a broken and charred region, wounded and blackened, humiliated with slaves turned rulers. It was a long way again from the new poverty and broken South to the modern industrial empire with its network of railways, highways, and factories. And it was to be a long and difficult road from the beginning of the new southern epoch of the first third of the twentieth century to its full contribution to the whole American epoch of the twentieth century and on. For the South, even as the nation, was still very young. And these stalwart southerners and their neighbors, with all of their strength and weakness, possibilities and limitations, were at once symbol and fact in the evolution of a people. It was as if there were necessity and prospect of more than Whitman's immeasurable self-extension: "To confront night, storms, hunger, ridicule, accidents, rebuffs, as the trees and animals do."

Not many miles from this quiet scene of the big man and the big black mule as of the old Major and his bay horse were other quiet scenes by the thousands. Some were similar to these, some were very different. Not very far away, a Mary Johnston, shy, modest, small, head of her father's family of several children, taking care of motherless children in the midst of a father's lost fortune, was cultivating deep the soil for new books to be harvested in the hundreds of thousands. Over on the other side, a quiet, unassuming Joel Chandler Harris was creating Uncle Remus and slipping quietly into the good will of the world. A little farther down was a Woodrow Wilson, and a little farther up a Walter Hines Page. And scattered here and there throughout the length and reaches of the South were the fathers and mothers of all that southern host who in the twentieth century were to build a New South upon foundations laid in the last quarter of the nineteenth century by elders ill equipped for the task.

In the quiet scenes of a rebuilding South there were few indications of the length and breadth and depth of the struggle that had been the South's, or that was to be the South's. It was as if, from this quiet midstream vantage point, the long and devious ways in the past, now in the way of being forgotten, were to be matched by the long and difficult ways of the future. What was to be the future distance, matching the lengths from Thomas Jefferson and his principles of freedom to the smoldering fires of southern intolerance and demagoguery, already breaking out in sundry places throughout the South? Or, again, from these latter-day leaders to a new leadership which should turn the southern potentialities into national power? But the ways were there for the going, challenging the South to make this quiet process of biological, economic, social, and spiritual rebuilding the forerunner of a new American epoch.

CHAPTER VIII

The Glory That Was the South

THE OLD MAJOR, much given to philosophizing on political and moral issues, strolled along before the White House in springtime on one of his few visits to Washington, enjoying its southern columns and plantings. He was prone to speculate upon what the South had contributed to the nation and might yet contribute if there could be a new balance of men and resources and culture in the different regions. There must surely be, he thought, a place through the years for some of the enduring values inherent in the glory that was the South. Could there be a blending of values such as Henry W. Grady had pictured to a great New York audience which cheered to the echo his eloquent picture of Lincoln as such a symbol? The thought was particularly fascinating when he contemplated the democratic principles of Jefferson, well wrought out into a practical society and dominated by his high standards for agriculture, science, education, and architecture. Speculation on this day was the more encouraged by a recent rare visit to Monticello, which had left upon him vivid impressions of what was and what might have been, and by his thoughts of Abraham Lincoln's southern heritage and national greatness.

There came to his mind pictures of innumerable colonial homes with the glory that was theirs. There came to mind also the contrast of that first American epoch of independence in which the South had provided the occupants of the White House for nearly fifty of its first sixty years and the barrenness of the South's contribution in a second similar epoch. He wondered what the third epoch would bring forth, but did not survive long enough to see the failure of certain heroic efforts of Woodrow Wilson and his southern followers to regain a long lost place, to be followed by a barrenness the length and breadth of which was still to be fathomed at the end of the first third of the twentieth century. In his vague way he was hurt because of the lost years of constructive cooperation and interchange between the South and the North.

He recalled that, at the end of this first epoch and with two governments instead of one, both presidents were southerners, born within a hundred miles of each other, and that the wife of the president of the northern republic had come from the South and the wife of the president of the southern confederacy had come from the North. It was all very complex and mixed, as it had been from the beginning. The problem was too hard for the old Major, who found musing and argumentation much more satisfying than finished conclusions, and so he turned again to reminiscences of the old days.

How many of the big-columned houses had there been to set that part of the southern stage? How many, and of what sort and variety, on the banks of the Potomac and the James and the Roanoke and down in the Carolinas?

How many in Georgia, at Athens, La Grange, Augusta, Columbus, and Savannah? In Alabama, at Greensboro, Montgomery, and Huntsville?

In Mississippi, at Natchez, Vicksburg, or Columbus?

In old romantic Louisiana, and back again to Tennessee and Kentucky? And in the regions and land in between?

Nobody has ever counted them; perhaps no one ever will. There have been notable samplings, to be sure, first among which would be the historic places of Mount Vernon, Monticello, Arlington, Shirley, Westover, Brandon, Sabine Hall, the Hermitage, and others. And of the others, what variety of names and what range of character: Belle Grove, Seven Oaks, Buller's Idol, Wormsloe, El Destino, Weldon, Springfield, Gainswood, Oak Grove, Log Hall, Level Green, Parlange, Forlorn Hope, the Forks, Mangorike, Rippon Hall, Rings Neck, Nomini Hall, Pocahontas, the Gland, Bolling Home, Bellmont, Pharsalia, Ash Pone, Snug Dale, Tyro, Somerset Place, Silk Hope, Gowrie, Hopeton, Elmington, Burleigh, Peach Point, Pleasant Grove, Retreat, Stratford, Tuckahoe, Homewood, Montpelier, Hunthill, Rose Hill.

But even these were but beginnings, while the naming of scores of others would still leave unnumbered hundreds with their characters of romance and tragedy unrecorded. The Oaklands, the Edgewoods, the Woodlawns, the Pleasant Hills, the White Halls were oft repeated in name and character. There was great uniformity in general type, great range and variety in detail: Hickory Hill, Scotchtown, New Market, Chelsea, Elsus Green, Horn Quarter, Upper Grandon, Greenwood, Sherwood Forest, Windmill Point, Berkeley, Bollingbrook, Centre Hall, Malvern Hall, Wilton, Rosewell, Palace Green, Kenmore, Ringfield, Timberneck, Warner Hall, Brompton, Eldham, Clover Lea, Laneville, Sherwood, Severnby, Lansdowne, Eagle Point, White Mast, the Shelter, Airville, Lowland Cottage, Glenroy, Toddsbury, Goshen, Waverly, Newstead, Mansfield, Hayfield, Moss Neck, Belleville, Dunham, Auburn, Dilchley, Poplar Grove, Chatham, Rosegill, Belle Isle, Edge Hill, Mount Airy, Stratford Hall, Bladenfield, Oaken Brown, Gaymount.

And what pictures they were! As varied and different as were the personalities of the masters who built and lived in them, and yet having the same sort of general similarity throughout. A big house on a hill by the river side or set far back from the road in the midst of great trees, white-framed with big columns, or a white-columned brick structure laid "in Flemish bond of alternately glazed black leaders and dull pink broadsides which give the walls solidity, distinction and a rich beauty." Or another mansion "with four huge rooms downstairs and a like number above, stood upon a terraced plateau, with a bowling green in front and a 'little handsome street' at the rear leading to the kitchen, bakery, dairy, and storehouses. The grounds, four acres in spread, were marked at the corners by schoolhouse, laundry, coach house, and stable, uniform in size and style. The first of these contained not only a schoolroom but lodgings for the tutor, the master's sons and a clerk, whence they were summoned to meals at the great house by a sixty-pound bell."

And another large rambling house "set in a magnificent grove of live oaks, the wide double gallery almost concealed by the luxurious vegetation. The central part is two-storied, with an attic, gabled; at one end an enormous addition contains two rooms, one above, one below, each forty-three by twenty-five feet. Some distance to the rear of the house, at one side, stands the great whitewashed stable with stalls for thirty thoroughbred horses; every stall is occupied; a small army of Negro hostlers bustles about it. Still farther away through the dense tangle of vegetation, which gives to the mansion its rather melancholy grandeur, a village of small cabins, brilliantly white in the sun; these are the quarters of the servants—the hundreds of servants who make the great plantation a little town."

Such were the plantation houses, while the colonial homes in the towns and cities had their marked characteristics scarcely less distinguished. They "stood back from the streets surrounded by heavily scented gardens, almost hidden by the semitropical sweet gum and the magnolia; here and there, although it was a little far to the north, grew a camphor tree. Over the small porticos of the older houses the sweet-scented honeysuckle ran uncut, wild; and the wide double galleries of the later dwellings, built in the recent spacious times, gleamed white through the great catalpa trees now coming into leaf. Voices, disembodied in the still air, floated into the street, as if the houses themselves had spoken."

The manner of building and the interior of the great houses were equally distinctive. Some of the rooms were more than twenty-four feet high, majestic in roominess; many, sixteen feet high and paneled to the ceiling. The reception rooms carried heavy cornices over walls entirely paneled, and the carved doorways and mantels were distinctive even for colonial houses. There were collections of books, plate, furniture, and portraits and pictures representative of an accumulation of many generations. Beautiful furniture and appointments with all the promise of priceless inheritance and antiques the mere listing of which would require great catalogues compiled with rare skill and portraiture. Priceless as heritage, rare as possessions, their aggregate would, even in the modern world, startle a sophisticated multitude.

The pictures of the southern men and women in these homes, and the plantation pattern of life which they led, have been painted many times, more often finished and framed in the romantic colors and setting of the past than set in realistic perspective. Nevertheless, whatever else they were, they were reflections of glory and grandeur, vivid, beautiful, and distinctive. In these pictures one sees southern men and southern women as the perfect flowering of American personality, and the plantation life as the best of American culture. Even a Walter Hines Page with his keen criticism of southern deficiencies could see the romance and virtue of the big house in the midst of the groves and the hundreds of surrounding acres, burdened with crops white for the harvesting by black folks, musical in the rendering of old spirituals, cheerful in song and story, polite, gracious, artistic beyond measure. The number of these slaves ranged from small units of twenty-five or thirty, through a common measure of one to three hundred, to the super-master with more than two thousand black folks doing his bidding. And of course "moonlight, the songs of the darkies in the distance, the flitting forms of beautiful maidens clad in ruffled skirts, their hair falling about their shoulders in ringlets, handsome, brilliant cavaliers bending over their hands, old gentlemen in black garments and black stocks walking with stately, meditative tread, white-haired matrons smiling indulgently upon the benignant scene, colored mammies, coaches-and-four and coats of arms . . ."

Around the place were the hounds and horses, the turkeys, chickens, and guineas, black and white children, uncles and aunties, and middle-aged black folks with varied rank and abundant pride. There were the elegant house servants, coachmen, butlers dressed in broadcloth, and women servants so well dressed that Solomon in all his glory might find a new proverb, and so numerous that often, like the lilies of the field, they toiled not, neither did they spin. Thus, at Nomini Hall there were carpenters, joiners, gardeners, postilions, "a bricklayer, a blacksmith, a miller, a tanner, a shoemaker, a hatter, a sailor, a butcher, a cook, a waiter, and a scullion among the men; and among the women three housemaids, two seamstresses, two spinsters, a dairymaid, a laundress, a nursemaid, and a midwife."

About the big house and the cabins were old-fashioned flowers—zinnias, dahlias, hollyhocks, prince's-feathers, honeysuckles, rambling roses, roses of Sharon, and farther out orchards and gardens and pastures. Variations of all these and other details were considerable, according as the big house was near the river with its own boat landing, or in the midst of the countryside estate, or on some Milledge Avenue in an old town.

There were vivid pictures of hospitality, high living and fellowship within these physical bounds. In such pictures, the master of the plantation lived in state, and extended his hospitality in great style. Visits were not by the hour or the day but by days and weeks. There were single meals for more than fifty guests with much variety of form, service, food, and drink. And there were the days and weeks of entertaining. For the eating and drinking and merrymaking there were soups, turkeys, chickens, hams, ducks, pigs, pork, venison, mutton, kid, wild fowl and animal, eggs, apples, sweet potatoes, hominy, greens, and all manner of vegetables; innumerable pies, cakes, and pastry, inimitably made; coffee, milk, cream, fruits, nuts, bottles of wine specially selected for the men, specially selected for the women; toasts, conversation, bowing men, departing ladies.

There was the estimate of food consumed at one of the great houses before the year was yet old: "twenty beeves, twenty-seven thousand pounds of pork, five hundred bushels of wheat and unmeasured corn, along with four hogsheads of rum and three barrels of whiskey, not to reckon the Madeira. For the twenty-eight fireplaces a cart with six oxen hauling four loads a day no more than sufficed for winter 'needs." And besides there were the luxuries that came directly from abroad, ships stopping at a planter's or neighborhood landing, in exchange for crops—silks, velvets, ribbons, and all manner of dress and household goods, jewelry and books, machinery, and, what was more, all manner of imported vintages for every course and occasion. And there were the contacts with London and Paris, with brilliant winters in New Orleans, Charleston, Mobile, and other places where were produced plays of Shakespeare before ever they were given in New York or Boston or Philadelphia. And volumes of Shakespeare, Scott, George Eliot, Johnson, Goldsmith, Greek and Latin classics, were often a part of the culture of these plantation masters, in spite of the complaints of Frederick Law Olmsted who failed to find them.

And there were the magnificent Mississippi steamboats sailing down the historic Father of Waters. A *Vesuvius*, an *Aetna*, a *Volcano*, an *Eclipse*, a *Caledonia*, a *Concordia*, a *Magnolia*, a *Grand Republic*, sailing back and forth with all manner of people, high and low, on board—with luxurious staterooms and saloons, excellent food, library, dancing, and all manner of "glory" characteristic of the romance of the Mississippi River. Boat races, adventure in flood tide at the many landings, the singing and scrambling of roustabouts, loading and unloading the bales of cotton, were a part of the never-to-be-forgotten historic Old South. And then on to New

Orleans, whence the rise of a peculiar civilization based upon clash of the Old World, upon mixed ethnic factors, upon slave labor, from which came Mardi Gras and the Carnival, and a distinctive society sometimes called the most American of the nation. Here were glamour, romance, and beauty from the inner Crescent City reflected over against that other city and era where "Negro slaves sang as they loaded bales of cotton from the plantation wharves onto the snorting steamboats of the Mississippi, while Creole dandies duelled under the famous oaks and Ursuline nuns fingered their rosaries."

The old plantation system was often likened unto a school in which society was molded into unerring patterns. Thus the plantation was often a community in which there were teachers for the children of the house, their relatives and neighbors, and special instruction for the talented Negroes in crafts, in routine skill, and even in reading, writing, and arithmetic. There were local government and citizenship, religious instruction and worship, agriculture and industry, entertainment and recreation, all centered around the various family units, so that many of the pictures of the Old South were indeed pictures of a miniature society.

What pageantry and variety were found in these old pictures! What portraiture in "the procession of plowmen at evening, slouched crosswise on their mules; the dance in the new sugarhouse, preceded by prayer, the bonfire in the quarter with contests in clogs, cakewalks and Charleston whose fascinations were as yet undiscovered by the great world; the work songs in solo and refrain, with not too fast a rhythm; the baptizing in the creek, with lively demonstrations from the 'sisters' as they came dripping out; the torchlight pursuit of 'possum and 'coon, with full-voiced halloo to baying houn'. dawg and yelping cur; the rabbit hunt, the log-rolling, the house-raising, the husking-bee, the quilting party, the wedding, the cock fight, the crap game, the children's play, all punctuated plantation life—and most of them were highly vocal. A funeral now and then of some prominent slave would bring festive sorrowing, or the death of a beloved master an outburst of emotion."

The leading man in the big house and its drama was of course the old southerner. Like the great houses which no man has ever numbered, he will never be measured by any man in all his variety and peculiarities and character. There have been many stories about him and many pictures presenting him as a type; but, like the plantations and plantation life, he had great variety, in the midst of what might nevertheless lend itself to typical portraiture. The old southerner was a gentleman and an aristocrat, whose character could be told at a glance by the measured dignity of his walking or riding or by the carriage in which he rode. His dress, like his manner, was distinctive, with perhaps a gold-headed cane, a great watch and chain of Geneva gold, the monogrammed prismic seal, the manner of his toying with chain and seal being, like the motions of a lady's fan, visible signs of the gentleman. He was proud, austere, impetuous, eloquent, and sometimes over-irascible, loquacious of tongue and pen, so that he appeared domineering to many northerners and to many a common man in the South. As man of leisure, politician, squire, manager of a plantation, or what not, he was the subject of varied stories, now pleasure-hunting the fox, raccoon, wolf, rabbit, quail, now visiting neighbors and arguing, now discussing philosophy and literature, and now fighting, according to his code of honor.

Leading lady, no less distinctive in her way, was the southern woman, grown from girlhood, full of larks and pranks and penchant for pleasures, into serious, gracious woman competent to meet the tremendous demands upon her body and soul; mother of old statesmen and soldiers, who led in the revolt against England, in the making of the new government, and later in the defense of the Old South. Such women were beautiful, gracious, commanding, setting new standards of their own, filling new books of romance for a new world to learn.

They were remarkable for perfection in mastery and service, creating and guiding their own large families, and taking charge of and dividing fortunes with sundry subsidiary families of black folks all around them. But perhaps the southern woman of all classes best reflected her glory through fortitude and heroic devotion during the War and reconstruction.

What if the Daughters of the Confederacy have overdone the southern woman? Was she not, they prove, "the *Magnolia grandiflora* of a race of Cavaliers? She inherited beauty—not alone of the kind which attaches to person, though in superlative degree she possessed that—but beauty of mind, beauty of soul, beauty of character. These combined to lift her attractions to a higher power and to give her the exquisite charm of loveliness. Hers were the Spartan traits of an Old South —endurance, courage, fortitude, superiority of mind—traits which compelled respect even from strangers, which inspired reverence in her children and loyalty in her slaves, and which secured for her the good-will of her neighbors. But she also possessed the strength which is born of prayer, the tranquil calm which comes from faith, and the serene smile, whose divine source is love. Whether in a pillard mansion or in a lowly cot, whether at home or abroad, whether in dispensing hospitality to her equals or in bestowing favor upon her dependents, she was everywhere and always a queen; and whatever she said or did, bore the baronial hall-mark of the old manor and told of the gentle molds of ancestry from which she sprang."

Not the least of all the pictures were those distinguished characters, the old slaves. These were not merely the sentimental "uncles" and "aunties" and "mammies," but men and women all, as distinctive characters as ever the South produced. They were able, charming, artistic, proud, so skillful and powerful in adaptation as to defy description and measurement by any art or science yet devised. Frankness everywhere compels the admission that here was a type the passing of which must always seem a tragedy of lost personalities in exchange for the greater gain of human freedom. The pictures showed clearly that "something of the beautiful loyalty in them which guarded the women and children with such zeal while husbands and fathers were fighting far away persisted in the early days of their freedom. Old slaves, with fruit and gobblers and game, would sneak into the house with an instinctive sense of delicacy and leave them in the depleted larder surreptitiously."

And what artists in manners and serving and in skill of vocations, on special occasions equal to any demand! Here was a neighborly gathering. And here "the old negro clad in his blue swallow-tail coat with big brass buttons, would appear in the library or the vine-covered house in the garden, carrying a silver tray filled with all the ingredients of his magic concoction. . . . Tender, fragrant mint firmly pressed with the back of a spoon against the glistening inside of a sterling goblet; the bruised leaves gently removed and the cup half filled with cracked ice; mellow Bourbon, aged in oaken staves, bubbling from a brown jigger, percolated through the sparkling cubes and slivers; in another receptacle, granulated sugar slowly stirred into chilled limestone water to a silvery mixture as smooth as some rare Egyptian oil, was poured on top of the ice; then while beads of moisture gathered on the burnished exterior of the goblet, old Nelson garnished the frosted brim with choicest sprigs of mint and presented the tall cup, with a courtly bow, to the nearest guest."

This glory that was the South was then of one pattern yet of many parts. The Kentucky glory different from that of Virginia, the Virginia from that of Tennessee, and there was none like that of Charleston or New Orleans. The southern poetry of Edgar Allan Poe or Sidney Lanier was different from the oratory of John C. Calhoun or Henry Clay. Southern politics was different from southern philosophy. Southern statesmanship of a silver-tongued Benjamin Hill, a fire-eating

Robert Toombs, was different from the force and drive of Andrew Johnson or the skill and artistry of Henry Grady. And thus one star differed from another star whether it were Washington, Madison, Patrick Henry, Marshall, the Harrisons, the Lees, and the other Virginians; Graham, Macon, Davie, Benton, Badger of North Carolina; Calhoun, Hayne, Laurens, Legaré, Lowndes, Pinckney, and the others from South Carolina; or Campbell, Jackson, Polk, White, of Tennessee; Houston of Texas; King of Alabama; Cobb, Forsyth, Stephens, Toombs of Georgia; Bibb, Breckinridge, Henry Clay, Guyot, Johnson of Kentucky; Livingston, Slidell, Taylor of Louisiana; Prentiss and Walker of Mississippi.

There were "giants" in the pictures of those days. "George Washington, Thomas Jefferson, John Marshall, James Madison were giants, as everyone admits; and the South in their day dominated the nation. Andrew Jackson, John C. Calhoun, and Henry Clay were no weaklings, either; such men do not spring from a degenerate race. In moral stature and military genius Robert E. Lee overtops George Washington himself, although Lee had not the statesmanship that secures Washington his primacy. And Stonewall Jackson, the two Johnstons, Longstreet, Beauregard, Stuart, Early, and Forrest were such soldiers as delight the heart of the romancer and flutter the maiden pride of any nation. Tardy Justice now begins to admit that Jefferson Davis and Alexander Stephens also were men of genius." And "before the war" there were times when the sons of the South enrolled in its colleges were more than all the sons of New England; and its college endowments were more than all of the region of the "Big Three" and their lesser satellites. And in later years there were times when the ratio of southern students, the influence and cordial relations of Yale and Princeton and Harvard were greater than at any time within the seventy-five years to follow the war.

Perhaps no pictures were more characteristic of the glory of the South than its military leaders, a veritable galaxy of stars, "picturesque individuals, flaming gentlemen at arms, who brought to this war sound military aptitude, and the color also, of the age of chivalry. But Stuart was something more than any of them. I think each footsore infantryman, each gunner pounding by, every hard-riding trooper, saw in Jeb Stuart the man he would like to be himself. Jeb Stuart was a symbol, a gonfalon that went before the swift, lean columns of the Confederacy. He served as the eyes and ears of Lee: his hands touched the springs of vast events. His Command- ing General said of him, at the last, the finest thing history records of any cavalry officer: 'He never sent me a piece of false information.'"

And there were yet other pictures of the glory that was the South. Southerners of unusual social and cultural heritage, of literary and creative ability, accustomed to wealth and dignity, standing or bending or breaking under the vulgar standards and edicts of carpetbaggers, scalawags, and Negroes. These were pictures unforgettable from any view- point. A bride concealing a beautiful diamond in her mouth: to the enemy, looking dumb for fear; in reality, storing up resentments and transmitting them to her children. Soldiers pouring oil and turpentine on priceless furniture and setting it on fire. Wealthy and cultured women crowded hither and yon, robbed of their silver and gold, and wandering in the streets of their home towns. Now and then a fortunate escape to Europe in a desperate effort to regain a little of the lost world of hope and self-respect.

A grand old man with no word of bitterness, robbed of his Arlington and without a home, astride old Traveler looking for a small farm. In the streets and highways thousands of Negroes swaggering with muskets and bayonets jeering former masters and mistresses, urged on by ecstatic whites glorying in the torture of a fallen folk. Straggling processions of crippled men, torn, battered and gray, day on day and week on week, passing drearily over country roads wending their way through the wreckage of homes and fields. Arriving home they found houses, barns, fences, supplies destroyed, mules, horses, cattle, sheep stolen or driven away, no money, no farming implements, no seed, no labor.

There were men and women destined to be citizens of the "gentle and fair republic of letters," smiling ironically over ruined aspirations, transcended by the work of farm and kitchen. Or, as Gerald Johnson paints it, "the most tragic figures in the South are the men who might have been artists had not their obvious duty compelled them to throttle their dreams and turn their hands to material labor. Every southerner knows them—wistful figures, a little apart from their fellows, even in old age, dimly aware that they have somehow lost, but not sure what, or why, or when." Again, pictures and pictures: "Many once wealthy families, especially in Charleston, parted with their plate and other heirlooms to buy bread; here, too, some actually starved to death. The fiery poet, Henry Timrod, whose lyrics had animated southern hearts during the war, suffered constantly from hunger during the latter part of 1865 and died two years later in utter poverty. William Gilmore Simms sold a few copies of Timrod's volume of poems to obtain money for the family, but Simms himself, with his country home burned down and his library destroyed by Sherman's troops, was ruined."

A great plantation sold for five cents an acre—and its glory was of the past, past. Of such was the kingdom of the Old South, the making and breaking of which were processes in the development of a region southern instead of national, current situations and dramatic scenes transcending all logic of biological and historical backgrounds.

And yet much of the glory that was the South was previewed in the South of the upper brackets of the middle-class folk who had attained a measure of wealth, and of those who came from the North to adopt the South as their new American home.

The old picture of Frederick Law Olmsted, wending his tedious and painful way through the slave states of the ante-bellum South, stood in vivid contrast to the picture of the swift-moving northern tourist of the 1930's speeding from the national Capital to the deep South, by train or automobile or airplane in a single sweeping trip. Olmsted complained vigorously of too plain hospitality and too meager civilization: no privacy, no freshness, no flowers, no fruit, no cream, no sugar, no carpets, no couches, no books, no thermometers, no piano-fortes, no sheets of music, no engravings, no works of art—no civilization. And had he postponed his visit until the post-bellum days of Uncle John and the old Major, his findings amidst scenes of desolation and want would have appeared even more discouraging. He did find, however, a baker's dozen of notable places, offering hospitality such as his experience and standards led him to expect.

This visit to the "Back Country" failed to reveal the best of the Old South; nevertheless, had he visited every great southern place and been welcomed into every southern gentleman's home, he would still have found but a fraction of the measure and range of the South's picture of 1930. Had he come again then, he would have passed thousands of homes and suburban places surpassing all that he had seen in the ante-bellum country. Instead of his crowded rooms, inadequate linen, and sordid conditions, he would have found comfort and surcease. If he had been invited to a private home, he would have been provided with his desired private room and bath, soft curtains and gentle lights, a warm house or cool according to season, music and books and pictures, recreation and conveniences, gardens and flowers and fruits. Indeed he would have appeared to be in a land of half-enchantment with gardens of flowers and fruits and vegetables in incredible abundance.

If, on the other hand, he had been entertained through the public hospitality, he would have found comfortable and well equipped hotels, with food from all the seasons and regions, running ice water in his room, the soft carpets which he craved, and all manner of luxury far surpassing the best of the Old South. Whether he appraised the southern picture in measures of money and material things, in numbers and quantity, in aggregates or individual excellence, or whether he measured it in terms of the higher culture and form, after eliminating current crude architecture and monstrosities, he would still have found southern wealth and resources far beyond the limits of any ante-bellum dream. . . . And yet he would also have beheld, mile after mile, area upon area, pictures of the same limited and sordid conditions of which he complained. For the New South was a kingdom of wealth, and it was a kingdom of waste. And it was to reflect not only the "glory that was," but also the "grandeur that was not."

CHAPTER IX

The Grandeur That Was Not

BOTH UNCLE JOHN and the old Major were enthusiastic followers of Jefferson and Jeffersonian democracy, but from different viewpoints. Uncle John, understanding only vaguely the general principles and ideals which he had heard were Jefferson's, was naturally a great believer in the rights and destinies of the people. The old Major, on the other hand, was perhaps naturally inclined to be a "philosopher," given to much debating and to the turning over in his mind of every sort of problem. He was particularly apt and eloquent in the discussion of general humanistic themes and politics. He had always doubted the efficacy of the old southern too-dominant autocracy. Part of this doubt had come from a fair reasoning about certain weaknesses of the southern economy, a certain amount of actual theoretical study, and considerable observations and study of the southern scene since the war. But perhaps a considerable part of his conclusions came from natural rationalization, since he himself, like Jefferson Davis and many another later southern plantation man, had come to his status quickly, developing in a single generation from a family of insecure small farmers into a great planter. With all his pride in the dignity of his expanded family, he could not see in the glory of the knightly gentleman who had developed from the restless pioneer, sturdy, plain, hard-working, any exclusive and permanent value differing from the earlier generation, pioneering, suffering, deeply religious, ambitious, honorable. He could see no aristocracy in the primitive days of the frontier, and he could think of the whole South in no other terms than series of frontier fringes, each great family at one time or another in its history having participated in the great restless drive for wealth and progress and superior class development.

Thus the old Major was inclined to think of Uncle John, somewhat undeveloped and unlettered but highly honorable and energetic, as an earlier member of his own generation. And Uncle John understood and esteemed the fortunes and family of the old Major and took great pride in the marriage of his sons to the daughters of the older family. The old Major recalled a similar understanding between the men who marched with Lee, where sons of aristocrats, side by side with mountain or flatwood folk, fought for and almost worshiped the great General. He had often wished that the South could have realized the possibilities of this greater understanding among its own people, both before the war in working out its own human economy and in later days with the bitter and pathetic struggle still going on among the classes in many communities.

Both Uncle John and the old Major were scornful of much of the false pride and hypocrisy of the Old South, and particularly of the remnants of proud folk on the one hand and the "strainers" and imitators on the other. There was much that was tragic and small alongside that which was tragic and glorious. It was difficult to decide whether pity or scorn was the predominant note in the conversations about the pathetic family of women in the neighborhood doing their washing in the attic and never hanging out the clothes lest the neighborhood might see the disgrace of their doing their own work. There was always this effect on southern standards and ideals of work, the lesser folk aping the bigger folk, the later generations imitating the old standards and old families. There was that pathetic case of another family having distinguished company from afar to dine, assigning one of the girls to blacken her face and hands and bring in the dinner in high fashion. And there was the family of unmarried men not knowing how to work, being too proud to work, aristocrats gone to seed, sometimes actually hungry, dressed in broadcloth, retaining fine dogs and horses on the place. Sometimes they actually called on the common-folks neighbors at mealtime and accepted their hospitality in the guise of neighborly honors from aristocrat to common man. And ever there was some hidden tragedy in the big house on the hill or in the grove: shutters never open, dark mysterious pride and mourning inside; tragic womenfolks, veiled, slipping out to buy provisions; bitterness, tragedy, pride, old age, broken minds, broken bodies, degeneracy, and decay.

The old Major had often maintained that the whole economic and cultural system of the South, although having many admirable features and at times approximating great possibilities, was neither well thought out nor well balanced. Just as the South could not or would not foresee the trend of events in its great embargo on cotton to England or the fallacy of its high-handed assumptions concerning the English attitude towards the war; and just as it could not or would not see the impossibility of slavery as a permanent institution in a rapidly changing social world, the South, instead of thinking out its economic problems and working out well balanced theories, had merely followed a temporary cycle, partly imitating English standards and partly following the same inclinations which looked to the present only. There were many others than the old Major who thought that the developing social codes and practices of the plantation South would have undermined its own civilization sooner or later. An unthinking aristocracy, a denial of education to the common folk and to women, an untenable attitude towards the Negro, a culture based on superficial acquaintance with the classics, an overemphasis upon luxuries and physical life, hard drinking, and dueling were all units in their count against that part of the old southern civilization. Evidence of the lack of foresight and grounding was plentiful in the chaos which followed such swift economic and social change as to throw a whole people into a new era untrained and undisciplined for modern movements.

There were imperfections and tragedies inherent in the old system at its best. If the women of the South during the war and the tragic aftermath suffered beyond any man's estimate, there were also many who suffered much under the old system, where perchance they learned well a discipline which was to sustain them in the decades to come. There was the beautiful, heroic, and tragic case of several wives of one master, each taking up the load where the last one fell, each succeeding one bearing her quota of stalwart descendants of gentlemen. Thus rode forth a great master, married to a beautiful mistress, who begat near a score of children, some of whom died at birth or later. But even of those who remained there was still a large family. This mistress of the big house not only had her own family to look after, to supervise, to direct their nurture and education according to high standards, but also was called upon to supervise and direct the many industries of the great house and the large number of Negro families with children all about the place. In exchange for her efforts on behalf of these black folks she received of course much service, the nursing of her children, and many loyalties of the categorical sort. It may have been, too, however, that these servants were part and parcel of her family in other ways as mothers of the great master's black children who, added to the score of her own, created a remarkable family indeed.

Thus to the glory and splendor and beauty of the mistress of the big house, with her remarkable mastery, was added much that was improper in any institutional order which claimed recognition for its glory and perfection. This woman, alongside the written and spoken eulogies of her beauty and grace, had little freedom of any sort. Her work, like the work of the woman among the common people, was never done. She was chaperoned and bound in by conventions and great tasks.

Education of the broader sort was not for her, and she, mistress that she was in many ways, was not supposed to interest herself in social, intellectual, and political movements. Many things she was not supposed to see or, if seeing, to record or, if recording, to let it see the light either in her own consciousness or in the records for posterity. Thus this remarkable character became a symbol for a certain type of hypocrisy, superficiality, and rationalization wherever reality was concerned, and this symbolism carried over into the reconstruction period and far into the twentieth century. For decades white children had been turned over to colored mammies, some through genuine continuation of the old custom, some through imitation, some through general unfitness, and some through the grand rationalization that children needed this discipline to make them gentlefolk.

So also had the women of the Confederacy preserved mass pictures of the Old South based upon romantic developments from individual incidences of beauty and glory, pictures that never were on land or sea or earth or sky. The Old South had nothing save perfection; its men were gentlemen; its women, ladies all. Any who criticized the old order or brought to light facts not conducive to its glorification either were not patriots or else were so uncultured as not to understand that all this new generation was neither to the manner nor to the manor born. Perhaps few things had militated so effectively against the South's facing reality as this pattern in which the lovely women of the South had tried to project an atmosphere of gentility, beauty, and glory through an overweening pride, bitterness, and narrowness.

The old Major, following his inclination to philosophize by linking institutions with morality, was wont to raise some questions about the consistency of the old southern emphasis upon the family and the sanctity of the home. Here, he would urge, sometimes sadly and sometimes half bitterly, was a great society with the family as its central unit, and with the glory of the home the glory of its culture, with the sanctity of its womanhood the measure of its purity. And yet in two larger ways the culture of the old institutional South set standards in violation of fundamentals of home and family unity. There was, in the first place, the extrafamilial relationships of the master of the big house with the women slaves in violation of all codes of chivalry toward his own family and the utter lack of respect for the personalities of Negroes. For this sort of thing Uncle John had less than no respect, and toward its standards he came as near profanity as ever his religious conscience would allow; while the old Major himself found it hard to defend even after the manner of southern logic.

In still another way the southern pattern contributed to the disintegration of the Negro family. Husbands and wives among the slaves were sold to go into different parts of the country, sons and daughters were taken from family settings and distributed wherever the buyer might decide. There was here also, then, another striking case of unreality, so much so that many of the southerners never even saw the rank inconsistency of their high morality for the purity of the women and the family in theory and their low morality in the practice of the opposite. Thus, the historians have estimated that "Tennyson's Dream of Fair Women pales into commonplace beside the picture gallery" of the southern woman, her family, and her purity; and "only in the Old South do we find that deference to women which was so innate and that chastity of honor which felt a stain like a wound." But, alas, the picture in reality, for posterity, left the dream of fair women paling not into insignificance but into tragedy, and the "chastity of honor" stained beyond the measurement of mortal. Behind the thin veil of glory were the deep shadows of tragedy.

The tragedy of the South's immoral morality and moral immorality was to project itself far into the generations—beyond the days of the plantation into a South clamoring for purity of race, enforcing its clamor through technical legislation in the midst of an increasing mixed race of its own begetting.

There were distinguished men of great families, handsome in bearing and powerful in influence, and their white sons alongside half-breeds. Their sons were often known in the community as brothers to the mixed, yet challenging unspoken penalties for the naming of the fact. Neither great politicians, nor great educators, nor great preachers, nor great merchants, nor any manner of leaders were exempt from the wild-oat sins of their fathers unto the third and fourth generations. For many years the extension of this relationship constituted a drain on much of the young manhood of the white South, conditioning their whole mental and cultural pattern, draining their energies, filling their minds with remarkable variety of filth, and resulting in the predominance of non-creative stimuli. Young boys and young men, no work to do, sitting around the stores, mingling in the cabins, colleagues in filthy song and story, the creative opportunity of the South passing them by unknown and unsung!

Both the old Major and Uncle John thought that the glory of old family and plantation as reflected in drinking and gambling had been overdone. Even before the war some of the students of the southern order, like the old Major, had begun to wonder whether the extreme ends to which the plantation led in the use of leisure time with much gambling, fighting, dueling, and drinking, were not detracting from the possibilities of creative work and substantial culture. The fact that drinking as a southern tradition had not left in the minds of its own people complete confidence and pride in its pattern was found in the almost universal verdict of bankers and money lenders that the prospect of the young man in question was always determined largely by whether he drank or gambled. The universal advice given to any such young man was that the road ahead was full of promise if only he didn't "drink and gamble." This was not merely later moralizing but the business verdict of the old men who sometimes came through southern communities in which not a single male descendant of the old families survived. And the glory of the old Christmas celebrations among the whites and blacks had its tinge of tragedy and tension and carried over into many later generations.

The magnificence of the old plantation life had its counterpart also in the stubborn individualism, noncooperative habits, violent tempers, feuds, duels, fighting, and isolation. How much glory there was in the heroic pictures of a stalwart statesman seizing the dagger of an opponent, attacking him in public meeting, splitting his head wide open to the brains, and throwing him over a wall into the river, then calmly coming back to address the crowd, depends upon the viewpoint and the standards of measurement. How much and what sort of glory were reflected in the shooting down by rule and institutional sanction of one great man by another great man depends again upon the measuring vessel into which the glory must be poured. If there was great glory and honor in the standards of the gentlemen and the chivalric codes for the settling of personal differences, such glory and honor appeared to later generations to be temporary and, at best, most wasteful. And the carrying of this glory, reflecting fighting codes of honor, into national House of Representatives and Senate, while providing plenty of liveliness and entertainment for the public, had left, nevertheless, a definite imprint not always an asset to the would-be southern statesman of the new day.

The old feudalistic ideals brought over from the English manor and imperfectly adapted also left much that was to be desired. The lack of definite disciplines of work and planning, the development of class feeling between the poor and the rich, between the country and the city, the brooding of the poor whites, competition of white and Negro labor, and many other effects, left in the wake of the war a chaos of ignorant, untrained, superstitious people ill prepared for the fierce struggle that was to come. The struggles of the overseers to become planters, the climbing of the newly rich, the bad manners of many plantation folks, lacking in social experience and provincial through isolation, yet honestly assuming great culture and urbanity, constituted heritages not altogether glorious. And there was cruelty to slaves, driving and beating and putting in chains. How much of this pattern remains today in the mob brutality and white-man defense of mob murder, no man can measure.

The old Major was quite critical also of the whole economic system of the Old South, which he claimed had never continued long enough on sufficiently stable conditions to prove its worth. His father and many relatives, he pointed out, had been forced to move from Virginia by overproduction and depletion of land; then malaria, mosquitoes, floods, had driven them east again; and even at the end of the war the ultimate inefficiency of the system was beginning to show in worn-out lands, in single money crop system, in a sort of fatalistic thriftlessness and wastefulness and the beginnings of economic decay.

Most people, the old Major thought, either did not know about or had forgotten the hundreds of "failures" and bankruptcies of plantations, from too much cotton, or vanishing rice, or vanishing indigo, leaving desolation in their wake. There were the sordid miseries of the migrating hordes, the restlessness and suffering of families, the failures never recorded. There were the vicissitudes of the plantation, disease among the slaves, difficulties with markets, destruction by flood and storm, all of which marked episodes much more important than have usually been recorded. And always there was the lack of scientific information and methods in agriculture, the monopolistic tendency of the big to swallow up the little, the hard competition with free labor, the cheapness of life in slaves, children, women, and the exaggerated claims of southern wealth, a large part of which were based on high evaluation of slaves, the per capita distribution being estimated only for the masters. Throughout all this dispensation a lack of economic training for the generations to come, so that when the war came and the system was destroyed there was no groundwork upon which the new generation could build its new life.

The old southern régime could not survive in an evolutionary world. Its philosophy and religion were not consistent with the development of social justice and democracy. Its economic groundings did not foresee the revolutions to come from scientific discoveries as well as social and economic changes. Its education and culture were not attuned to the modern era of science and the new mobility. The Old South's wounds were deep; not only wounds to its glory and grandeur, but antagonisms left from class distinctions and discriminations of the old order. The extreme snobbishness which the imitation aristocracy manifested had left its mark, and remained as a conditioning influence. No adequate pictures had been painted for the mastery by southern folk of the art and practice of condescension. Later bitterness and antagonisms of the common folks and the poorer whites toward the more wealthy, as well as of the Negroes toward the whites, manifested themselves in politics, religion, education, intersectional and interstate quarreling and conflicts. A modern cultural region in which one class could not mingle socially with another, or recognize its existence socially, although sprung from the same ancestry, could not thrive in that form.

Of the tragic power of the other level of caste in the South—namely, the race-sex chasm between white and Negro and especially Negro man and white woman—neither the old Major nor Uncle John was as yet conscious. If they had thought about it there would have been some such feeling as the Greek verdict about the gods. Nobody had ever explored the realms and reality of their habitat on Mount Olympus or had seen them with his own eyes and returned to tell the tale. But if ever one did return he would know better than to talk about it. On this subject of sex and caste as related to white women, a man could not think. If he thought, he could not talk. The white man had more sense than to talk. For the Negro man it was death.

In later years the glory that was *not* was to be continued in the South's treatment of the Negro. It was not only exploitation, such as was common to other parts of America in their treatment of the immigrant or other disadvantaged groups. It was not only in unnecessary segregation and discrimination. It was also in the total attitude that mistreatment of the Negro was not wrong, and in the action patterns of physical brutality. This was, of course, partly the result of the slavery heritage and the feeling that the Negro was scarcely human. But it was also something more in the cumulative process of irresponsibility and brutality. There could be no southern glory in the spectacle of Negroes shot and hung, hanged and shot to pieces, dragged over roads, cut up and burned. There was no American glory in the insulting by white civilians of American Negro soldiers and sailors. There was no American glory in the beating by police of Negro college youth for no other reason than that they were educated. There was no American glory in the low estate of the Negro woman in the hierarchy of southern values.

CHAPTER X

Middle Folk and Common Man

THROUGH THE PROCESSION of years while the South was con-
valescing from its tragic wounds and sickness, from hunger
and fear, and from grief and bitterness after the Civil War,
there was again this universal power of the middle folk and
common man as Nature and Society were growing a new
generation of men. Buttressed by the great middle class of the
prewar era, the destruction of much of the old planter aristocracy, and the merging of all the folk elements of a new and
mingling South, the "rise of the common man" in the nation
was being recapitulated in the South again.

For, here again, there were the common threads running
through the history of the South; namely, its "American" character and its folk quality. There was, for instance, an English-
man in Pennsylvania begetting sons and daughters of a Dutch
mother, and one of these sons, symbol and reality of the great
American common man in the making, transferring from his
mother's farm where he saw the "Dusty Rebels" of the South
marching to Gettysburg, "reeled down across the continent
into the reconstruction South—a strange wild form of six feet
four—and a rolling tide of rhetoric, a preposterous and comic
invective, as formalized as classical epithet." Down South,
married to a vividly daring daughter of a mixed Scotch clan,
here again was American common man, siring the Thomas
Wolfe symbol of southern common man become genius, writing in powerful portraiture to reflect the "sum of all the movements of our lives" in symbol of *Look Homeward Angel* or
again more powerful in *Of Time and the River*. And always,
over and over again, of time, of geographic factors, of the
culture and behavior of the people in a region.

Some such big common man, six feet four or perhaps of smaller, sturdier stature, maybe five feet seven, full of the mysteries and complexes of nature, was forever explaining much of the character and behavior of the South in the annals of struggle following reconstruction. And like many another sturdy common man, along with the hazards of accident and tragedy "whatever he touched in that rich fortress of his soul sprang into golden life: as the years passed, the fruit trees—the peach, the plum, the cherry, the apple—grew great and bent beneath their clusters. His grape vines thickened into brawny ropes of brown and coiled down the high wire fences of his lot, and hung in a dense fabric, upon his trellises, roping his domain twice around. They climbed the porch end of the house and framed the upper windows in thick bowers. And the flowers grew in rioting glory in his yard— the velvet-leaved nasturtium, slashed with a hundred tawny dyes, the rose, the snowball, the red-cupped tulip, and the lily. The honeysuckle drooped its heavy mass upon the fence; wherever his great hands touched the earth it grew fruitful for him."

A thousand farmers multiplied by other thousands were symbol of man and land, of nature and frontier, of rugged ruralism and stanch stubbornness that knows no surrender. They loved the land and the crops. They fought with the weather and its hardships. They became hard with the ways of winter weather and skeptics and conservatives taught by Nature to watch and wait.

And there was again the forgotten woman, middle folk *de luxe*, mother of the backbone of the South. What she "endured in pain and fear and glory no one knew." As she "marched down these enormous years of love and loss, stained with the rich dyes of pain and pride and death, and with the great wild flare . . . her limbs faltered in the grip of ruin, but she came on, through sickness and emaciation, to victorious strength."

Much of the glory that was the South and of the grandeur that was *not* was found in the experiences of the millions of middle folk not commonly recorded in the annals of the 'heroic or in the stories of submerged groups. Much that went on in the South "was too completely tragic to furnish material for theatrical tragedy, far too high in spirit for written romance which crawls along the beaten paths of life, too stark for poetry." Indeed the culture of the Old South and of the New was found exclusively neither in the romanticism of its aristocratic gentry nor in the tragedy and comedy of the much described poor whites, but in the living drama of its common folks; for there were more, many more, of the people represented by Uncle John than in the combined aggregate of the old Major and the remnant poor across the river. And in their life and labor particularly were to be found not only the fabric of the New South and its civilization, but much that was in the Old as well.

Pictures of Lee's army, the best fighting units of the whole Confederacy, reflected the complex structure of the Old South. Scions of aristocratic houses marching alongside conscripts from countryside, backwoods, and mountain coves, fighting a common battle, reflected much of the glory of the common man, "their beards unkempt, their uniforms torn and patched with clumsy hands, their feet upon the ground, devoted men, ironsides after the fashion of Cromwell's army two hundred years before, their commander second only to God himself." So they marched and fought during the war; so also they marched sadly back—common men but with heroism a sort of commonplace virtue within them: armless sleeves; crutches, ragged, gray uniforms, in battered hats and caps; remnants of flags; relics of a brave army; wrecks of men—common men who had borne the physical burden of a nation for its error slavery, plain countrymen, blameless victims of a sectional wrath. Nevertheless, a part of their story was found in the fact that they "had miraculously survived and crawled to barren homes from the clash and slaughter and from starvation and such deadly vain endeavor as no other men have ever known and lived."

Back home they had been the backbone of the Old South even as they must be for the New. Thousands of them: "humdrum, but honest, pious, substantial and numerous . . . no pretense to spectacular living . . . not given to ancestor worship . . . not aristocratic in political view . . . not aristocratic even in the religious preference . . . moderate landholdings . . . few slaves . . . small planters . . . a great element of society, its solidity if not its ornamentation, with which the glamorous plantation legend failed to make connection. Such an inaccuracy is not a casual one; it is not meaningless; it is basic." Here, then, was the picture of one type of common man of the South, the small planter, "living in a modest home, tilling a hundred or so acres of soil, earning by the sweat of his brow and a very little Ethiopian perspiration a none too luxurious living, courteous, hospitable, withal simple, frolicking in mild fashion on rare occasions, voting for Jefferson and those he felt the followers in spirit of the great democrat, genuinely but not painfully pious, after a Methodist, Baptist, or Presbyterian fashion, raising—not rearing—a family of children, and sleeping at last with his fathers."

The mosaic of the Old South was made up of nonslaveholders and the small slaveholders scattered everywhere, as well as of the larger owners. At least three-fourths of the white population had no proprietary interest in the Negro. In the cotton counties of the Mississippi delta, men without slaves were to be found largely as overseers and perhaps woodcutters to supply the steamboats with fuel. On the other hand, "In the mountains, in some parts of the pine barrens, and on the borders north and west, they comprised nearly all the population. Everywhere else they dwelt as neighbors of the planters and of well-to-do townsmen. Their standards of comfort and propriety, their manners and morals, varied with the vicinage, with health and wealth, with education and opportunity, and with individual proclivities and predilections. Joseph E. Brown, wartime governor of Georgia, emerged from a mountain farm with a yoke of oxen as pay for schooling; a contemporary as governor of Virginia, began adult life as a carpenter; C. G. Memminger, Confederate Secretary of the Treasury, was an orphanage boy; and Andrew Johnson a tailor's apprentice, illiterate until a wife took him in hand. These and their fellow millions cannot be lumped as 'poor whites.'"

The picture reveals many log houses alongside the mansions. Allen Tate has described the small farmer dwelling in a log cabin such as Jefferson Davis was born in: "If the farmer prospered he made a hall of the passage and added porches front and rear or even raised a second story. Most of the household activities went on in the large bedroom in which the farmer and his wife and the youngest children slept. The cooking was done before the huge open fireplace. The family dinner, consisting of bacon, corn bread, mush and molasses, was spread on a checkered tablecloth, sometimes on the bare boards of the pine table which stood in the center of the room. The farmer's wife washed her clothes out of doors, heating the water in an enormous pot over a fire made of chips or the smaller sticks of wood from the woodpile. If the farmer owned a Negro family, as was frequently the case, the mistress 'minded' the young pickaninnies along with her own children, in order that their mother might be released for service in the field. A small farmer, like Samuel Davis, worked as a rule side by side with his slaves."

Walter Hines Page saw in this great class of sober-living and thrifty proprietors the economic backbone and the moral fiber of the southern states. Largely unsung by poets and romancers, they cultivated their lands themselves, frequently working their own plow, like industrious New Englanders. "Their establishments were well and neatly kept; their toil yielded a sufficient income to provide most comforts and certain luxuries; their sons and daughters had a good schooling, and occasionally instruction in the higher branches at a denominational college." There was glory enough among these substantial middle folk if glory and romance are seen as realities in the midst of difficult situation. Here again there was much of the Old and the New South mixed, much of the dividing line between old aristocracy and the common man being obliterated. There had been many southerners who distrusted slavery and had great loyalty towards the Federal Union. There had been great national patriotism in the South, and credit was due to the double patriots.

Of the men and women in this great middle group there were many and notable pictures. A clan of eleven brothers and three sisters with the patriarch father of them all living to the ripe age of ninety-five, every man among them a powerful worker and fighter, and every man looking a red-bearded giant. Of the group, one was a singer who taught his music lessons far and wide and published songbooks galore; one was a blacksmith, always hankering after new inventions; one was the greatest horse trader in the community; the others were farmers, each inclined to some special excellence, whether it be a brag patch of cotton, the heaviest display in hog-killing time, or the fastest horse in the community; and to the last one they were militant Populists just before the turn of the century when southern Democrats and Populists came to grips. The old patriarch bellowed eloquently that he had shouldered his old musket one time against the damn Yankees, and he would be damned if he wouldn't just as soon try it again against the Democrats! Such were the later pictures of a developing southern Populism among the common folks.

And there was the picture of the sons and daughters of a Walter Hines Page antecedent, every one grown to vigorous maturity: "huge figures frequently gathered at the place for family celebrations . . . the Reverend Jesse . . . the theologian of the family . . . 'Uncle Jim,' famous especially for the mighty volume of his singing voice . . . Pascal, the family scholar . . . politics also represented . . . 'Uncle Rufus,' a

Whig leader before the Civil War . . . Malvina married to a Methodist preacher . . . Ann Eliza also the wife of a Methodist preacher and Araminta suggesting an acquaintance with Elizabethan poetry."

There was the youngest daughter of Uncle John whose earliest experiences centered largely around the privations and hardships multiplied by the Civil War and its aftermath. This little girl in her first years especially seemed a symbol of all that was beautiful and pleasureful. She sought out the simple flowers and shrubs and rocks on hillside and bluff and by the edge of rippling waters. She sang almost incessantly and danced and played with rare imagination. Then 1860 and the war. Then enlistment of father and brothers on a battle front in which they were little concerned save as patriots or conscripts, united in a cause to which they had given little attention, and drawn into a war for which they were in no wise responsible. Then hardships and long suffering. The song of the little girl turned plaintive, nature became fields and rows of cotton and corn. She grew up; pleasure was translated into service, religion became a merciless tyrant demanding all pleasure for itself. Love of Jesus was substituted for love of youth, the beauty of the spirit transcended the beauty of the body. Then marriage and the family, many children, three dead, and the love of the beautiful was translated into the pictures of the promised land; aspiration turned toward meeting the children on the golden shore; continued hardships, after-the-war poverty holding on, always frustration of all aspiration for the beautiful. Then typhoid fever, interpreted as punishment from God because of her secret aspirations for beauty and companionship. Then more suffering and conflict until in the latter days of her short span of years in the service of the Lord, in the search for life and beauty, there came the bitter confession that no longer would she sing,

> Gladly will I toil and suffer,
> Only let me walk with Thee.

She might toil, she said, but of suffering she had had enough.

Another daughter of the old Major married a bright young farmer, and they both started out without property. The first years were full of fruitful effort, in the development both of the family and of the farm; the man was a good man, perhaps a little too much inclined to drink the juice of the corn, but a "good provider" and a good father of his children. There were seven children, of whom the oldest was a daughter upon whose shoulders was to fall the burden of the household. The next oldest was a boy. As he grew up, it was clear that he was a sort of physical giant, the best wrestler and runner among all the children at school, good-natured, lovable; and following in his steps was the next oldest boy, like unto him. They came to be known as defenders of smaller children in trouble. There were next two daughters of rare personality and enthusiasm, overflowing with wit and humor, and reflecting a fine composite beauty of country girlhood and simple gracefulness. And the younger boys, somewhat after the fashion of the older children. Typical country folks, quick, fair work, fair mischief, the whole family of nine presenting rather an attractive picture of middle folk in the after-war South.

Then hardships of sickness added to the struggle for existence. The family was stricken with typhoid. The father was taken, the mother stricken, and for twelve unbroken weeks there was always a member of the family "down"; then the mother invalided, in bed for six years. It was never reported of her that she failed in humor and good cheer. Throughout the community, neighbors came to see her, forgot to cheer her in their habit of being cheered by her. Then the broken family made a new start in the mill village. A new home, with new ambition, more money, and again cheer and optimism abounded. The older daughter, much after the disposition of her mother, turned leader and nurse, Sunday-school and church worker for the small village and community, until she became a sort of symbol of that which was beautiful and good. Then the white plague, too much work to save money and to save souls, and an aristocratic spirit among the common folk succumbed in the unequal struggle. It was a picture of a promising family of middle folk, with all manner of promise to community and state, placed in an unequal struggle in which they never had a chance.

There were the pictures of individuals—farmer, doctor, teacher, preacher, common men in a common cause struggling to rebuild a civilization. There was the picture of a physician come up from the Confederate army while still a stripling, and contriving to get a medical education. For forty years "he carried on a practice so immense and so widely scattered that it would drive three modern medicos into nervous prostration in six months. The horses the man drove to death would have remounted a regiment of cavalry; and in the vast, poverty-smitten region over which he ranged, not one patient in five could ever pay him a cent. He could hardly buy a decent coat, not to mention expensive surgical equipment; yet I doubt that he slept a single night through for half a lifetime. Through sleet and snow on many a bitter night alcohol carried him through when he must otherwise have failed some suffering pauper in the remote wilderness. Alcohol got him at last."

There were other pictures of simple living, and gala occasions, all-day singing and church meetings, Thanksgiving and Christmas, as times began to grow better. The southerner, whether from plantation or from farm, well-to-do or poor, was wont to draw heavily upon nature and whatever supplies he had. Wasteful but enjoying himself. Mixed pictures again. There was many a cheerful picture of Christmas in home and farm of middle folk and common man. "Long strands of red peppers hang to nails outside the kitchen door. . . . Shoats growing fatter each day on the sweet acorns falling from the live-oak trees, and on the peanuts and potatoes, peas and ears of corn which were left in the fields when those crops were gathered. . . . In the wild-crabapple thickets fruit covering the ground. . . . The sugar-cane mills with their bright fires making shining red stars at night, the fragrance of the boiling syrup steaming up from the brown gallons which simmer and thicken in the wood-lined vats. . . . Sweet potatoes in banks . . . hay in stacks, corn in the barns, most of the cotton picked. . . . Cotton gins run at full tide. . . . Axes swing and ring in the woods . . . fat rosiny pine knots. . . . Wild broom grass ripe enough . . . for brooms. . . . Quail in the fields."

And throughout the land simple farmhouses with front yards clean-swept with broom and wind. . . . Box borders . . . large box-woods in formal array inclosing the little paradise of flowers . . . old-fashioned flowers—zinnias, petunias, vari-colored phlox, red feather plush, blown in the wind, hollyhocks, stately, graceful, majestic, guardians of home and tradition . . . and the honeybees always in profusion and all manner of birds and butterflies . . . harmonies of nature and life, realities of the bucolic scene . . . and figs and grapes, big round red plums, blue little plums, apples, May apples and June, Yates and Winesaps . . . peaches, early June and Georgia Belle and golden Elbertas . . . scuppernongs and muscadines . . . watermelons and muskmelons . . . Spanish peanuts and goobers . . . popcorn and hickory nuts . . . chestnuts and chinquapins . . . jellies and preserves . . . backbone and spareribs . . . sausage, haslet, and chitterlings . . . new wheat bread and water-ground meal for corn pone with cracklings . . . milk and honey . . . blackberry wine and apple cider . . . locust and persimmon beer . . . and inside clean rooms, simple in old-fashioned plainness and elegance . . . mottoes over the doors . . . Bible and family portraits . . . feathery beds of ease and sheets of immaculate whiteness . . . family prayers . . . the singing of hymns . . . simplicity with natural loyalties and emotions . . . "loyalty, liberty, and service." . . . "God bless our Home."

Other pictures of the mountain common man abounded in the southern highlands . . . Blue Ridge hills . . . ridge country of Virginia . . . eastern Kentucky . . . eastern Tennessee . . . western North Carolina . . . northwestern South Carolina . . . north Georgia . . . northeastern Alabama . . . a hundred and twelve thousand square miles . . . New York and New England combined, or England, Ireland, Scotland, and Wales put into one . . . young life in its prime . . . energy and daring . . . leaping from childhood into manhood . . . gambling squarely upon the benevolence of soil, growth, and weather . . . planting crops, hunting game, catching fish, harvesting fruits and berries . . . self-sufficiency. The wife cooking, churning, making the clothes, keeping the home, and picking the geese for feather beds . . . midwives, herb doctors, basket makers, carders, millers . . . water mills, farm boys with bags of shelled corn swung over their horses' withers . . . shirts open, lips pursed for whistling, bodies asway to the leisurely, plodding gaits of their mounts . . . surprisingly free from awkwardness and uncouthness . . . an unpresuming dignity, a quiet courtliness, unspoiled by the conventional forms of etiquette and politeness . . . a genuine, unhurried serenity . . . old-time, homely ambitions . . . folk romancers and romantic rascals . . . moonshiners . . . Robin Hoods . . . Friar Tucks . . . Maid Marians . . . Little Johns . . . greenwood revels . . . sheriffs . . . Saturday night gambles and gambols . . . handcuffs, jail houses, penitentiaries, and buryin' grounds . . . the Land of the Sky . . . azure walls of the Blue Ridge . . . the cool spicy breath of shady glens . . . swift streams . . . overhanging masses of mountain laurel and rhododendron . . . the banjo . . . Monkey Simon with his tambourine . . . the master instrument of music, the fiddle uncramped by books and black notes of the masters . . . sentimental songs, sung by lovely women and gallant men . . . intricate circles of the country dance, weaving and swinging in graceful winding figures through the trampled stubble of the darkening field . . . the voice of the caller, borne far into the evening air . . . the "old-time fiddler" an institution.

There were still other pictures of the common man. There were the tenants and the small cotton farmers, with more than half of the sháre tenants in the United States found in the southern states. Of all the farmers to whom cotton was the chief source of income, more than two-thirds were tenants. Thus, with a percentage of tenancy in the United States of less than 40, eight states in the South had a rate of over 50 per cent. In the United States a fifth of all farms changed occupants. In eight cotton states more than a third of the rented farms changed their tenants. December and the tenant in the Cotton Belt "takes a mind to move. . . . Over the neighborhood he rides, holding conferences with this and that landlord about a place for next year. . . . Landlords looking for good tenants and tenants looking for good landlords . . . in country stores, at crossroads, in backyards, and on front porches. The landlord asks questions about "the crop made under the renter's former landlord, his reasons for leaving, the number in the family able to work, the acreage to be planted in cotton. The tenant wants to know the kind of house on the farm and the details of supplies to be furnished. The deal may be closed verbally, or a lease may be signed. If the renter is satisfied that he can better himself by moving he agrees to terms and announces to the family on his return home that next year 'we are going to live on the old Brockton place over across the creek.' "

Some of these tenants came to their lot by the hard way of misfortune and the turn of war and reconstruction. Some fell naturally into the new southern share and crop renting economy. Some evolved from mountain migrants. Some just grew. And some were the issue of that small portion of the white South without slaves who were "wretchedly 'po' white trash,' scorned even by the slaves. Any crops they might plant were likely to die of neglect, any jobs they procured were apt to be lost by default, any lands to be taken for debt. They commonly fell to drifting as tenants or squatters in wilderness clearings unless they chanced upon barren lands where they might cluster in communities of their own squalid kind."

Something more of the portraiture of southern tenants may be found in other pictures of the rural and mill-village South. Thousands were illiterate, most of them were poor: "Hit's mighty hard to work all year and then not have a new pair of shoes for Christmas," or to end the year in debt and in want. And so it was inevitable that some of these ever migrating tenants would join that large group of mill workers. And there were the new pictures of the mill-village common folk of the South, a tremendously important part of the southern fabric. Many of them of the best of stocks, many from the best of common-folk families, many of them of the essence of America. Here again were mixed pictures. Early morning, and thousands of mill folk rising and going to work at the call of the mill whistle. Day in and day out for six days in the week, Sunday alone excepted, responding to this blast of the mill whistle. It was as if the religious rules and early hours of the old New England children's homes were in force again! There was the morning whistle: "The mill worker's wife dresses hurriedly, kindles the fire in a little wood or oil stove, and hastily prepares breakfast. The mill worker, meanwhile, and his children are making themselves ready for the more than daily dozen. Sometimes the mother goes too. At five-thirty there is a second warning of the mill whistle, this time telling the worker that in twenty-five minutes he must be at his spinning frame or loom. By this time he is eating his breakfast. Fifteen minutes later, or a quarter to six, another warning is sounded, three short blasts of the whistle, which means that ten minutes more remain and the worker must be on his way."

Pictures of moving activity; here they come to work. If it is summer, the morning is light and one sees men and women, girls and boys, coming hurriedly from every direc-

tion. In the adjacent countryside the mill workers' kinsfolk on
the farm start for the fields. If it is winter, the workers are
heeding the call of the mill whistle though the visitor cannot
see them because of the darkness of the early morning. Five
hundred, one thousand, two thousand, five thousand strong
they come. These people of ages from fourteen to fifty, of farm
and mountain heritage for the most part, come teeming in to
their new-found work. The men come clad in overalls, or a
three-dollar pair of trousers and a coat which does not match.
The women and girls clad in dresses of gingham or of similar
material, the older ones sometimes with the cotton lint from
the previous day's work still clinging to their hair, hurry to
the spinning or spooling department, or to the weave shop.
And back home again, and tomorrow like today, unless to
move to another mill.

And the never ending pictures of the Negro common man.
No South, no Negro—no Negro, no South. Black Ulysses and
his compatriots . . . Negro worksters and songsters, un-
changing scenes . . . local community laborers . . . road
and construction gangs . . . trucks loaded with black worksters transferring from town to camp and from camp to town
. . . quick-shifting labor and faithful keepers of homes and
grounds and stores and cars . . . now the ramblin' mind, the
shiftless loafer, the quarrelsome Negro always complaining
. . . now the faithful worker, distinguished in folk character,
builder of gardens and houses and towns and wealth . . .
labor turnover and changing jobs . . . Negro workers averag-
ing a job a month . . . others, like Black Ulysses, aggregating
over the years seemingly innumerable tasks . . . trouble with
the "captain" . . . trouble with the "walker" . . . trouble
with the work . . . too much expected, too little pay . . .
rest periods and wanderlust . . . untrained and unskilled
hordes . . . no guidance or wholesome direction . . . lack
of dependability and reliability . . . characteristic light-

heartedness and subtle humor . . . reckless abandon and folk freedom . . . road and construction camps . . . railroad and highway scenes . . . black drivers of mule teams . . . six-mule wheelers and Mike and Jerry teamed to a scoop . . . black men and black songs . . . builders of a material progress . . . grading down hillsides . . . tunneling through mountains . . . raising up buildings . . . rain and shine, hot and cold . . . good workmen and bad. . . .

Other pictures from *Rainbow Round My Shoulder, Wings on My Feet, Cold Blue Moon*. Evening in southern towns and cities, Negro quarters teeming with life . . . evening song and blues . . . pianos jangling with phonograph concerts . . . much coming and going to and fro . . . lighthearted and talkative Negroes alongside silent and sullen souls . . . fine clothes for the Jew and perfume of Arabia . . . loud talking and easy walking . . . dancing and banjo singing . . . rising action till late into the night . . . sound slumbers and a world of work and struggle forgotten in a deep sleep . . . Black Ulysses, a veteran two-timer moving on to new places . . . a little-scarred love-legionnaire a part of all that he had fought . . . holding his own with zest in the midst of sex conflict and strife—heat, passion, and ruthless survival . . . blood and pearls, razors and hearts . . . now New Orleans, now Vicksburg, now Memphis, now north again to Cincinnati or Detroit or Chicago and back "home" . . . social episodes in the Negro scene . . . church meetings and picnics . . . church suppers and socials . . . country and village dances . . . corn shuckings and quiltings . . . courting and quarreling . . . Christmas and holiday gatherings . . . lodge and fraternal events . . . men, women, and children, dressed in Sunday best . . . high spirits and serious business. . . . And, more serious, "I'm conditioned up like this: I can do what I have to do . . . Ain't no time, ain't no place, ain't nothin' but me an' my feelin's . . . Been mighty change since I been bo'n, change where I been. Never changed me."

Yet middle folk and common man were still more than all these. The occupations and the professions were all there, dynamic in their processes of struggle and expansion. Leaders there were of many sorts and on many sublevels of common man. And there were common folk of the vintage of all the rest of the nation. Indeed the story of the common man is reminder that much that is called "the South" is not unlike human nature and common folk everywhere; and this fact must be kept constantly in mind. The backbone of the people in middle folk wanting to be let alone, stubborn in their convictions and folk-ways. Common men professing Christianity and democracy, willing to fight for their "principles." Common folk defending their women, proud of it: "I wouldn't want to belong to a people who wouldn't defend their women, would you?" Common folk, high and low, with race prejudices, common folk strong in body vigor and lusty natures. Common folk weak and sickly and suffering "miseries." Common folk proud of their American common folk, preachers and teachers, doctors and lawyers, farmers and industrialists, men and women, rural and urban, all human beings first and foremost, the stuff of which society is made.

And middle folk of the middle folk, common men of the common men, often the leaders of the people, are the most vivid reflectors of the great level of mankind that makes the folk culture. Perhaps members of state legislatures are, after all, most characteristic of the folk. Too numerous over the years to name and characterize, it is possible, however, to note their general qualifications and occupations as indices of working local "democracy." Here, again, the states vary greatly, although showing general homogeneity in religious affiliations, occupations, education. Of the eighteen hundred members of state legislatures in the southeastern states, 95 per cent were Democrats. Over half were from rural homes, and only one in nine came from cities. Nearly 90 per cent were church members, of whom two-thirds were Methodists and Baptists. More than three hundred different occupational combinations were represented in the southeastern states. Samplings to balance the lawyer's portion: farmer and planter, evangelist and preacher, carpenter and editor, sheriff and jailer, football coach and barber, and others of, for, and by the common folk. The lawyers, however, represented the largest number in each of the state legislatures.

Here again the role of middle folk and common man in the life of the South is best portrayed by what the common folks did and what they believed. Already in the "way of history" something of the role of the middle folk and poor whites has been emphasized. Now we come to sense the power of middle folk and common man in their religion and song and in their education and politics, as well as in the products of their racial attitude and behavior. And, first of all, is the role of religion.

CHAPTER XI

In the Name of God, Amen

IN THE BEGINNING of America, as the United States was to constitute this America, and as this nation has continued to be the symbol and reality of the American Dream, faith in divine guidance was the seed of the first plantings, and a stern Puritan religion the first fruits of the New World. "In the Name of God, Amen" began the Mayflower Compact, in which the new compatriots sought to covenant together for the better ordering of the new society through those "acts as shall be thought most meete and convenient for ye general goode of ye colonie." It was thus that this covenant, meeting the first crisis of dissension and survival, started the new world on the long American Road "solemnly and mutually, in ye presence of God and one of another."

And there were other "articles of agreemente in ye union and Confedderation" of similar essence. Witness the eloquent Bradford's History: "Whereas we all came into these parts of America with one and ye same end and aime, namely, to advance the kingdome of our Lord Jesus Christ, & to injoye ye liberties of ye Gospell in puritie with peace . . ." "In the Name of God, Amen," too, was symbol of salutation and signature in solemn letters back and forth to the Old World and to the New, letters of personal intimacy or letters of public affairs. It made no difference what sort of letter or document, there was salutation and signature always with the sign of devout reverence to God. Thus, one Richard Andrewes signs himself "Your Loving Friend" and "So comending you & yours, and all ye Lord's people, unto ye gratious protection and blessing of ye Lord, . . ." And one Charles Chauncy writes: "The Lord in mercie directe & prosper ye desires of his servants that desire to walk before him in truth & right-

eousnes in the administration of justice, and give them wis-
dome and largnes of harte."

This early American religious conditioning in reality set
the stage and gave continuing incidence to the religious South,
which has continued this particular way of culture more literally and more aggressively than any other region of the
nation. There were again Ben Robertson's kinsfolk, symbolic
of the great mass of middle folk and common man, militantly
proclaiming the religious nature of the southern folk, believing that their religion was worth fighting for and practicing
the credo on many an occasion. "We were southerners, native-
born and of the heart of the South," they would say; but they
got their Christianity from Salem and Plymouth. "We are
southern Jeffersonian Puritans. Sometimes I think there is
more of Salem in our southern hills today than is left in Salem."
And again, "We are stark northern people, bitten in spirit by
frosts and hard winters, hampered in memory by darkness
and ice, and our country is warm and sunlit and southern
. . . To live a religious life is hard." Yet the South, religious
scion of its New England parentage, is willing to fight to enforce its religion. Even as many a noble Christian was put
into stocks or ostracized as witch or disgraced as "dirty atheist"
in Puritan New England, so the Ku Klux Klan of the later not
so noble South has attempted to pass its own violent judgments upon the nonconforming of the third and fourth generation of them that worshiped not as the fathers did. And even
as New England worshipers thanked God that through His
divine interference they were able to burn and slaughter
hundreds of Indian women and children, so southern Chris-
tians counted the Negro as beyond the pale of human beings
and, therefore, outside the Christian code of brotherhood of
man and fatherhood of God.

There were other ways in which the South patterned after
the early American religious influence. One was in the found-

ing of colleges and universities. Even as Harvard, America's
most distinguished university, was founded for the education
of ministers, and even as Columbia's King's College and Yale
and Princeton's earlier heritage were bottomed in high religious purpose, so the South's oldest universities were
modeled after them—North Carolina on the Princeton influence, Georgia on Yale leadership, and the others following
in their time, save Virginia's Thomas Jefferson motivation to
keep state and church separate. Yet the South carried its religious education much further, developing a standard pattern by which in each state there was to be a church college
for each of the three major denominations, Baptist,
Methodist, and Presbyterian, with smaller institutions galore
representing the lesser constituencies. Yet the South has also
followed the rest of the nation in minimizing the religious
influence and control. Thus, Vanderbilt University and Duke
University passed from religious control to secular. There was
the common folk saying that the state universities were God-
less institutions devoted to the teaching of evolution and to
the irreligious nurture of rich men's sons; and for many years
it was generally claimed that the church colleges provided
most of the teachers and educational leaders of the South.

Another way in which the religious South parallels the
earlier religious New England is in the predominance of
ministers among those who lead the people. It is generally
known that New England long had the largest ratio of distinguished men in the nation. It has perhaps not been so
generally observed that religious leaders constituted the
largest ratio of them all. Vance calls attention to the fact that
in the earlier period of development the Northeast provided
357 notables in the field of religion, or 16.4 per cent of all
their great recorded in the *Dictionary of American Biography*.
While the South's distinction in leadership as recorded by
the national verdicts was in the fields of political and legal
attainment, at its state and regional levels religious leaders
seem preeminent if we add to the powerful influence of the

ministerial leadership that of leaders in religious education and the lay-religious business leaders. In every state where a popular census was taken of leaders who influenced the people most, there has been strong representation of religious leaders.

In the total story of the South, the Protestant minister of the gospel has constituted perhaps the greatest single influence other than the political leaders and orators. In the earlier days the circuit rider was a power, and in both earlier and later days the evangelical revivalist exerted a powerful influence. Still later not only the Protestant leaders but the Catholic groups began to take important parts in social service and public affairs in relation to race, crime, vice, and citizenship. Of especial significance has been the rise of women religious leaders, with influence not only in church affairs but in the improvement of race relations.

So important has this religious influence been that it may well be said that the way of the South has been also the way of religion. Already in the chapters on the way of the folk and of culture we have emphasized the elemental place of religion. Now we have noted that the South has carried over the American religious heritage much as its culture reflects the continuing frontier heritage. That is, in many ways, measured by religious indices, the character of the South in the first half of the twentieth century still resembled that of all America in the century before. This might be illustrated at any length by the American Sabbath and its observance, by the influence of the church in all culture, by the attitudes toward evolution, and by the close association of the church with the upper brackets of the wealthier groups of Americans. The South has all these, and also the emotional power of the evangelical religion among the common folk and its use as a tool of demagogic appeal in politics.

Yet all of this is in character with the folk culture of the region and with the powerful psychology of the religious conditioning. An essential part of the picture, therefore, is the story of the folk quality of southern religion and of its negative influence in the life of the region. Here again there is the usual contradictory situation: to millions of the folk of the South religion has been the sustaining power in times of tragedy and diversity; and, on the other hand, the church has had its limitations and its weaknesses, like other institutions. Of the grandmothers whose symbolism of courage and strength and faith we have featured as a powerful influence in the biography of the South, let Ben Robertson one more time give the picture: "My grandmother and many Southerners like her became serene in their old age because during their days they had faced every sort of tragedy and desperate trouble and had survived—there was no terror left that could try them. They had fought a gigantic devastating war and had lost it; they had seen the country stripped and looted, had lived under the unreasoning despotism of soldiers, under a radical black government; almost starving, they had taken the law into their own hands, had ridden at night and terrorized, had not hesitated to vote tombstones in elections; they had nullified an amendment to the Constitution, had reconstructed a state, and in their old age their strength was firm; they were stoic in repose."

The religious life of the South was of two sorts in its elemental manifestations. One was the creed and the faith of the Christian evangelical gospel and its expression through formal worship and church support. The other was the elemental power of song, shared somewhat also by the lover of the secular folk song and music, which constitutes a separate folk influence in the life of the South.

Of the religious character of the folk there is perhaps no better example than the multiple, yet simple, experiences of Uncle John and his compatriots of the common folk. Uncle John's tent at the camp-meeting grounds was a mecca for preachers; his home and the homes of his children always kept open house for the local pastor, who often brought good cheer and inspiration, and sometimes entertainment to larger households. To the tired mother, a visitor, new thoughts, a joke, and a benediction were ample recompense for the additional work of killing the chicken and frying it to be served with hot biscuits made from the spare supply of white flour. "Well, now, let me see, Sister Southern," the man of God would drawl out, "this boy looks like a judge. See that bump on his head." And: "Ah, yes, this one will sholy be a bishop. Look here at this bump." And: "Aha, look at this little queen of a girl! Ain't she sweet?" And so the mother was cheered, the children were entertained, and Uncle John felt better for having the preacher "break bread" with him and say a "word of prayer" before bedtime, albeit no preacher was ever found who could pray more eloquently than Uncle John himself. There was vitality in that simple otherworldly religion.

And as for the annual camp meeting, there were pictures challenging all resources of descriptive art. It was a forerunner of summer camps in the mountains or countryside, of Chautauqua, religious conferences, and of Billy Sunday's tabernacle and sawdust trails. It was a composite of the regular summer revival meetings, and special Pentecostal showers. Once each year during "laying-by time," the community reveled in one great feast of worship, of rest, and of eating. About the old church and the big "arbor" tabernacle were the tents, rows around. They were made of rough lumber, simple and comfortable after the manner of forest tent-cottages. Tables and bed frames were made, rough and strong. Each tent had its bedroom, its dressing room, its big dining room with the long table, and often the "preacher's room." A week before the meeting all hands turned in for such a cleaning as only a camp-meeting ground, unused for a year, could demand. The inside of the building was swept and washed. Fresh wheat straw was scattered thickly on the ground floors and made into mattress ticks for the beds.

Coops were made for the chickens; back home, lambs were killed for mutton, pigs for pork, and neighbors cooperated in killing a beef. Cookstoves were set up, wood was cut, and all was ready. There was thrill and excitement to it—whether more for the children or the elders, or the ministers, the records do not tell.

And so forgathered the hosts. Some had tents. Others came for the day. Others were invited as guests of those who had tents and guest facilities. From far and wide they came, kinsfolk and friends, the earnest and the curious. City folks arrayed in fine clothes came to impress, and to enjoy religion in their own way. It was a season of rejoicing and courting and comfort. And what meals were served in the tents! . . . Long table, at one head the senior preacher and around him brethren in profusion of numbers and spirits; at the other head Uncle John, and round about him members of his clan and their guests. The women, for the most part, busy with serving. And such serving! The second noon dinner of the week. There were fried chicken, and steak, and roast beef and mutton, and boiled vegetables and fresh potatoes, and all manner of abundant dishes, pickles, jellies, and jams. And pies—apple, and egg custard, and sweet potato—and cakes of many kinds, products of choice family recipes. Much talk and enjoyment. Fine food, nectar for the gods.

Then on to the big tent—the "arbor"—tabernacle. A bell ringing, people gathering for the preliminary service. A song and prayer. Couples walking around, strolling down to the big spring of incomparable cool water, strolling back. Gathering crowds, the sermon begins. A fair sermon and success. Dismissed congregation and supper. Then the first *real* service with the big preacher brought from the conference's best ranks. A big sermon, responsive singing, and the camp meeting is on. Tomorrow a little more fervent and tomorrow and tomorrow increasing crowds and religious fervor until the meeting has assumed the proportions of a genuine revival.

Earnest, tired people seeking after God find him. Young, wild youth seeking to avoid him, escape. Others are caught in the sweep and "saved." Couples in love seek God together. Others draw apart, alienated the one from the other by the Holy Spirit. Exhortations, showers of blessings, shouting and praying, some years the spirit moving more than others, but always a tired, hungry people going home exhausted, but somehow satisfied.

These camp-meeting scenes were reminiscent of much of the fabric that was earlier America. On the psychological side they were powerful combinations of physical and spiritual stimuli. Sweet-smelling wheat straw against songs of exaltation; hard benches against ease in Zion; pungent odors of well cooked food and the eloquent "blessings"; new-smelling smoke of cigars from the city, lemonade in the shade of the trees, watermelons in abundance, the Tom Watson and the Georgia Rattlesnake unbeatable! And genuine, honest, and sincere religion, still remnants of the pioneer and wilderness of the frontier South, still reminiscent of the circuit rider and his powerful and picturesque influence over a people. For few figures have been more interesting and unique than the circuit-rider type of preacher, whose life and influence molded powerfully the destiny of the South. His was a guiding hand frequently more powerful than all the economic forces often adjudged to be the determinant factor in southern economy. His was the influence paving the way for the later religious South, still emotional and Pentecostal, but expressing itself more in objective attacks upon men and causes than in the subjective old-time religion that was "good for Paul and Silas."

As a matter of fact, the old-time religion was not good enough for the folks. The camp meetings evolved into such mongrel mixtures that a son of Uncle John took steps which ultimately led to their abandonment. Year by year the meetings grew larger and less orderly. A summer hotel was built, advertisements were spread abroad, a temporary drugstore and soda fountain was established. Couples sat out in buggies more than in meeting, preachers lost their power, and so the gathering had to go. To an old-timer it was a tragic picture later to see hotel and tents used for the fattening of steers for the markets, and the son of Uncle John was roundly abused for his part in the breaking up of such an institution. He could see, they told him, before his very eyes the fatted calf which was brought forth not for the prodigal son, but for a golden image to be worshiped of Mammon. No longer echoed shouts and hallelujahs, and songs of glory; instead, bleats of calves and bellows of bullocks. Even Uncle John himself was almost persuaded that his son had made a great mistake, for he loved his religion well and wanted it in as much variety and effectiveness as was possible.

There were, however, always the "protracted meetings" which every local church must have sometime during the year. There were special weeks set aside for reinforcing the faith of the members, and they lasted as long as they were successful. Uncle John's participation in these was simple and sincere, and they wrought no havoc upon his soul or conduct. They were occasions for worship and expressions and for social gatherings. They had not yet developed into the professional revivals of later days when maddened campaigns wrought havoc with the souls of men or with their fortunes and standing in the community, if they happened to be Jews or outside the faith. Nor had the professional evangelist yet swept down with such devastating effect.

In later days some of the cheaper revivals often joined hands with the Ku Klux Klan, the white-robed leaders strutting down the church aisles impudently to bless the preacher and to tell him what to do. The revivals came also to be a fanning breeze for the fires of bigotry and intolerance, and the revivalists used a powerful mob psychology to warp the minds and souls of thousands of children and youth who were never to recover. One night, long after midnight, a ten-year-old grandson of Uncle John, tormented by the terrors which a leading evangelist had painted for his soul that evening, sought out an older brother, wide-eyed and weeping. "How can I know," he implored, "that God and hell are like he says? And when I haven't done wrong, why must I go to hell?"

It was a sorry, pathetic occasion when a small boy must become helpless before fanatical onslaughts which made men, women, and children accept all sorts of "propositions" and do things for which they would later feel ashamed. Even Uncle John could not approve of these later evangelists; his son, the father of the small boy, waxed eloquent in denunciation; and some of the grandchildren of Uncle John, and many of the grandchildren of the old Major, were to fight shy of the churches and their revivals.

That same son of Uncle John, representing the rural and common man of the South, lived a great deal more than his threescore years and ten. He never gave up his work with the church or his faith in God. They gave him purpose and they gave him worship, and often they gave him work to do. He never lost faith and would comment, as a matter of fact, when crises came, "Well, they always have—the Lord must know what He is doing." "I am not afraid to live, and no more afraid to die," he would say. He was forever thanking God that he liked to work and had work to do. He just could not understand why people couldn't see the value of the good life and of righteous behavior. In practical affairs he held that a man could not hate his neighbor if he loved God, and "any one who says he loves God and hates the Negro is a liar." And he was always puzzled by a South that professed Christianity and treated the Negro in an unchristian way. He talked and prayed well in church, and his teachings were of the simple godliness of those who feared God, did justice, and walked humbly.

His wife was equally devout and perhaps had a more literal faith, as did her sisters and all their families. They believed in and communicated with God, and all this had a profound influence upon their lives and their morality. There was the family rule that nothing, unless good, should be said about the preacher, who was literally considered a man of God. When in earlier years some of the children died, there was faith that God took them, and that they were better off in the other world. And when the First World War came there was the mother's faith telling her that the two boys who died young would, if they had lived, have died now in European battle. There was always that sort of faith that rationalized life into something of peaceful adaptation and endurance. Religion was reality in the common experiences of life.

This same son of Uncle John was representative of many common men in another way. He came to criticize the church as striving more for form than for worship, more for show than for service. He felt that the preachers and the churches, in the midst of the needs of their people, were failing in their mission, and that the churches had little to offer the common man. He observed that no one of his descendants, children and grandchildren, had found in the church any primary interest or activity; and he was continuously wondering what the future of the church would be if it continued to develop into superficiality and a hypocrisy resembling that of the scribes and Pharisees. In all this, and in the chaos of troubled times, his inner heritage of religious faith kept him strong and cheerful so that, in the way of the folk and rich living, he appeared to have something more than the cynical folk who criticized the simpleness of his religion.

The diagnosis of the religious South was a difficult one. Yet, contrariwise, it was logically explained through historical and cultural backgrounds. The prevailing elemental factors included the power of the religious folkways among all people and especially as applied to the South; the structural place which religion has had in the institutions of America; and the organizational and institutional power of the church. Religion and its institutions, like education, was more often the creature of a society than the creator or director. The South was "the Bible Belt," and it was more Protestantly religious than the rest of the country at different time levels of its biography. Its orators and writers quoted more Scripture, its business men advocated church membership, its people believed that there was somehow a Divinity that shaped their ends.

The South was always paying word tribute to God. It opened its conferences of whatever sort with prayer, began its public dinners with a blessing, had its prominent public leaders teach Sunday-school classes, and predicted dire things for those who forget God. William Allen White said that the dominating elements in the making of the culture of the West were the little church and the little school in the community. Scarcely less true was this of the South. The church was the field for community activities, for certain social relationships, for marriage ceremonies, for the training of ministers. If it followed the leadership of the dominant professional and business men, that was natural. If it let the sweep of technology negate many of its teachings, so did the other institutions. If it measured its goodness by the number of its members, the size and quality of its edifices, so did the school and other institutions. If the church was in a transitional stage, so were most of the other institutions as well.

Perhaps the most important fact to note at this point is that, if it is not possible to diagnose the South's religion and church life adequately, no more is it possible to understand the South apart from its religion. This is the essential fact of importance and must be kept in mind as one of the essential keys to the understanding of southern culture. It was an essential part of the folk culture, even as were the songs which the people sang and the folk music which they loved. And all of this again is, of course, a part of the essential Americanism of all the earlier folk now mirrored again in a hundred religious radio programs of song and prayer from coast to coast. So much for the common man. In the upper brackets of the white South and in the urban centers the church was the chief institution next to the family and the school. Southern towns and cities were well churched, and proud of it. Ministerial associations worked hard on both positive measures and negative protests. Auxiliary church groups of young people, women, and laymen's organizations functioned widely.

Even as the total South has long had the heritage of early America, so it still clings to it with great persistence and naturalness.

CHAPTER XII

Southern Symbols in Folk Song and Music

THE SOUTH of the new century continued particularly susceptible to music and song, the power and influence of which appear deeply imbedded in the folk backgrounds and folk life. Their influence was constantly being accentuated through religious and emotional patterns, developed further through the sweeping hymnological modes. Here music and song not only brought forth the sweep of social heritage and individual memories but touched deep the chords of old moralities and loyalties, mingling actual association with whatever poetic aspiration might be found in the suppressed, hard life of individuals or the roaming, carefree individuality of the lovers of liberty. "Here old melodies are born anew, songs of long ago are revived, new songs of the soil come forth like wayside flowers when the sun sends winter backing off."

Yet, strangely enough, the way of the South here was the way of earlier America. For many of the hymns and much of the singing that were characterized as southern abounded among the New England folk a long time ago and still continued to some extent. This was true of the hymns sung by the white South, but it has also been shown that many of the Negro spirituals are evolutions from the older American religious songs in which the Negro has outdistanced the whites in the distinctiveness of his creations and their renderings. None of this, however, affects the main fact; namely, that in these songs and the singing South, both white and Negro, will be found an important explanation of the way of the South.

There were, for instance, the favorite hymns of Uncle John, his children, and his children's children. They were sung at church, at home, at school, at singing classes. They came to be a part of the environmental forces under which the children grew up. And years later, no matter where any of them sojourned, or under what circumstances, the singing of the old hymns would bring their thoughts and emotions back to the old scenes and the old influences. They were music so interwoven in the fabric of the children's experiences and emotions that they were never-dying. Their singing was effective, partly because they brought back memories, emotions, or experiences as unerringly as the phonograph needle reproduces a recorded song, partly because they represented patterns and techniques of worship, inspiration and longing, born of hardships, struggles, and idealisms. The associations of the past and the aspirations of the future were inseparably bound up in these psychophysical expressions of self and environment. What the words were, made little difference. It was the imprint that counted. No picture of the religious South could be presented without giving a large place to this powerful psychological force of religious songs. The singing of the old hymns in congregational fervor, or alone in solitude, carried a sense-sweep of rare importance.

Here was power in simple but vigorous expression and in pictures: rest for the weary on the golden shores, in "a land where we'll never grow old"; a home "far beyond the skies," "where no storm clouds rise"; a land of "cloudless skies"; a "land of an unclouded day." Otherworld pictures accentuated by mass feeling against a background of hardship and religious faith. Or "gathering home," after tragedies of death and disease and thwarted hopes, or ambition for something better, but yet in unrealistic aspirations.

> Up to the city where falleth no night,
> Gathering home, gathering home!
> Up where the Savior's own face is the light,
> The dear ones are gathering home.

Or gain to sing "on that beautiful shore, the melodious songs of the past" was promise enough.

> There's a land that is fairer than day,
>   And by faith we can see it afar;
> For the Father waits over the way,
>   To prepare us a dwelling place there.

And so there was the abiding faith in the sweet by-and-by to meet on that beautiful shore . . . And peace . . . peace . . . rest.

> There I shall bathe my weary soul,
>   In seas of heavenly rest,
> And not a wave of trouble roll
>   Across my peaceful breast.

Noble sentiments of devotion and loyalties . . . worship and adoration . . . surrender and self-effacing pleasure in worship . . . men and women . . . God and people. Contrast enough to the realities of a conflicting world.

> Let me love Thee more and more
> Till this fleeting, fleeting life is o'er,
> Till my soul is lost in love
> In a brighter, brighter world above.

> Near the cross I'll watch and wait,
>   Hoping, trusting ever,
> Till I reach the golden strand
>   Just beyond the river.

And the blood power had its peculiarly strong appeal, strangely inartistic and crude and contradictory to many of the elements of Christianity, yet full of the sacrificial heritage of formal religion. And the love power, transporting many a maiden into rapturous worshipful emotions, strangely mixed —a fountain filled with blood, drawn from Immanuel's veins . . . sinners plunged beneath that flood . . . lose all their guilty stains . . . Or,

> There is power, power,
> Wonder-working power
> In the precious blood of the Lamb.

Love and endearment: "Jesus has His way with me"; "I'm true to Him, I'm true to Him"; "I love Him"; "Still sweeter every day"; "A little more love"; "He hides my past"; "A smile from God above means so much to me"; "Just when I need Him, He is near," And

> The half cannot be fancied
> This side the golden shore,
> Then He will be
> Sweeter than He ever was before.

Surrender, aspiration, hope, prayer, grandeur, victory are all on the wings of song. Favorites all—powerful, spiritual beyond measurement . . . reality after all . . . Or again:

> I rode on the sky,
> Freely justified I;
> Nor did envy Elijah his seat;
> My soul mounted higher,
> In a chariot of fire;
> And the moon it was under my feet.

And there were the old standbys of all congregations, "Rock of Ages," "All Hail the Power," "Blest Be the Tie That Binds." In and through them had been expressed not only much of the religion and philosophy of the common man, but in the cities and larger churches and over radio many of the more beautiful and dignified hymns had had a large part in musical programs and organ recitals. They were an important part of the culture fabric. This, too, was American, especially as reflected in radio in the rural areas. There had been some new emphasis upon the dignified beautiful hymns, in opposition to the cheap ragtime, revival, and Sunday-school songs. This was reflected in church musical programs and in calls which came to the radio centers for the playing of favorite hymns . . . Sidney Lanier's "Into the woods my Master went, Clean forspent, forspent." Old dignified favorite hymns: "Our blest Redeemer," "For the beauty of the earth," "Praise, my soul, the King of Heaven," "O breath of God, breathe on us," "Jesus,

Thou joy of loving hearts," "Jesus calls us, o'er the tumult,"
"Lord of all being," "Fill Thou my life," "O love of God, how
strong," "Dear Lord and Father," "I sing the Almighty,"
"Spirit Divine! attend," "We love the place," "O worship the
King," "Gracious Spirit, dwell with me," "Lord in the fullness,"
"The day Thou gavest," "At even, ere the sun was set," "Break
Thou the bread of life," "Summer suns are glowing," "Praise
ye the Lord, 'tis good," "Holy, holy, holy," "All things bright
and beautiful," "O Master, let me walk with Thee."

Or take the opening exercises of a village school. The lusty
singing of youth, morning enthusiasm and zest, older boys
and girls, younger children, starting early in the religious
mood, "look away from the cross to the glittering crown."
Beaming faces, swelling voices, sparkling eyes, carrying parts,
admiring glances.

> Just beyond the rolling river
> In that land so bright and fair
> Pearly gates on golden hinges
> Will be standing open there.

And there were pictures of the all-day singings, community
vying with community, prizes offered, choruses, teams, individuals. Religious fervor, community competition, personal
exhibition, courtship, recreation. Young girls singing with
abandon like golden-throated songbirds. Hard-to-be-forgot-
ten pictures. Young men admiring from far or near, or an
occasional bold fellow trying to pitch his song high enough
or low enough to become attuned with the singing of his beloved. Singing in parts. Men on the right side, women on
the left.

This folk singing was part both of the past picture of the
South and of its present fabric, full of meaning. To the uninitiated it was a mystery. "The key to the riddle lies in the
relation of the Sacred Harp to the outstanding characteristics
of early British music; namely, the form of notation retain-

ing the primitive triangle, lozenge, diamond and square note forms; the popularity of counterpoint, the tenor as the fixed melody; the terms crotchet, minim, and breve to describe time values; the love of chorus singing; the significance of the harp as a symbol of the highest function of music in worship; and finally the hymn as the triumphant belief that

> God will not forever cast us off,
> His wrath forever smote,
> Against the people of His love
> His little chosen flock.

Still other pictures of the magic power of the singing of hymns by a group of Holiness folk gathering in the evening darkness under the trees around the lighted lanterns hung on lower branches of trees. Here were primitive scenes and primitive norms which beggar description.

Tired from day's work in field or store or shop on the fringe of town, the gathering worshipers come together in the quiet of a valley under the spreading trees for worship and solace and expression.

> Oh, there's peace and rest and love
> Where the healing waters flow.

In the light of the lanterns, still forms are silhouetted against the distant valley or hill, creepy effects of song and prayer and shouts: "Glory to God in the highest," "Blessed be the name of Jesus," "Bless His name," "Look away from the Cross to the glittering crown." Song and intoned singsong prayer and sermon far into the night. Swaying and rhythm, O Lord God!

And there were the remarkable pictures of a great political convention, white folks' of course, for which people began arriving on the evening before, camping near by, and in the early morning streams of automobiles, even some wagons and buggies, pouring in from all radii, until perhaps ten thousand people have come together for great political speech-making. And then the songs: "Onward, Christian Soldiers" as a starter, followed by "On Jordan's stormy bank I stand and cast a wishful eye," quickly balanced over against "When the roll is called up yonder I'll be there." Tension, excitement, enthusiasm, emotional conflict, such as only a southern political audience of this sort can generate. Then a song started, "In the sweet by-and-by," then another, "Will there be any stars in my crown?" and so on until the crowd has reached the revival stage ready for the preacher of political gospel. Hymns of praise, "America," and sentimental homemade songs carry the day and the crowd.

And millions of copies of the revival songbooks and Sunday-school editions, everywhere literally setting culture patterns of a people. Blood and the Lamb, crowns and stars, glory for me, fast-stepping music, and pleasure-loving tunes. And new editions. And for everybody, everywhere. Here was a big stalwart member of Cleveland's cabinet, twice governor of his state, and United States senator, writing his testimonial: *"Dear Sir: I have used your song book, Revival No. 2, for three years. I now use your Revival No. 3. I have never seen any song books which, I think, give more satisfaction than yours."*

These pictures were of the white folks of the South. Negro pictures were even more vivid. It was not necessary to recall that the Negro had long since taken over many of the hymns of the white man, and so far outstripped him and surpassed him in their execution as to make many of them appear as the Negro's own spirituals. In "The Old-Time Religion" and many other favorites of the revival mode, were found songs common to whites and Negroes. Thus, very much like "Ain't gonna study war no more," there was a popular hymn of the old camp meetings and revivals of the southern white folks:

> If you get there before I do
> Down by the river;

Tell all the folks I'm coming too
Down by the river side.

We'll end this warfare
Down by the river,
We'll end this warfare
Down by the river side.

The Negroes and the whites vied with each other in hymns painting pictures of Heaven's bright home, too, more vivid than Greek mythology, more concrete than a "Tannhäuser" chorus, or more compelling than the English poet Noyes's imagery of the world beyond. In both the Negro and white songs, Heaven is glory land, blessed promised land, that blissful shore, the unseen shore, Beulah Land, goodly land, Canaan's happy land, the golden strand, the land divine, that land so bright and fair, Canaan's fair and happy land, the blessed homeland, glory land, beauteous fields, those mansions fair, home, a mansion in the sky, an eternal home, a better home, the home of glory, a city, beautiful city of gold, a city high eternal, that great kingdom, yon bright heaven.

The Negro songs had been portrayed so often that it was scarcely more than necessary to recall their vividness and the important part which they had had in the development of the southern picture. And songs, the enumeration of which had never been made and probably never would be made and the variation of which surpasses all recording and notation. Heritage of the old scenes. Beautiful but impossible of perpetuity. An older generation of black folks, artistic in manners and souls. A black epic in a white world. Memory of old bards and singers of rare personality-charm to the race, creative art in the southern scene, long ashamed of its sorrow songs. A Negro church on the village hillside, eventide to darkness, late-gathering worshipers, toil-tired from road and field and kitchen door. Lights dim by pulpit and altar, native hewn rugged benches askew. Quiet sittings in accustomed places. The gathering spirit of worship, night contrast to day, self-expression and solace, feeling that "De other world is not lak this." A leader opening song, swaying body, closed eyes, head backward, face heavenward, rhythmic swing of arms, slow pat of feet, rich vibrato voice, now swelling in ascendancy, now softening to appeal:

> Steal away, steal away to Jesus,
> I ain't got long to stay here.

There were still other pictures of religious singing in the South. There were the itinerant white singers, sometimes blind, sometimes carrying banjo and harp, sometimes accordion, and sometimes playing on the church or home organ. More often they were near the mountain country. They sang and played hymns, but they sang more from the vast store of general folk songs. If religious songs were wanted they could sing them. If hymns were wanted they could sing them. And they rendered many a ballad of religious import or moral teaching, exercising at times as much temporary spell over their listeners as the revivalists. And always they were carrying on the folk-song patterns of other days and making new ones for new incidents and new lessons.

> Come, all you young men, and listen to my rhyme,
> I'll tell you what you're doing at the present time,
> You are taking from your parents, your time and useful days,
> And spending them in folly and many wicked ways.

Among the most popular of the semireligious songs were those aimed at the church and the preacher. On court-week days or special occasions, such as county fairs or the Dayton-Scopes trial, these songs brought smiles and nods and dimes to the singer. And a good time was had by all.

> In this world of frills and fashions where the churches are so fine,
> And the trade mark on religion is a classic dollar sign,
> There's a rule that never faileth, you will always find it true,
> Where the dollar rules the pulpit, there the Devil rules the pew.

Yet religious songs were not all of the picture of an emerging South. There was a fiddling, foot-patting folk, symbol of the natural in emotional expression and in the spiritual forgetfulness of hard reality and the sentiment-binding power of the folk music. One master fiddler of the Old South and of the New wrote: "You asked me for a list of all the tunes I have ever heard played. It would be a hard matter for me to furnish you with a list of all the tunes I know as I know so many it would take me weeks to think them all up. However, I will try to make up a list for you, but it will perhaps be two or three months before I can get it made up." The list was never completed; and yet some of the samplings with their natural spelling and setting are indicative of favorite tunes and vivid in their portraiture: "Devil in the Wood Pile," "Arkansas Traveler," "Turkey in the Straw," "Fishers' Horn Pipe," "Pop Goes the Weesel," "Wild Goose Grace," "Wild Horse," "Whistling Rufis," "Leather Breeches," "Logan's Hoedown," "Mississippi Sawyer," "Mocking Bird," "Cackling Chickens," "Dixie Land," "Tarked Deer," "Rickets Hornpipe," "Nocking Around the Kitchen," "Cumberland Gap," "Drunkards Hichoughs," "Boney Parts of Retreat." Some later favorites included: "Silver Threads Among the Gold," "When You and I Were Young," "Choe Taw," "Red Wing," "Dixie Darling," "Roving Gambler," "Prisoners Song," "You've Got to See Mama," "Chicken Reel," "Honey Succle Blues," "Will You Ramble," "The Troubles of the Potomac," "Wabash Blues," "Boll the Jack Blues," "Lonesome Road Blues," "Honey Where You Been So Long?" And even slow tunes included favorite hymns and slow songs of sentiment: "The Old Rugged Cross," "Nearer, My God, to Thee," "The Battle Hymn of the Republic," "Rock of Ages," "A Boy's Best Friend Is His Mother," "Fare Well to Thee."

This man, representative of thousands of fiddlers throughout the South from many walks of life and from every region of its wide expanse, was symbolic of one of its most vivid pictures. There was one who boasted that he could fiddle all

night and call dance figures until midnight and never repeat
any save the most elementary. The fiddler was an institution, "and the cheerful scrape of his bow sets the feet involun-
tarily moving." This music drew its power from many sources
—its technique, the personalities of its fiddlers, its association.
It seemed irresistible. It was as if some magic would "strike
the auric nerve, run down to your feet and put motion into
your toes in spite of the strongest resolution against it. Men
who had lost their feet affirmed that it set a-going the toes
which had been buried years ago. It seemed to be dangerous
to play those tunes in the presence of marble statues, unless
they were securely fastened to the floor. The old revivalists,
who wished to wean their converts from the vanities of the
balls, felt compelled to proscribe the fiddle as the Devil's instrument. When I was a boy it was a general religious tenet,
that playing it was a sin equal to dancing, horse-racing, cock-
fighting and gambling."

Fiddling and dancing just naturally seemed to go together.
The spirit of the old folk dance and the old folk songs was
abundant in thousands of country places and closely adjacent
to towns. There was about the fiddle and the dance "a love
of the open, of the vigor and joy of activity for its own sake,
of cooperation with others in exercises of rhythmical beauty.
There is that sense of balance and proportion that is related
to all real art." And Miss Burchenal has spoken of the folk
dances as "the wild flowers of the dance world, unspoiled by
the hand of man. They have sprung naturally from the hearts
of simple, wholesome country folk in response to the human
need for self-expression."

And thus might be interpreted the pictures of the southern
fiddlers and dances. They were of one body, yet of many kinds.
They made unforgettable pictures; and indescribable as well.
Here was a crowd slow-gathering at the home of a neighbor:
a few standing around outside, a few inside, dull conversation about the weather and illness and food; a few "settin'

down," a few walking around, more coming. Here on a week-day evening men and women, older and younger, who in town, work, or Sunday meeting seem so staid and mechanical and uninteresting, are now suddenly shifting to a new pulse of life. The musicians arrive, and dancers file in—an assembly of friends and kin. The dance begins. "Two fiddlers of evident renown in those parts were seated in a corner of the big hall. Their hats were kept on. They soon fell into the preliminary tune medleys and then—as though suddenly infused with the spirit of the hour—drew out a full and vigorous call to the dance. The dancers fell into the circle and began as spirited and delightful exhibition of folk dancing as I ever witnessed. Simpler than the Russian and Eastern Europe folk dances, they are equally as racial and rich in Anglo-Saxon content. Characterized by a physical vigor and cleanness. There is small chance for sex morbidity or individual exhibition in the cotillion and reel. The beauty of flashing figures and rhythmic freedom produced on the spectators the same joyousness that the dancers radiated. Drudgery of the day and crudeness of the house were forgotten in the pleasure of the dance. All ages took part. It was a genuine surprise to see the young moderns as versatile as the elders in the intricacies of the old dances."

Here was a description of old times in Tennessee, remnants of which still remained in many places. The pictures of the old days and amusements abiding as a part of the southern heritage. "When the day's work was performed, the yard was swept, covered by the flowers of the forest, and the dance commenced. The old-fashioned Virginia break-down reel, where twenty couples faced and eyed each other, as they moved through the mazes of the merry dance, while the bow was drawn across the strings of the violin (we called it a fiddle) discoursing sweet music. Then the 'band' would give us 'Jenny put the kettle on,' 'Molly blow the bellows strong, we'll all take tea', then 'Leather breeches, full of stitches,' and by way of variety, 'Billy in the Wild Woods' or 'Nappy

Cot and Petty-Coat' and 'The Linsey Gown,' 'If you want to keep your credit up, pay the money down.' The dancing was really enjoyable. In old times we had a favorite reel called 'Mrs. McCloud.' When the word was given, 'Hand all around, set-to and face your partner,' giving to each full space to display their activity and gymnastic skill in the various steps of ancient times, the scene was a magnificent one. I have seen several sets at the same time, both boys and girls, cutting the single and double pigeon wing, which caused a thrill of excitement and emotions equal to the brilliant flight of an eloquent speaker."

A real fiddlers' convention such as those held in Atlanta or Birmingham or Columbus, where thousands of people greeted the "champions" from many regions beggars description. Old gray-haired fiddlers, super-excited through competition and cheering audiences. Young fiddlers boasting the third and fourth generations of fiddling champions. A father and son. Another father and daughter. Three brothers. An uncle and nephew. Teams from the same community. For the time being all the world's a fiddlin' world. And the audience looks upon it and finds it good. Competition in groups, in pairs, in solos. Shouts and exclamation. A snatch of song. Quick movements. Mimicry and pantomime. Fiddles across the knees, between the legs, on top of the head, across the back, upside down, horizontal parallel, fiddling like fury, vibrant with life, reaching out and reaching back into and beyond the beginnings of music.

The fiddle and the banjo were constant accompaniments also of the great mass of old ballads, general folk songs, new ballads, comic and common supplements to modern tunes. Here were emotional appeal, narration and story, pathos and humor, the magnifying of simple virtues, moralizing against vice, love, hate, sung to the accompaniment of simple folk motions and folk music. From Kentucky to Texas, from Virginia to Florida, from Georgia to Mississippi, and the hills and woods and farms between, the old ballads were still living. Thus, in an Alabama ordinary rural county Thomasine McGehee found scores of songs, replicas and variations of the whole Child collection. In a single county in Mississippi, Hudson found remarkable variations and similarities as well. In the mountains of North Carolina, Campbell, Greer, Sutton, and many others found wonderful counterparts and equally wonderful variations which checked back to the old collections, revealing the very soul and process of folk music and folks songs in their making and preserving. In Cox's "Folk Songs of the South," Davis's "Traditional Ballads of Virginia," Smith's "South Carolina Ballads," and many other collections were found hundreds and thousands of songs and their variants never ending in their pleasure-giving power. A single Tennessee blind itinerant singer thought he knew more than a hundred. A single North Carolina mountain man has been known to render fifty songs, each different from the published ballads. Like the singing of hymns, these ballads become a part of the pattern and structure and function of the people, reveal immeasurable characteristics of the folk and recapitulate much of the folk and race history. Samplings of these songs would fill a large volume. They represent something of the American musical idiom just as the Negro song has come to represent an American contribution. And they represent a part of certain character such as led Sidney Lanier to say: "I know that he who walks in the way these ballads point, will be manful in necessary fight, fair in trade, loyal in love, generous to the poor, tender in household, prudent in living, plain in speech, merry upon occasion, simple in behavior, and honest in all things."

There were ballads of sorrow and ballads of joy and all manner of life and experience. They sang of the family—the place of the husband, the wife, the children, women, orphans, mother. They sang of love and courtship—love of nature, maternal, paternal, conjugal, sweetheart, filial, fraternal, sex, courtship, marriage, separation, reunion, elopement. They sang of morality—virtue, temperance, courage, loyalty, the beautiful, the true, the good, the bad. They sang of God, of heaven and hell, of life and death and suicide and judgment and mystery. They sang of men and of animals, of work and play, of homesickness and wanderlust, and memories, of patriotism and cowardice, of wealth and poverty, of mountains and the sea, of justice and cruelty, of style and show, of robbers and heroes. And there were hundreds of variants and hundreds of remarkably "pure" specimens. Davis found in Virginia no fewer than 122 titles of traditional ballads distributed in every one of the one hundred counties and with 148 musical variants with a total item-variant count of 420– 440. They conformed well to Child's classification and presented variants of the well known "Barbara Allen," "Barbara Ellen," "Bonny Barbara Allen," "Robin Hood's Death," "Robin Hood and the Tanner," "Robin Hood and Arthur O'B'loved," "Robin Hood Rescuing Will Stully" and other old favorites. Checking with Cox's folk songs of the South, Smith's collections from South Carolina, Hudson's from Mississippi, McGehee's from Alabama, Campbell's from Tennessee and North Carolina, Greer's and Sutton's from North Carolina, reveals a similar abundance with faithfulness to traditional patterns as well as variants. They were an important part of the southern picture.

There were the mixed songs and ballads of all kinds. There was the itinerant bard with his harp and guitar traveling hither and yon singing his songs: now entertaining the crowds at the courthouse or county fair or picnic, now entertaining the individual or small groups, now singing at the great house. A single bard running the whole gamut of southern folk song —conventional ballads, Negro songs, popular medleys, current blues, homemade ballads of the day, church hymns. Here were favorites sung with characteristic folk manner, now picking his banjo and singing, now suddenly combining banjo, harp, and song, his harp being attached by way of a wire, easel-like frame, so that he could reach it with his mouth: "The Arkansas Traveler," "The Baggage Coach Ahead," "Be Kind to a Man When He's Down," "Bill Failed to Keep Peace with Sam," "The Blind Man's Lament," "Black Sam and the Ghost," "The Boll Weevil," "The Bugs and the Bees," "Casey Jones and the Kaiser's Fight," "The Clansman's Creed," "Come and Jine," "The Dollar and the Devil," "The Hell-Bound Train," "Jesse Was a Gentleman," "Johnson's Mule," "Just Before the Battle, Mother," "Kansas," "The Long-Tongued Woman," "My Mother Is Dead in Heaven," "The Murder of Miss Laura Parsons," "No Disappointment in Heaven," "Poor Girl Long Ways from Home," "The Ragged Jacket," "Railroad Bum," "The Sammies Are in France," "Song of the Black Sheep," "*Titanic*," "The Traveling Man," "Uncle Sam and the German Submarine," "The Woman Suffrage," "You Will Never Miss Your Mother Until She's Gone," "The Truth Twice Told," "The Prisoner's Song," "Advice to a Boy," "The Business End of a Bumblebee," "I'm Gonna Let the Bumblebee Be," "Lizzie and the Bumblebee," "Mother's Old Red Shawl," "Sarah Jane," "Down in the Coal Mine," "Tender Recollections," "The Feller That Looks Like Me," "The Wabash Cannon Ball," "The Little Tin Lizzie," "Kaiser Bill," "Jesse James," "The Billy Goat," "Frank Dupree," "John Riley," "The Roving Gambler," "Little Sadie," "Warning to the Gambler," "Three Months in Prison," "House Carpenter."

Perhaps the favorites were the sentimental sorrow songs and the new-made ballads narrating current and recent happenings. The dying soldier, two little orphans, the baggage coach ahead with the dead mother of a crying child, the mother who is gone, the little girl gone wrong, death and suicide, all were powerful themes. Thus the song of many stanzas of the Slate Stone Horror, when on a cold December day, dear Papa was taken away, comes easily to grips with the simple emotions:

Oh, Papa, dear Papa, where are you tonight,
With a face so sweet, so fair, and so bright;
With eyes so brilliant, so soft, so blue,
A heart so manly, so kind and so true.

Oh, Papa, dear Papa, we all miss you now,
Our living was made by the sweat of your brow;
Poor Mamma and I are so sad and so lone,
We still live together in our sad, sad home.

Though our eyes may be dim, our hearts may be gay,
We are coming, dear Papa, to see you some day;
To dwell with you forever on that Heavenly shore,
Where sorrow and shadows will come no more.

Such songs spring up overnight, sometimes picturing local tragedies, sometimes comedy: Floyd Collins, buried for days in the coal mine; Mary Phagan murdered (a million records sold); the murder of Miss Laura Pagoris, Pine Mountain schoolteacher; the assassination of J. B., leaving the sad wife and children; the Scopes trial, and the death of William Jennings Bryan, epitome of the simple religion, philosophy, and mental set of the folk:

William Jennings Bryan is dead, he died one Sabbath day,
So sweetly was the king asleep, his spirit passed away;
He was at Dayton, Tennessee, defending our dear Lord,
And as soon as his work on earth was done, he went to his reward.

He fought the evolutionists, the infidels and fools
Who are trying to ruin the minds of children in our schools,
By teaching we came from monkeys and other things absurd,
By denying the works of our blessed Lord and God's own Holy
  Words.

Later there were the ballads of Ella May Wiggins of Gaston County, North Carolina, which were made vivid for the nation because of her death at the hands of a rioting community. The folk picture was a vivid one:

We're going to have a union all over the South,
Where we can wear good clothes and live in a better house.
Now we must stand together and to the boss reply
We'll never, no, we'll never let our leaders die.

And so the long story was told in ballad form. And many another and another like it. Then there was the "Song of Life":

We leave our home in the morning,
   We kiss our children goodbye.
While we slave for the bosses
   Our children scream and cry.

It is for our little children
   That seems to us so dear,
But for us nor them, dear workers,
   The bosses do not care.

But understand, all workers,
   Our union they do fear,
Let's stand together, workers,
   And have a union here.

Among the hundreds of songs were other conventional folk improvisations. Some about the First World War and Kaiser Bill—doomed eternally to smell of American corpse. The Kaiser's dream of being kicked out of hell to make a hell of his own . . . Some one in France . . . Uncle Sam and the submarine . . . Casey Jones and the Kaiser's fight. Bill failed to make peace with Sam.

Later there were many about the depression and the WPA and God and Roosevelt and the folk, and some about the Second World War and Hitler and the Japs.

Roosevelt with Hitler
He tried to live in peace.

.   .   .   .   .   .

Hitler tried to fool the Negroes,
By sayin' they ought not to fight.

They have no home and country
No flag or civil rights.
But the Negro knewed the best,
They deeds did prove the rest.

Then there were the whoopee and funny songs in which the bard would have his listeners smiling, cackling, perhaps howling in glee. And subtle suggestion and ribald rhymes so fascinating and rippling as to cast a spell over his audience. It might be forty-one rhyming couplets and chorus of "It Ain't Gonna Rain No Mo'," ranging from good-natured humor through gentle sarcasm and Aristophanian jokes to unprintable rattle-rhymes. Improvisations were abundant and natural, so that verse grew on verse and new songs grew where old songs had been before. And the seeds of these songs smoldered in the ground to spring up in the years to come in a thousand radio hillbilly tunes or "Pistol-Packin' Mamma."

Or it was a parody—always popular with the folk; perhaps a parody on the preacher or the society woman or the rich man or Kaiser Bill, and sung to some rapidly moving tune. Listen to "Little Tin Lizzie" sung to the tune of "The Little Brown Jug":

One Ford car with piston rings,
Two rear wheels and one front spring,
Has no fender, seat, or plank,
Burns lots of gas and hard to crank.

.   .   .   .

Got lots of speed, runs like the deuce,
Burns either gas or tobacco juice,
Tires all off, runs on the rim,
A darn good Ford for the fix it's in.

There was the picture of the rural South given in the twenty-seven stanzas of "The Boll Weevil." Hard he was to kill. He always had a home. The farmer put him in the hot sand (not so hot as he could stand), in a red-hot pan (he could stand it like a man), hit him with brick (well, it's liable

to make him sick), put him on the ice (surely was nice),
plowed him under deep (right out he'd creep).

> The farmer says to the boll weevil,
> "I'll burn you up with fire."
> The boll weevil says to the farmer,
> "You are a dog-goned liar,
> I've got a home, I've got a home."

So the boll weevil tells the southern farmer's fortune for
him and challenges the whole South as well.

> The farmer says to his children,
> "I'd send you off to schools,
> But since the boll weevil struck this land
> You'll grow up like durned fools,
> And stay at home, and stay at home."

> The boll weevil says to the farmer,
> "I'll learn you a little sense;
> I'll learn you to raise your own foodstuffs
> And cut down your expense.
> I've got a home, I've got a home."

This folk-song portraiture was not complete without other
pictures. There were songs of southern women in all their
beauty, purity, and glorified virtue. And they were powerful
like all the songs of the nineties—"My Little Georgia Rose,"
"She Was Bred in Old Kentucky," "The Girl I Loved in Sunny
Tennessee." There were ballads of girls and ladies in traditional folk song. The pathetic Mary Phagan songs of a later
day and others typified the unfortunate girl. Again, there were
the songs of the outlaw, Jesse James, even as there were among
the Negroes; and songs of railroads and boats—the *Fannie
Fern* river boat and others—white railroad songs differing
somewhat from the Negro railroad songs.

> The Cannon Ball she run so fast
> Couldn't see yourself in looking glass.

There were the inimitable boys who played the mouth harp, costing a nickel—a very fine silver-shiny one for a quarter. It was a wonderful instrument in the hands of a youngster learning or in the prideful mastery of an artist, and no preachers ever made war against the harp, as they did the fiddle! A boy with a nickel harp blowing "Turkey in the Straw" or even "Home, Sweet Home" or

> Who's been here since I been gone?
> Pretty little girl with red dress on

was a perpetual envy to the uninitiated. He represented pleasures unequaled, attainments superlative, capable of the full development of the wholesome personality.

If there be those who doubt the efficacy of these songs as conditioning factors in the South of the second period of its evolving biography, there is need only to sense the extraordinary sweep and power, the range and the kind of folk songs and imitation folk songs, and of folk fiddlers and imitation folk fiddlers on a hundred radio stations. Tune in, tune in, dial in and dial out, early morning to wake you, midmorning for housewife, noon for the workers, and all through the evening hours, alternating with New York's and Los Angeles' and Cleveland's night-life symphonies. Catalogue them, analyze them, enjoy them, suffer with them, sad imitation of normal twang folk singing, realistic rendition of old and new variations, the multiple-millioned rendition of "Pistol-Packin' Mamma," symbolic of the power of the folk song and the eager search for rhythmic easing of the inner-charged emotions.

CHAPTER XIII

Leaders, Followers, and Politics

IN NO ASPECT of the South's culture, perhaps, has its heritage been more influential than in the total field of leadership. There was, first of all, the colonial period, with its distinctive contributions to the national picture. Next there was the period before the Civil War, in which Calhoun symbolized sectional philosophy in the national setting. The third period in the South, following the Civil War, was very different from either of the earlier periods, and showed little resemblance to them in the nature, equipment, and influence of the leaders. Earlier, the South had a frontier, and a growing way of culture, and a participation in the national scene that was broad and positive. In the Old South there were character, dominance, and vigor. In the New South, of the reconstruction period, there were poverty, disaster, sorrow and bitterness, and an isolation from national affairs that left its leadership limited and negative.

In the Old South, the Negro was a part of the growing economy, helping to build a southern structure of distinctive quality. In the New South the Negro constituted a new people; he had become an economic problem and, besides continuing the old conflict in ideologies, had set the stage for a new sort of leadership. Who should lead him, and who should lead the whites in an entirely different world? The Negro had so conditioned the white man or, more accurately, the white man had so conditioned himself, that a new world of fear and prejudice had made the South a place where prevailing leadership in the years to come either would be afraid of the race issue or would use it in demagogic appeal for votes. In the Old South there were generations in the upper brackets who

196

were trained for leadership, while the upper middle brackets of white families were working out their own philosophy. In the New South, youth had been decimated by the war; there were few who were experienced or trained for the new tasks, and they were handicapped by a carpetbagger northern leadership that would negate any normal program of leadership. In the Old South the preponderance of noted leaders was found in the field of politics, while after the Civil War there was the invisible Klan, and aside from that the pattern was woven around the Confederate military hero and the glorification of the past.

Once again, after the Civil War the primary field of leadership was narrowed down to rebuilding a region, finding ways and means of surviving, evolving industry that would give employment to millions of disadvantaged whites, adjusting the Negro to free labor, and defending the southern people. Leadership was, therefore, local, state, and sectional rather than national. In the meantime, the South's experience, its education and training, its science and skills had lost the high place they once had held in the total national picture. And the southern leaders turned more and more to the old pattern of oratory and words in which they undoubtedly excelled, but in which they no longer had adequate content and purpose. Rupert Vance calls them spellbinders, and they were a remarkable lot of orators.

So, too, if one wanted to know who were local leaders in town and country, let him catalogue those who gave the Memorial Day addresses each April in honor of the Confederate dead, what time the children carried wreaths of flowers to a thousand cemeteries. It may well be doubted if ever there were more gracious speech and beautiful words in the annals of any people. Yet it was a leadership looking backward, and one which in time came to substitute ideals and superficial ideology for the hard work of planning and creating a new world.

Thus, it came to pass that in the stern realities which the South faced through the years there grew up a sort of stock pattern of substituting recognition for what the South had done in the earlier years of the nation for continuing achievement and leadership. Symbolic of this was the argument that the nation should elect a southern man as President as reward for its past contributions. "For seventy-two years [1789–1861]," so the argument ran, "there were fifteen Presidents of the United States and nine were from the South. In nearly every Cabinet of the fifteen Presidents, the Attorney-General was a Southern man. These nine Southern Presidents made such excellent ones that five of them were reelected and not one from the six remaining ones from the North was reelected. For sixty-four years the Chief Justices of the United States were Southern men. The obligations of the Nation to the South are great. Richard Henry Lee, of Virginia, offered the resolution of independence. Thomas Jefferson wrote the Declaration of Independence. George Washington established it. James Madison largely created the Constitution and was instrumental in having it ratified. John Marshall was Chief Justice thirty years. These men with Alexander Hamilton may truly be called the Founders of the American Nation." And on and on the claims extended, ending with the query, "Will the Nation be fair-minded enough to honor the South again?"

The picture might have been painted brighter if the record had been extended to include all the South's earlier contributions to politics and statesmanship. For the South had contributed generously to the practice and theory of American government. With the American political personages estimated as worthy of permanent biographies in the *Encyclopaedia of the Social Sciences* as a background, what was the South's early contribution? Of the twenty Presidents listed, eleven were born in the South. Of the forty-seven figures "important in domestic affairs before the Civil War" listed, six were of foreign birth. Of the forty-one born in America, all but fourteen were born in the South. Here were actual

pictures, standard measuring-rods of achievement: Thomas
Hart Benton, Montgomery Blair, Richard P. Bland, John C.
Calhoun, Henry Clay, Howell Cobb, Jefferson Davis, John
Dickinson, Robert Y. Hayne, Patrick Henry, Sam Houston,
Arthur, Charles, Henry, and Richard Henry Lee, William
Lowndes, Nathaniel Macon, John Marshall, George Mason,
John Randolph, Peyton Randolph, Robert Rhett, Spencer
Roane, Alexander H. Stephens, Robert Toombs, William
Yancey. Of the "figures important for development of political
theory," the South had twenty-seven as opposed to twenty-
five from all the other states and fifteen from foreign coun-
tries. Among those not included in the previous list were
James G. Birney, George Fitzhugh, James Hammond, Hinton
R. Helper, Andrew Johnson, Hugh Swinton Legaré, Henry
St. George Tucker, Nathaniel Beverley Tucker, George
Wythe. There was none listed from the South among the con-
tributors to "social theory," but the South's contribution to
the Supreme Court was large.

If, however, the picture was to be made up of figures important in domestic affairs *since* the Civil War, there were listed
only Joe Cannon, Champ Clark, and Tom Watson! Vivid
pictures they were, but in great minority of numbers if not in
picturesqueness. Many of the vivid southerners of before-the-
war distinction continued to achieve, but their efforts were
toward the rebuilding of a section rather than participation in
the national picture as such; and southerners now living may
yet attain such ranks. Nevertheless, the later record of the
South in producing creative leaders in the field of practice and
theory of politics has not compared well with its earlier record, so that its place in the national honor must be won again
rather on merit than on past laurels.

It was still difficult for the South to realize that its earlier
leadership and culture had not been successful, and especially
that the old standards, even where successful, would not apply
to modern conditions. Students of history and culture were

constantly asking why Virginia in the earlier days had made the richest contribution of all the states; what they were not yet asking with sufficient earnestness was why Virginia had not made more recent contributions. And so it was, in lesser measure, for other southern states. There were reasons a plenty, of course, but what were they? And were the real reasons commonly assigned? The South, in the midst of its "growing pains," with its rapidly expanding industrialism, its suffering agriculture, its growing cities and modern highways, still seemed to insist that its leadership in religion, education, politics, industry, should conform to the same standards which had failed in both the earlier and more recent past. The South had followed its religious leaders a long time—what were the fruits of its following? It had followed its political leaders— where were the Jeffersons, the Washingtons, the Madisons, the Marshalls, the Calhouns? The South was a third of the nation—where was its third of outstanding leaders?

It appeared as if the South with its phenomenal physical development, in the midst of phenomenal social and economic changes, still insisted that it needed no new leadership; or as if, in the difficult ways of reconstruction, it had become so involved in survival that its leadership was still suffering the long lapse. And so once again its leadership was of a mixed pattern—distinguished leaders of the Old South, mid-channel Memorial Day orator-leaders and program makers, loyal defenders of the lost cause, later translators of this loyalty into demagoguery, religious leaders, Ku Klux Klan leaders, political leaders of various kinds, and a new type of southern critic and liberal. All these and more contributed to the colorful mosaic of the South of the first third of the twentieth century. In so far as leadership was vested in political leaders, there was a tendency to mix Protestant religion and politics and at the same time make separation of church and state a chief anti-Catholic issue. This resulted naturally from making personalities the subject of debate instead of issues, abstractions instead of realities. Yet it did not alter the nature of the leadership.

The first quarter of the twentieth century is near its end when a late summer political campaign reaches the eve of its final great day. People are gathering, in a steady stream of cars, buggies, and wagons, far into the night—Uncle John's clan and kind, mostly, but many also of the old Major's, and of the thriftless neighbors across the way, and people from near-by mill towns and small cities. Camping nearabouts.

On the morrow nearly ten thousand people gather, waiting for the chief candidate: walking about, sitting in automobiles and buggies; menfolks talking about crops, weather, and politics; womenfolks preparing dinner on the ground, taking care of babies and other children, talking about health and sickness, weather and food, when to start back home. The crowd mills up nearer and nearer the speaker's stand. Lemonade and Coca-Cola, hot sunshine and soft breezes. A song leader starts the crowd—singing slowly some good old tunes. Then more. Then gospel songs, "When the Roll Is Called Up Yonder," "Onward, Christian Soldiers," with rising fervor, increasing volume and power, revival symptoms: "Will There Be Any Stars in My Crown?" and "In the Sweet By-and-By."

The candidate-idol appears on the platform, the gospel hymn stops, suddenly as if by magic, and instead there go up shouts and shouts. Tension and emotion break forth into pandemonium. Hats in the air, shouts as of victory and encouragement—glory in the highest—then silence. Silence. "Boys, let's hear him." Silence, then the candidate, in preliminary greeting—"Well, boys, we're gonna give 'em hell, ain't we?" That is all. Shouts. Hats in the air, laughter, glory in the highest! Then the gospel songs again whilst the candidate rests a moment for his speech. And the cause of the party has become the cause of God, even as the voice of the people is the voice of God.

There were, just before the turn of the century, thousands thus listening eagerly to the sandy-haired Tom Watson hurling his philippics at the Democratic plutocrats in Washington.

The pictures were vivid ones. Wild cheering, hats thrown in the air, while the silver-tongued orator pictured the idle rich with their silver-lined bathtubs, their luxury and high living at Washington and New York. To Uncle John and the thousands of his compatriots, without experience in leadership, here was a new prophet of Jeffersonian democracy. He was, he told them, fighting against the intrenched interests on behalf of the common man. And the students of political history agree that he was. What Jefferson fought for as against Hamilton, Watson fought for as against the recalcitrant Cleveland, long since surrendered to the plutocrats. Watson, they said, was the full-fledged Jeffersonian. What a picture, could he only have fought his fight without personal bitterness! Was it the southern atmosphere, or defeat, that made him the archetype of demagogue?

For, a little later, the selfsame orator was fighting "against" something else; he was always against something or somebody, inflaming his followers into a white heat of emotional loyalties. Now it was against the Democrats, now against the Republicans, now against the Negro, now against the Jew, now against missionaries and now against the Catholics, and then against Woodrow Wilson and Herbert Hoover. And always with the brilliant half-truth technique of the master demagogue. Once, in the notable Frank case, it fanned his following into such a flame as would lynch the governor of a state and did later result in the lynching of the accused. It was one of the South's most dramatic illustrations of a leader and his followers and one of the most dramatic that have appeared on the American scene. No one who has not heard the murmur of a vast mob swell into a terrifying roar could understand the power of this sort of leader.

The story of how this leader came to be what he was, and how his followers swore allegiance to him is one representative of the whole Southern picture, more particularly perhaps in South Carolina, Georgia, Mississippi, Alabama, Texas, Arkansas, and Florida. The picture of the evolution of this leader was one of the most vivid in all America. His native state "was a wretched land and it had brought to the ruin of the Civil War a population already ground under by economic shifts. The people had found a philosophy for their necessities. They were kindly, loyal, and in their way aspiring; and Watson's association with them taught him that they were worthy. He was a passionate soul, and he resolved then that something must be done to relieve the abuses they were subjected to. He was early in life the emotional fighting southerner. Speaking, he was irresistible, swinging his audiences delightfully down the dizzy transitions he made from impalpable illusion, to stories of a man who could smell the gravy and know the sex of a hog—and then back again to what seemed the final citadel of erudition. Among his chief targets were various ecclesiastics, particularly Catholics, and those Protestants who busied themselves with foreign missions. He would not give any of those brethren any rest. His Catholic animosities, indeed, soon blazed into an obsession, the prosecution of which cost him, before all was done, some $200,000. Tried for alleged indecency in his lampoons against Holy Church, he was acquitted. Upon being threatened with a change of venue to some place out of Georgia, he sent word succinctly to the authorities in Washington that he would wait upon his doorstep, with pistols, any extraordinary officer sent for him." Then there was the Frank case: "The fact that a fusillade against the Yankees in the affair would inescapably set loose an unreasoning racial hatred and that it would in great likelihood result in a violation of Georgia sovereignty graver than any Yankee violation, did not check him. He took that risk unblenchingly, and the hatred he released, along with a little hemp rope, did the rest. And he looked upon his work and—for all he ever said to the contrary—found it good."

Yet here was a man who had produced competent historical work, had given promise of rare ability, and was considered by many southerners as the greatest living American. Jefferson had mellowed under the influence of success and an earlier southern atmosphere; Watson had become almost maniacally bitter through failure and a later southern atmosphere.

It was from such episodes, with their bitter unreasonable and unreasoning denunciation of men and causes, that the North gained many of its pictures of the South. Leaders and followers—in the bypaths and dark hidden ways of demagoguery. The South protested that these were not representative leaders, and that their antics and their explosions received undue publicity. Nevertheless, if they had thousands of followers, and if they represented always the balance of power in religion, politics, and education, then they must be accorded a chief place in the leadership of the South. To measure this leadership was to measure the following of preacher and governor of Texas; of long-haired senator and local preacher-governor of Mississippi; of preacher-governor and Blue Shirts of Florida; of a Tom-Tom senator and Ku Klux of Alabama; of a willy-nilly congressman and Baptist-Methodist combine in Georgia; of a firebrand senator and fundamentalist governor of South Carolina; of various religious demagogues throughout the South headed by an intemperate bishop; and of the later worse demagogue represented by the Georgia-Mississippi-Louisiana trinity of Talmadge, Bilbo, and Huey Long.

It was not enough to say that the masses would have followed better leaders. The tragedy was that they wanted good leaders and would have followed them; and the further tragedy was that the people often thought their leaders were good. But, whatever their characteristics, most critics of the dominant pattern seemed to be powerless, afraid, or not to know how, to fight for a change. Many professional and business men and women, as well as many special groups, appeared to feel that too much energy and trouble were required to interfere with the prevailing mode. It was, they felt, easier to go along without "hurting people's feelings."

Thus it happened that such leaders exerted a dominance

entirely out of proportion to the esteem in which they were held. This applied to various aspects of southern life—religion, politics, education. And later the problem appeared in the industrial world. Here was a minority group of dominant and domineering types, not so much esteemed and followed by the better industrial leaders and the common folks, but somehow helping to determine the southern pattern and to give the South its reputation in the field of industrial leadership. And just as there had often been pictures of a solid phalanx of ministers unreasonably attacking institutions, measures, and individuals, with none among them to break the ranks, so there had appeared pictures of closed ranks among textile folk, with no man among them apparently able, or knowing how, or bold enough to break the unfortunate spell.

Some of the elements which appeared oftenest in the picture of domineering and demagogic leaders had been ignorance, naïveté, disregard of truth, hypocrisy, and unfair methods. Thus a single editor of an important industrial publication over a period of years was known to have published literally hundreds of falsehoods about individuals, institutions, and movements when the facts could have been verified. The published statements ranged from libel to naïve misinterpretation of commonplace utterances. Yet for a third of a century this man had proceeded on his way with little interruption or exposure, hundreds of leaders in the industrial field denying that he was representative of their group and yet all the time believing what he had to say and repeating his falsehoods. More than this, in his later years he was rewarded by election to the board of trustees of his state university and assignment to prominent posts in committee work.

These pictures of demagogic leadership were contrasted with the old types of leadership in which the South excelled. Thus, the great body of leaders of the South of the early twentieth century had neither experience nor training outside the atmosphere of political strife, economic limitations, educational and social deficiencies, and general mediocrity in many aspects of life. How, then, could they lead with distinction or govern well? Or how attain an equal place in the last half-century of rapid development? Who were the old southern leaders, the lawyers, the mayors, the judges, the statesmen? Consider then the same communities, towns, cities, states in which they held forth; how many of their children occupied the same positions of leadership as their fathers? If their children had not come into the succession, then others had. Who were they but the chance representatives of a new diffused leadership, whose potential abilities had in no wise been brought out or tested? Some there were of the same heritage as the old leaders; more there were of the common folk, mixed here and there and everywhere in a varied composite of the land.

Whatever else might be said of the old southern leaders, whatever their shortcomings according to democratic standards, such as attitudes toward the Negro and the workingman, they stood forth as examples of distinction, charm, order, force, character. They led. And while the younger leaders did have many ideas in advance of their predecessors and might have in them the making of another generation of distinction, they did not stand out. They were a generation with limited experience, limited training, and limited leisure but with an abundance of energy, enthusiasm, and small-town adolescent zest for participating in politico-social activities and for enacting righteousness.

Thus the responsibility and promise of the South for the development of a better leadership was reinforced both by a need and deficiency and by the heritage of a South of which the pictures of the old leaders were vivid enough. It was not a new thing for the masses of southern people to follow their leaders. Dodd estimated that only twice in the history of the country had men felt so keenly the loss of leaders—at the death of John C. Calhoun, and at the death of Lincoln. Of Calhoun "today the people of a great state think of him as of

no other American and linger sadly about the tomb where
their fathers laid him—a people who still feel more keenly
than all others the weight of Sherman's terrible blows of 1864
and 1865, who still insist that their cause and his was just."
And of all the southern qualities, their loyalty was perhaps
most characteristic. In terms of loyalty to leaders and causes,
coupled with ideals of defense from outside criticism and
stimulated by eloquence and mass meetings, the result is
easily understood.

There can be no doubt that the type of southern leadership
was chiefly responsible for the South of the period after the
Civil War, the character and heritage of which were powerful
factors in molding the continuing Southeast and Southwest
of the first half of the twentieth century. There were oratory
and eloquence, humor and invective, stubborn allegiance to
ideals set in the midst of folk loyalties, and the virtue of neighborliness and good will. Surely these types and symbols of
leadership should have availed much. What then was the
name and nature of the old leadership, and what did it trans-
mit to later leadership?

Yet in all these there was only the symbol and reality of the
white South. The Negro's part, through the cultural condition of the South, by default or by intent, was largely forgotten. Among the most vivid pictures of the South, the Negro
leader presented a challenge for special portraiture. He was
a rare picture, hard to paint. He was here, there, and everywhere, his skill the envy of many a white man. The picture
included not only statesmen such as Du Bois, Washington,
and Moton, who stood out among both whites and blacks, but
also the composite of thousands of Negro teachers, professional men, business men, preachers whose vividness and
artistry are worthy of a major effort to portray. Skill, patience,
courage, humility, poise, frankness, these and many other
qualities made the measure of their success all the more remarkable. And in this area of the South's development at least

there was a real New South. By the time of World War II, there were Negro leaders in many southern states who were listed by both whites and Negroes among the first twenty in influence. Their leadership and their character were symbolic of the new Negro culture and its challenge for opportunity.

In the South as her culture was maturing in the contemporary world there were a number of important considerations that related to its problem of leadership. One was that there had developed certain patterns of leadership which seemed to *represent* the people rather than guide them. Another was that the range and quality of this leadership were everywhere the key problem in understanding and planning for the regional-national integration of the South in the national culture and economy in the postwar world of the 1940's. There was needed, therefore, a new inventory of southern leadership since the Civil War, and such comparisons as would indicate the changing patterns between the old and the new. In the preliminary studies that have been made, the contemporary leaders of the South appear to be increasingly anxious to please or pacify public opinion rather than to blaze trails for the people to follow. There appears to be a well-nigh universal fear of what the people will think or say. This is not just in the political field. Even more the fear exists among educational leaders, church leaders, business leaders. This fear seems to be somehow also a heritage of the past, bottomed in a fear of radicalism, of the Negro situation, of outside interference. It is not so much a fear of these things as it is of what the people will think about what the leaders think, and will say about them. In every aspect of planning in the South, whether in education or agriculture or industry or labor, it is difficult to find a bold and united leadership above the level of defending the South and of a demagogic profession of faith.

There was one phase of the South's heritage from the time after the Civil War which might well have been continued more effectively for the better understanding of the region and its more articulate integration into national life. This was a continuous interchange of fellowship and leadership between northern and southern leaders, as in education. Perhaps the chief statesmanlike application by the best of the endowed foundations of their funds is for this interchange and cross-fertilization of ideas and research. Thus, through the national agencies of the three great fields of learning, the humanities, the physical sciences, and the social sciences, this interrelationship of scholars is promoted in regional and national conferences and in the learned societies in the many fields of science and education. There is, however, evidence that only a beginning has been made.

In leadership, as in most aspects of a regional culture, the portraiture would be different if it could be envisaged apart from the conflict with the larger national picture, and if the situation could be analyzed altogether in the framework of the South itself. The South presented an extraordinary array of local leaders and of state leaders in education and in agriculture and industry, whose influence was superb. From Henry Grady on down to the mountain folk who preached democracy, from the progenitors of Walter Hines Page and his few colleagues on through the catalogue of courageous editors and teachers, the roll call would show a galaxy. In rural life and agricultural education there was the Bradford Knapp movement, and later the congressional legislation for vocational and extension education, and demonstration in agriculture and home economics.

There were women leaders in these fields, and there were eloquent women leaders in the "lost cause" whose personalities still symbolized the South. There were southern congressmen and senators who rose to the occasion. But in particular, there were schoolmen and preachers who led the people in positive philosophy and encouragement, and who built institutions of learning that stood high in the estimation of the people. And there were educators whose names will always stand as symbol and reality of the New South.

In the later crises of depression, World War II, and reconversion, southern leaders were prominent in cabinet, court, and directives; and in the Armed Forces the South's ratio was high, so that here as in other aspects of southern culture there was great contrast.

CHAPTER XIV

Southern Education

IN THE JUDGMENT of many observers, public education has been the most American of all the institutions which have flowered from the maturing nation; for public education, and later college education, came to be the open sesame to opportunity and status. This meant not only the people's confidence that education would give them democracy but also the faith of the people in what education could do for them and their children. As proof of this verdict may be offered the figures which show how the United States excels all other nations in the ratio of its total population who have the opportunity for public education, the nature and amount of school facilities, and the total expenditures for public education, which exceed all other expenditures except those for war.

In this greatest of all American concerns the South again reflects its complex pattern of contradiction and paradox. Strangely enough, education came to be one of the South's main traditions. It is in some ways the most American of all the regions; and yet its education reflects the peculiar quality that distinguishes the South from the rest of the nation. So true is this that the term "southern education" connotes something special and different in more ways than the regional. Yet, since the Civil War, the South has often excelled in the democratic way of providing public education for the white children, and for all youth eligible for college and university education and for special training schools. It advanced rapidly to make public education in the elementary and high schools a new shibboleth, following its revolt against the culture ideals of the planter aristocracy; and it almost outdid the great middle states in allegiance to the state university, later to the land-grant college as offering to all the people equal and practical opportunity for democratic education.

The extent to which the South has followed the American pattern may be seen from the growth and development of university education in the United States. First of all, we recall the earlier religious bottoming of our American universities from the founding of Harvard to give deeper learning and understanding to the religious leaders of the new world, down through the founding of Yale, the College of New Jersey, King's College, to the chartering of our state universities, most of them led and manned by scholars from the great eastern universities. Always the thread of religion and piety and humility ran through the fabric of scholarship and learning. This was what the people wanted, and what the leaders of those days, conforming to the early American pattern, wanted and voted.

There was then the powerful influence of European culture and the example of European universities in the classics, in science, in philosophy, molding and conditioning the ideals and patterns of America's growing college and university life. This was, of course, in line with the earlier European influence on American culture in the East and in the South.

From this development the universities tended to become, like the European universities, more and more aristocratic in their assumptions that only a small minority of the people were capable of a thorough education and thorough culture, and it must be bottomed in the learning of the past and in pure science.

Now, no matter how realistic education based on such assumptions may have been, it was contrary to the basic assumption of the "American dream," which was to make public education a sort of *religio poetae*, and the open sesame to good citizenship and equality of opportunity for all men. Consequently there developed another level of university education, symbolized in the rise and rapid development of the state universities, starting in the great Middle West, spreading southeastward and then to the farther West. This was a movement toward democratizing university education. As Frederick Jackson Turner pointed out, the state through "the university offers to every class the means of education, and even engages in propaganda to induce students to continue. It sinks deep shafts through the social strata to find the gold of real ability in the underlying rock of the masses. It fosters that due degree of individualism which is implied in the right of every human being to have opportunity to rise in whatever directions his peculiar abilities entitle him to go, subordinate to the welfare of the State. It keeps the avenues of promotion to the highest offices, the highest honors, open to the humblest and most obscure lad who has the natural gifts, at the same time that it aids in the improvement of the masses.

"Nothing in our educational history is more striking than the steady pressure of democracy upon its universities to adapt them to the requirements of all the people. From the State universities of the Middle West, shaped under pioneer ideals, have come the fuller recognition of scientific studies, and especially those of applied science devoted to the conquest of nature; the breaking down of the traditional required curriculum; the union of vocational and college work in the same institution; the development of agricultural and engineering colleges and business courses; the training of lawyers, administrators, public men, and journalists—all under the ideal of service to democracy rather than of individual advancement alone."

The development of these great American state universities, founded on the basis of democratic service to the people, in many ways followed the same trend and level of university education as the great endowed eastern universities and later universities such as the University of Chicago and Stanford. They tended therefore to become again aristocratic, with their enrollment and their curriculum following the pattern of America's leading universities. So true was this that when the second level of democratic state university education took form in the great land-grant colleges of agriculture, engineering, and mechanical emphasis, it became the common mode to seek legislative funds for these institutions on the ground that the state universities had become institutions for rich men's sons and for classical education; and in those states where the land-grant college was merged with the state university, the new college took on the name of "cow college" and the standards of the university were considered to be greatly lowered. Then followed the further extension of the democratic education policy in the establishment of special teacher training institutions, normal schools and colleges, and special technical institutions. Many of these in later days were to seek full recognition and standing as standard colleges and universities, thus multiplying the units of state higher education and complicating the problem of the university.

It was, therefore, logical if not inevitable that the next trends in university development were quantitative, toward giving university instruction in all the multiple fields demanded in the modern world both by the people in general and by special interests of varying sorts. This quantitative university education made greater and greater demands upon the financial support of the people, thus bringing the university system nearer and nearer to the procedures of economy and efficiency in the use of public funds.

The universities had moved naturally on what might be called a popular level, in two ways. First, they sought to provide ways and means for every high-school graduate to attain that university education which the people had come to consider an open sesame to success; and secondly, they competed for popular support and for alumni loyalties through adult education, extension work, and public athletics.

Now, manifestly, these several university trends were not necessarily exclusive of one another; nor was there always a clear demarcation between them. Rather, they represent the university's effort to adapt itself to a modern, technological world which was reshaping every American institution. Alongside the state universities, interwoven with them into the fabric of American higher education, were the hundreds of notable private colleges and universities seeking nobly to maintain standards and at the same time to meet the qualitative needs of the people, and particularly of their religious constituencies.

So, also, the cumulative heritage of these great university epochs reflects a major part of the biography of the United States of America in the rise and development of its great prosperity as measured by the crest of the 1920's. The biography of American colleges and universities is in many ways the biography of America.

The South, when it really got started in the field of higher education, made what was in many ways the most remarkable record of any region in the country. Its failure to reach a higher level than it did, or to excel in the development of great universities, is in character with its relative achievements in other cultural fields. Some of these are revealed in the story of the South's technological resources, and others in the general culture of the region. Yet certainly the limitation in achievement was due in part to the earlier handicaps and to the lack of wealth with which to endow and support educational institutions of the first order. Before the Civil War the South got a slow start toward public education because its aristocracy did not believe in education for the Negro and for the masses. The old heritage was influential far into the new century, so that many people still believed that education would spoil a good worker, whether white or black: education, as they conceived it in classical terms, was beyond the capacity of more than a small proportion of the people. As we have said, this belief was a part of the general university heritage from Europe; yet it played a special part in southern public education on the elementary and high-school levels, and in the entrance requirements which the universities and colleges set for students from the high schools. Then there were, after the Civil War, the problems of exhaustion and recon- struction and of starting anew all education without capital and of the coexistence of two races. These were logical and inevitable in the southern culture and economy, and were highly important in the southern story.

In spite, therefore, of the extraordinary efforts long after the Civil War of leaders North and South to develop educa- tion of a really national level and quality, the South has dif- ferentiated itself from the rest of the nation in education as in other fields. In spite of the fact that the South has made more progress in public schools in recent years than any other region and has spent a greater proportion of its public moneys on them, it still reflects the regional quality in its measures of public education. In spite of the fact that Thomas Jefferson was prouder of founding the University of Virginia than of any other achievement, and that the two oldest state universi- ties in the nation were in the South, the region has failed to reach the national level either in standards or in participation in the educational work and scientific research of institutions of higher learning. All this, too, is in the light of one of the most inspirational episodes of American development and in the light of the South's major efforts both in imitating the nation's patterns and curricula and in pioneering on new fronts.

The reasons for all this again are apparent in the complex cultural heritage and fabric of the South. Measurable reasons are in the technical handicaps of a remarkable series of dichotomies in educational organization and functioning. These, appearing more and more clearly and powerfully, are increasingly important for the understanding and direction of the future South; but so vital is the reality of the situation that the total handicaps present tend to fade into the picture. Knowledge of the growth of the southern educational system but heightens consciousness of the problem of strengthening it where it is weak.

We begin again with the higher education. For the South has not one, not two, not three, but at least four levels of education in colleges and universities, combined with an uncertain capacity to support one adequate system. These double-multiple levels of education are, first, the dual white and Negro education; second, the male and female dichotomy of colleges; third, the state-church dichotomy; and, within that, the liberal arts, technical, and agricultural institutions often stand over against and separate from the state universities.

Little more need be said about the dual system of white and Negro schools, which obtains on all levels of the public school system. Manifestly, this makes unavoidable problems of finance and administration and of social and cultural relationships—all a part of the tragic heritage and continuing dilemma of the South seen in every phase of southern culture and economy.

Yet the folkways of coeducation between men and women were such as to set up another great dichotomy which made the South different (in the Northeast there was a similar pattern).

In the South not only state-supported institutions but denominational colleges were often separate for men and women. In each state there was, as a rule, one men's college and one women's college for the Methodist, the Baptist, and the Presbyterian denominations (six such colleges in all). Here we will pass over the distinctive quality of the education they offered and their major influence on the education of the South, and will only indicate their importance in the South's educational attainment.

In particular, there was the oft-recurring power of the folk culture to have education as the people wanted it. On the one hand they insisted that it be in the framework of the religious South, with denominational colleges. Then there was the later conflict between the state universities and the land-grant colleges; for the democratic way of appealing, often in demagogic

emotional patterns, to the people led to the agitation to transfer
support from the state universities—characterized as country
clubs for rich men's sons—to agricultural colleges for men and
normal and industrial colleges for women. This conflict went
on far into the first third of the twentieth century.

Then, carrying the democratic analogy further, and on
admirably logical premises, the movement for junior colleges
and district agricultural schools sought to educate all the
youth, in the communities in which they lived, in subjects
which would fit them for life. Needless to say, the point here
is that the multiplication of schools in local areas was manifestly at the cost of the higher schools and was for the most
part regardless of standards, and of ways and means of support. Although many advocates of the local schools made a
fine impression upon the people, often pioneering in satisfying a great need, the total result was to increase the demand
upon the people for financial support beyond their capacity,
and to diffuse effort so as to preclude the best results.

In all these advances in education, politics and appeals to
the people played a larger and larger part, coloring the whole
educational fabric of the South. Something of this may be seen
from later references to politics and the solid South, in which
again the prevailing culture was more southern than national.
Suggestive of the character of the folk culture and the ability
of the South to do what it wanted to do in education, was the
spectacle of college and university football, which, the South
came to boast and the nation came to admit, was probably
played better in the Southeast and Southwest than anywhere
else in the United States. The South could have the highest
type of football and it could bring in coaches and forget the
folkways of anti-Catholic Protestants what time they sought
the best of Notre Dame's stars to win national recognition.

Many of the states, with their dichotomy of colleges and
universities, competed in football and football attendance
with one another and with the other regions. There was

Louisiana, with Tulane and Louisiana State University; Alabama, with its University winning Rose Bowl awards and Auburn knocking out the winners and winning its interregional contests. In Georgia, first Georgia Tech and then the University, both winners of Rose Bowl games, made football history. In Tennessee, Vanderbilt and later the University led the South and distinguished themselves in the national arena. Not very far behind all these were the University of North Carolina and Duke University, keeping big-time football on the southern map. In the Southwest, the game became almost a distinctive enterprise in which the folkways of football seemed to be about to take a place above the folkways of education; for there were not only the University of Texas and Texas A. and M. but the church colleges, making themselves known to the nation through football more than through scholarship. In Oklahoma there were the University and the A. and M. and Tulsa.

Nevertheless, the story of education is inseparable from the whole biography of the region in its American background. The composite cultural character of the South transcends any single aspect of its culture and any single institutional influence, and transcends completely the glamour and tragedy of the Old South. Appraisal is not so simple as a formula with merely so much religion, so much politics, so much education; or so much backwardness, so much progress, so much ignorance, so much enlightenment; nor again so much plantation and so much poor white. This conclusion is supported by the sound theoretical considerations which show all cultures as evolving through the folk-regional processes. It is supported by the realistic pictures of much southern culture as it reflects a regional cross section or chronological stratum of universal cultural development. It is indicated further in the interlapping and overlapping of many of the indices which characterize the special institutions, such as the church and religion, the state and politics, the school and education, rural life and culture, industrial development, and most of the general southern folkways. Thus, many of the characteristic indices in the catalogue of politics apply in the field of religion; many in politics and leadership apply in education; many in education apply in industry and agriculture; and so on for the others.

From this viewpoint, it is clear that education, for instance, can no more carry the whole load of direction and reconstruction than it can give character to the whole region and its people in all aspects of enduring, continuing culture. So the attempt to analyze and direct the region's politics without understanding and directing its agriculture and tenant economy or its educational background would be quite as futile as to reconstruct its agriculture and economy without coming to grips with its folk culture and attitudes. The regional culture must be broken up into its several elements before we can see the whole picture, and make the needed comparisons in time and regional quality, and appraise the prospects of redirection and reconstruction. In no other way can we appraise the folk culture of the region realistically, avoiding the stereotypes and stage characterizations which prevail throughout the country. In no other way can the picture of the region in the national development be projected into the future.

Here then is double and triple dilemma. It must be clear that the all-dependence so often placed upon education as the single institutional approach to progress was not enough. On the other hand, every major problem from farm tenancy to political democracy is bound up with the regional culture, or system of economic and social ideologies and arrangements, which in turn represent the realities of recent historical development more than the possibilities of the region under different conditioning and expansion. Manifestly, also, the strategy of mass attack upon the culture of a whole region conforms to neither common sense nor scientific specifications. Nor does pride or acquiescence in a regional culture as superior because of its history or its variation from national type or its conformity to certain early American traditions satisfy any of the practical requirements of the present time. The more realistic approach as stated in the objectives of the Southern Regional Study, in addition to understanding the "exceedingly complex nature of the regional cultures involved and the immensity and time-quality of cultural reconstruction," was "to focus upon a relatively small number of elemental factors toward which practical study and planning may be directed," to the end that the whole culture might be best readapted to the needs and possibilities of the nation and of the region. The premise would be that this region need not lag on the one hand nor, on the other, follow blindly the paths of a hectic, urban, technological, transitional period of civilization.

In the field of education, perhaps the most significant approaches to modifying the general culture through special avenues are found in Negro education, in the Federal grants to land-grant colleges for extension service, research, and experiment stations, and in the endowments and grants made by the larger foundations. In Negro education the change in status and attitude appears to be gradual, a normal outgrowth of regional development, but accelerated—mostly through the influence of Negro colleges, Negro teachers trained in other regions, grants from private individuals and foundations for Negro education, and the Negro's own significant achievements. Among the evidences of change are new attitudes and procedures in race conferences and contacts, appreciation of the achievements of superior Negroes, greater respect for Negro personality, the rise of Negro college youth, the evolving of a new Negro culture. The land-grant colleges, long standing afar off from the people, have come to take the lead in many aspects of realistic education and have made inroads into many of the old procedures in diet, home economics, farm management. Evidence of the forces involved may be seen in the figures for home and farm demonstration agents, faculty members, and in specific results in livestock farming. The national foundations have functioned broadly in the fields of higher education, public secondary education, Negro education, and in health and child-welfare activities.

Perhaps in most of the general educational development in curricula, administration, buildings, and hygiene, the region has largely imitated the form and mechanics of the nation with little visible effect upon the regional culture. Something of routine imitation has been manifest in the overemphasis upon illiteracy, and in the weakness of adult education. It has been apparent in the overemphasis upon wholesale consolidation, and in the curriculum. The end results are probably as stated in spite of the large number of educational ideologies, experiments, and "schools," enumerated elsewhere, which have marked the region's creative efforts. Many of the original proposals have taken form as ambitious plans, sectional schemes, or outlets for personal expression of leaders.

In colleges and universities, the influence of faculty members trained in eastern and western universities has been great; but few of them have modified the southern culture in any fundamental way. This is one example of the dominance of the regional culture, which has been especially apparent in race relations and attitudes. The strength and integrity of the southern culture have been more and more effective as the southern men and women trained in other institutions and returning to the faculties of southern colleges have increased to the point of displacing natives of other regions from major posts. This and other factors—such as a revolt against industrialism, technology, and urbanism, the romanticizing of the old southern culture, the experience of northern capitalists in southern industry, the attempt of northern idealists and reformers to coerce the region, the experience of the Negro in the North and West, and a revivification of sectional antagonisms—have contributed to an apparent solidifying of the regional culture. So powerful is the "solid South," and the Civil War Republican tradition, that the older order continued unabated through the depression and into the Second World War, sustaining itself for the most part on party and sectional differences over issues and men.

Turning next to the several modes of institutional organization and achievement in the South, perhaps relatively little more on education is needed except to point up certain key situations. Certainly, there is no need to repeat the long catalogue of low rankings and deficiencies. Certainly, enough of the facts are available; their continued repetition may well be a smoke screen for realistic action. Of mere cataloguing of mechanical, self-evident indices we have had enough. What is needed, however, is to focus upon whatever elemental factors are basic to the understanding and direction of the region in its next period of development. One such factor is a relative retrogression of education in the region since the rapid gains of the first third of the century. The other way in which the region lagged most was in the influence and standing of its educational institutions and leaders in the nation. Here are facts which, for the most part, the educational South appears to be both unwilling to face and resentful at having presented. It is not only that the region has no university of the first ranking; it also lacks college and university scholars and administrators of the highest distinction, by the usual standards of achievement and recognition. The statistics here, of course, measure status, not potential, and there are no data to indicate what scholars or administrators might have done under different circumstances or in equal competition; but the fact is incontrovertible that the region does not rank. Yet a wealth of evidence indicates that this region greatly needs such leadership, not only to develop its own incomparable physical and human resources, but to tie its institutions into the national culture and obtain a commensurate part in the nation's support, which it does not now have.

There is one exception to this appraisal. The South has gained in its Negro higher education, and has in its institutions the best scholars and educational leaders of the race. Yet this is a combined effect of assistance from the outside, and of the failure of colleges and universities in the East and West to appoint Negro scholars on their faculties; since they do not permit of separate institutions, the Negro scholar and teacher has nowhere else to go. In the meantime, the Negro is making an extraordinary contribution to the regional culture.

Compared with the regions of America which have achieved most distinction in higher education, the South has a shortage of universities sufficiently free from state or church dominance to function independently and at the same time sufficiently well endowed to set the pace for other regional universities and keep interregional and national influences and participation constantly effective. It has no institution comparable to Harvard or Yale or Chicago or Stanford as a pacemaker or independent university influence of sufficient strength to maintain a continuous presumption for the best in education. The premise, of course, assumes that these institutions in the other regions have, by measured fact, contributed largely to the standards, achievements, and status of university education in those regions and in the nation. The conclusion might be naturally drawn that one sure way to insure a continuing low standard and status in the Southeast would be to do nothing about the shortage of pacemaking universities. That the South must set up its own pacemaking institutions is not in accord with historical developments. Differing from the other regions of the country, the South has a powerful handicap in the imbalance of trade and wealth which go to enrich these other regions. Yet none of these considerations alters the fact, that the South has no institutions sufficiently endowed to lead the way.

A common answer to the urge of the South that it needs a few strong universities comparable to the best in other regions is about as follows:

The South is neither capable of nor deserving of such universities; and it would not support them in funds or in cultural constituency if it had them. Furthermore, instead of becoming national universities they would become sectional, concentrating upon the regional culture and drawing a large proportion of their students from the same sources as the other universities. The present enrollment of southern students in northern, eastern, and western universities is perhaps the chief interregional cultural contact and should not be disturbed. Furthermore, it has not seemed possible to reach satisfactory agreements upon the universities to be endowed and the method of endowing them; and some of the results of endowments and grants have not been convincing of the wisdom of these. The alternative proposal has been that in both federal equalization funds and in foundation assistance the functional approach is the only feasible one. That is, there must be broad equalization of opportunity in science, in rural education, in higher education, in agriculture, to the end that the best results may be distributed most equitably.

The answer to this realistic situation and to these logical arguments is equally realistic:

If the nation and the region, after appraising the extraordinary facts pointing to the abundance of natural, cultural, and human resources, still remains convinced that the region should not and cannot have its first-class universities, then the region must remain continuously deficient. Such a final conclusion must reflect upon the national program and capacity as it must reflect upon the region. It must inevitably result in continued sectionalism and drain upon the national unity and resources. From any viewpoint of adequate culture and effective democracy the position is untenable. The record is one of defeatism. The more realistic and difficult the situation is, the greater the need for working out an effective program of regional equilibrium, of balance, and of enrichment of culture. Equalization funds and supplementary endowments will still be needed as they are projected on the functional framework of statesmanlike programs.

Moreover, when it is suggested that the region have first-class, privately endowed institutions comparable to Yale, Harvard, Stanford, Princeton, and Chicago, two assumptions are inherent. One is that the institutions will be in reality first-class and national universities, taking advantage of the many regional opportunities and equipping themselves with facilities and personnel such that their enrollment would be to a considerable extent interregional. The statistics of the last ten years, which show that the leading southeastern universities have a larger ratio of students enrolled from outside the region than those of any other region, indicates the practicability and the reality of such a premise. The assumptions provide further, as has been set forth in various memoranda, that one basic need in such universities would be provision for interregional exchange of students and faculty as an essential part of the university system. In addition to this, the assumption is that these universities would tend to have the same effect in the southern region as in other regions—accelerating at once, through example and competition, and in very appreciable measures, the development of standards and support in the state universities.

One of the points of immaturity of many of the national programs is found in the failure to balance values, resources, opportunities in the region with those in other regions. When the accrediting agency and the endowment advisers insist that standards of achievement must be equal they are, of course, following the only reasonable course. What they have generally not sought, however, is a fair equilibrium between the ends sought and the available means. Here, for instance, are some handicaps of the professor or administrator in all institutions of the Southeast: he is required to carry heavy teaching and administrative loads; to work with many local and state committees; to function without known or understood standards; to fight against inertia and antagonism; to combat racial and religious conflicts; to stand for or against his own people in the midst of violent outside criticisms; to get along with less money, less intellectual contact and companionship, and with fewer pacemaking institutions or leaders to give him leverage on his load. And back of all this he has had less training and experience upon which to build his structure of scholarship or administration. It is, of course, an impossible basis upon which to plot comparable standards and achievements.

Some notable features of southern education are the extraordinary amount and quality of work and achievement done under these circumstances. This has been reflected especially in the output of graduate students for other institutions, South and North, of educational and religious leaders of the smaller colleges; and in the educational ideology of southern culture. The denominational colleges in particular, for both men and women, are examples. Those for women have been particularly successful in preserving and developing the southern culture. Because of the multiplicity of smaller colleges and their significant part in the past, because of diminishing financial support and of the changing trend toward state education, the problem of standards and consolidation appears to be an imminent one. In strengthening weaker centers, consolidating institutions, and seeking the most effective regional balance of colleges and universities, the Southeast might well have developed one or more well supported municipal universities.

Once again, the story of the South and its education, if viewed from the vantage point of the region alone and without unfavorable comparison with other regions, reflected extraordinary progress. There was much of romance and something of epic quality in the South's militant expansion of its schools and in its enthusiasm for new efforts. The actual ratio of increase in educational expenditures was far greater than that for the nation, and the increase of enrollment in high schools and colleges was creditable from any viewpoint. Symbolic of the extraordinary progress made is one state which, in the year 1930, appropriated more money for Negro education than it did for all education in 1900. So, too, the several state educational associations, school journals, and membership and leadership in the National Education Association reflected a dynamic movement that, in retrospect and in comparison with the high national standards, is likely to be forgotten. It is a record that is worth remembering.

CHAPTER XV

"North" and "South" Again

DURING THE 1920's and the early 1930's it was commonly assumed that "North" and "South" were no longer valid realities in the new America that was developing, except as they reflected a tragic past which the nation wanted to forget. The First World War had relegated the term "The War," meaning the Civil War, to an outmoded past that took its place alongside other epochs of "only yesterday," or that represented steppingstones on which the nation had already risen to higher things.

Before that, perhaps during the whole of the first third of the twentieth century, there were very substantial trends toward a genuinely realistic reintegration of the South in the nation as, in the regional balance of America, the southern states adopted higher standards of achievement and participated more largely in the total American culture. The South, as Southeast and Southwest, was taking its place dynamically in the nation, even as the Far West, the Northwest, and all the other regions were making America strong and united by developing their separate diversities of strength and seeking a new economic and cultural balance.

There were several reasons for these important trends, perhaps about equally balanced between the regions and the nation as a whole. The leaders of the South had inventoried her resources and her deficiencies and had begun to face the facts in preparation for genuine progress. A new school of historians in the North had rewritten the history of the nation, appraising the South fairly, and had also made realistic diagnosis and criticism of the northern administration after the

Civil War. The South had also made extraordinary strides in nearly all phases of its culture and economy. It had developed industry, paved great highways, increased its urban civilization in both the Southeast and the Southwest faster than any other regions. It had pioneered in some aspects of public welfare, public health, and education, and had, with the cooperation and support of the Northeast, strengthened its colleges and universities. It had begun to develop research in both the physical and the social sciences and to apply the results to agriculture and industry, and it was increasing its representation in the national councils of leadership. The South had assumed a new sort of leadership in literature and had become the best documented of all the regions. In all this, the South had liberal cooperation from publishers and educational leaders and philanthropists in the Northeast. And there was pride of achievement not only in the South but in the other regions, particularly in "the wests," for what the southern regions were doing.

All this was especially marked in the period immediately following the First World War, from 1918 to the early depression years. Then, once again, both the Southeast and the Southwest took larger and more positive part in the affairs of the nation as the Democratic administration developed the New Deal. This was true in two main ways. One was the natural and logical larger southern share in the federal government under a Democratic administration. The other was the southern share in the measures of relief and reconstruction during the depression years when the region was sometimes worse off than other parts of the nation. At any rate, the southern states put their hands to the task, and through state planning boards, through various technical ways of cooperating with New Deal agencies, through public works, work relief, agricultural adjustment, through educational cooperation, and other ways were assuming a new sort of normal and logical participation in the total national effort. Southern personnel, both in political and in appointive arrangements, was large.

Then a strange thing happened, happened twice, once because of the depression New Deal pressure and once because of the pressure of war; namely, a sudden revivification of the old sectional conflict and the recrudescence of the terms North and South. It would have been unbelievable if it had not actually happened that this, together with special and intensified revival of the old race conflict, would bring the South to its greatest crisis and the nation again to one of its chief domestic problems since the Civil War.

First, the realistic researches into the resources, deficiencies, and needs of the South, and then the action of the New Deal administration, caused the nation to rediscover the South as an example of backwardness and later of badness, and to undertake to remake it overnight. The revival of the term South, in so far as the national administration was concerned and in so far as it began to be used universally by editors and critics, came about in two ways. One was typified in the now noted slogan that the South was the nation's "Economic Problem No. 1." The South was Tobacco Road. It was again missionary territory. But, whatever it was, it was "The South." Secondly, the South came to be synonymous with conservatism or reactionary policies because southern senators and congressmen and state governors and leaders opposed many New Deal policies. "What else could you expect? He is a Southerner," came to be a common refrain. And then the South, with its usual sensitiveness, revived with a vengeance the term North, charging that section with again "trying to make the South over."

The second intensification of the North-South conflict was brought on by the war, which was expected to unify the nation, and in which the southern states led in enlistment and in all-out support, as a result of the South's racial segregation culture and laws. The nation realized suddenly that the American Dream guaranteed to all its citizens equal rights and opportunities, and that, while it had gone to war for global democracy, two of its own great regions contained a negation of democracy. It realized further that this negation and this segregation policy applied to the armed forces, because the Army and the Navy and the Air Corps were a part of a white man's world, where the Negro was discriminated against through no fault of his own. And so there was the ever recurring question, "What can be done about the South?" Increasingly, individuals and agencies, private and public, set themselves to the task of "making" the South change. This is a long story which we have already discussed in the chapters on folk, race, culture, and regions. Yet the net result was an unbelievable revival of the old bitterness attached to the terms "North" and "South" what time the South resented "northern interference," and what time the North tried to coerce the South again.

Then there was another factor. There might be no new South nor new North in these conflicting areas, but there was a new Negro of such force and vitality as to make compromise well-nigh impossible. The Negro himself had changed tremendously. It was not only that he had developed important upper and middle classes; it was not only that he had developed a magnificent leadership, and thousands had taken advantage of higher educational opportunities. It was not only that Negro youth, sensing the epochal spiritual change and racial attitudes and led by Negro leadership of the North and South, was minded to experiment with every type of equal opportunity; it was all this and more. It was as if some universal message had reached the great mass of Negroes, urging them to dream new dreams and to protest against the old order. It was as if there were pathos and tragedy in their misunderstanding of the main tenets of a bitter Negro leadership, and as if many of the northern Negro leaders of limited mentality had confused them with the idea that any sort of work or courtesy or cheerfulness was an index of subservience to the white man. In all of this, whether it was pathos and tragedy or admirable idealism and noble effort, the net result was a new Negro facing the old white man and joining with the North against the South.

In studying the annals of the South and the nation, exploring their cultural development and the present situation with a view to next steps, two considerations are important. First, not all of the attack by the North upon the South was specifically against the South. Much of it was the good old American way of criticism. It was the way of the intelligentsia and the reformers. Many of the later intelligentsia, severe in their denunciation of all America and extreme in their devotion to European culture, were ignorant of the realities in America and limited in their outlook on life. Much of the criticism of the South had the same American quality as the old New England and Northeast, and much of it was symbolic of a thousand national voluntary organizations in New York which gave livelihood and high motivation to thousands of workers whose field was the nation's reform. A part expressed the phenomenal ignorance of the newer generations concerning American history and the different American regions. The West is still the land of the wild jackasses.

To test this premise it is only necessary to note similar attitudes toward other folk. There is no hesitancy in telling England what to do with India, Europe what to do with its powerfully conflicting folk cultures, South America what to do with its mixed heritage and growing pains. The level of criticism is one of intellectual and moral isolationism, in which the merits of abstract ideological concepts or untested moral assumptions have very little to do with the action patterns of reality. On this level of intellectual isolationism there is a failure to understand the realities of the folk wherever found with their perennial problems of life and culture in all its aspects of growth, sex, race, work, aspirations, imperfections, drama. So, too, much that is ascribed to the South is scarcely more than old man Human Nature and frontier America or rural folk in nature's setting. If the South could understand this, it would do more work and be less sensitive.

The other explanation is found in the historical background of the terms "North" and "South" and in the heritage of both regions from the Civil War. In his two epochal appearances before the eighty-first anniversary celebration of the New England Society of New York in 1886 and the Boston Merchants' Association in 1889, Henry W. Grady appealed to his distinguished northern audiences for a fair understanding of what he was calling "The New South." "Will New England," he asked, "permit the prejudice of war to remain in the hearts of the conquerors, when it has died in the hearts of the conquered?" And at Boston: "We need not go one step further unless you concede right here that the people I speak for are as honest, as sensible, and as just as your people." And while Grady was cheered to the echo on both occasions, it was clear that the South had not forgot its bitterness and the North had not changed enough to look upon the South with sympathetic understanding.

In reality, in spite of the glorified eloquence of Grady honestly and devoutly rationalizing that there was a new South, the South was new only in the necessary changes which come through time and technological and industrial progress and in the noble ideology of patriots, South and North, who sought to rebuild it and bring both sections together on enduring American principles. The South might have forgot and forgiven had there been a different sort of reconstruction; but it never did, and threescore years and ten after the reconstruction there was to be an unbelievable recrudescence of the bitterness that had brought on the Civil War and resulted in the continued conflict of brothers, reminiscent of the European folk conflicts, stranger than fiction or more realistic than the age-long personal and family feuds of fighting folk, and a strange thing happened among the youth of both North and South. In the early 1940's it was a

standing joke that, wherever northern and southern youth
came together in camps and cantonments, the Civil War had
to be fought over again. To the southern youth it was as if
the northern soldiers always brought the attack; and they in
turn ran true to form and defended vigorously.

In all other aspects of Americanism there was great progress toward united ideals and higher standards. The South
made startling advances in nearly all phases of modern civilization—in public health, sanitation, education, welfare,
building, in physical and chemical science. In the North the
sweep and tempo of life gave the people little time to think
of the past, and they scarcely thought of the South except
incidentally in achieving the world's most sensational progress. Yet, as in the South, whenever the old issues of race and
religion and sectional competition rose they brought the old
intense reactions. It was an extraordinary spectacle, in which
the nation could take little pride. It was essentially a new
problem of education and adjustment in the interregional
balance of America. It was not merely narrowness or liberalism, something to be dismissed as unimportant and provincial.

Here are two examples of the northern viewpoint. One is a
letter from an instructor in one of the most distinguished New
England colleges, and the other from a young anthropologist
in the service of the government. Neither is exceptional, and
both state the problem so vividly as to make it a part of the
contemporary story of the South. The young instructor writes:
"I am a Northerner, born and bred. New Hampshire was
my birthplace, New England is my home, and I have lived
in other states strung out from here to California. But I have
always felt a profound antipathy to the South and most that
it stands for. This was no unreasoning prejudice inherited from
a childhood of post-Civil-War hatreds. I acquired no 'attitude' toward the South from either of my parents, or from my
schooling or my environment in New Hampshire. My profound scorn, not to say hatred, for the South I created myself.

I created it out of the knowledge that I acquired during the passing years, years of study, graduate work, teaching, years in which I found that the South held the lowest record in the country in all those things which I cherished and believed in: the lowest record in public schooling; the lowest record in higher education; the lowest record in public health, in civil liberties, in housing, in crime prevention and treatment; the lowest record in tolerance and freedom and justice in all this land. Oh, it was easy to account for some of these: northern economic piracy, effects of the Civil War, the Negro problem, and so on. But not all of them. It seemed to me that it must be the caliber of the people themselves that was at fault: their intelligence, their character, and their good will."

One thing this instructor had not done, and that was to see the South for himself.

The other letter, from a young anthropologist in the services of the government's far-flung community relationship, is not exceptional. First, there is the verdict that "to northerners, particularly to those whose thinking like my own is conditioned by the currents of life in large cities, the South is the problem of our commonwealth." Further: "We northerners possess few facts about the South, and do not understand her. We imagine that she fell out of step with the nation after 1865, and that she then turned in upon herself. Her subsequent internal developments have been a mystery to us. We have no inkling of the motives that drive her people, of the logic that supports their judgments."

The South complained that there was no adequate way in which the northern youth could learn of the southern regions. There was a brilliant young woman graduate of a prominent eastern college who had got her main knowledge of the South in college, through a Negro woman from Georgia who visited the class and told of her difficulties. When she married a young southern doctor and was about to go to Memphis, all her friends consoled her because she would be leaving civilization. Later she was unable to convince them of their ignorance until they visited her. This is in line with the continued verdict of the young anthropologist, who writes:

"A northern child's, and many an adult's, first awareness of the Southland comes from meeting occasional migrant Negroes who work in our kitchens and live in our ghettos. The reaction is a confused one. There are uneasiness and fear, and we seldom clarify our relations with individual Negroes. The Civil War and reconstruction years are so presented to us in the schools that we can make no dynamic connection between those times and upheavals and the presence and status of Negroes in our northern cities; no philosophy of interracial conduct has been presented for our use. Films and best-sellers, on the other hand, provide us with a definite if special outlook. They offer beguiling picturizations of the ante-bellum South as some country of Cockaigne where men were chivalrous and ladies glamorous, and their former slaves were attached to them by silken bonds. Yet the creed of the North contains a fierce repudiation of slavery in any form, and the schools do teach us that this principle was sanctified by our blood in 1865. Thus the fairy-tale South looms also as a menacing sinner. We condemn her on the antislavery principle alone, not knowing more about her, and unaware of the extent to which she has actually influenced us in our own unfair treatment of Negroes. The economic and other necessities of the southern slave period are unimportant to us, interesting though they may be. We view the defunct institution of slavery and the present unhappy state of race relations by themselves, ripped from any context. They are an absolute evil, blamable on the South."

The South is either all bad or all fine. "And yet there remains an ineradicable feeling of appreciation for the South. So vividly do we recall the tremendous contributions her great men made to the young Republic that today she still carries prestige, even after secession and crushing defeat, despite the horrible disorganization of the reconstruction, and the chronic

disaffection she has shown ever since. The careful hearings
she receives, from the halls of Congress to jive sessions in
Tin Pan Alley, are often gilded with some sentimentality. This
accolade is rendered even in the Negro world. We northerners
play at adopting southern nicknames and accents and tones
of speech, we dream of warm, magnolia-scented nights and
sing songs about Basin Street and the poetry of bayous we
have never seen."

But deep down in the mind of the North, it is still the bad
South. "The stresses of war now rouse all our sleeping mistrust
of the South. We see that race relations are worsening, conflicts becoming widespread by contagion, and overt. Southern
spokesmen refuse to honor federal regulation of an increasingly intolerable situation. They caution their supporters
against the 'carpetbag' and 'bureaucratic' agencies of the federal government that allegedly threaten to demolish the democratic processes of the land. We wonder how they mean
their words, how they view their own oligarchical methods
of control, their unfairly applied literacy clauses, their poll-
tax system, their controlled primaries and other methods of
assuring favored elections. We wonder why southern spokesmen reiterate the language of democracy when they are eager
to withhold the vote from even their own relatives in uniform
in order to exclude uniformed Negroes from southern ballot
boxes, all being done in the name of the doctrine of States'
Rights. We wonder at the devious southern mind."

Now the anthropologists in their study of culture give us
here a stark contrast. First of all, they teach us all the fundamentals of studying culture objectively, looking at it from the
viewpoint of no time, no "good" or "bad," but just culture as
it is seen in cross section of here and now, as it has developed,
and as it is in reality. Time, place, values are only for identification. For here, they say, is culture, and it must be looked at
objectively, all cultures examined with the same scientific and

careful observation and analyzed with the same dependable methods.

The contradictory appraisal comes from their oft repeated ignoring of these fundamentals whenever they turn their attention to the South. The most distinguished of all American anthropologists, for instance, cautioned and exhorted his students always to be patient with the conflicts and cultures of Europe, people in travail and in quarrels, because forsooth culture is of the long-time process and of great environmental conditioning. Nevertheless, time and again, in a noble enthusiasm and adherence to pure science, asserting that nothing counts but the facts and that there are no inherent racial differences, he seemed to forget the powerful facts of relationships, of race prejudice, slavery, and postwar reconstruction conditioning, the power of caste, and join the caravan which sought to remake the South in one generation. From the vantage point of this story of the South, there could be no doubt that he was eternally right in his interpretation of race; but culture and folk, they were another matter, when and if they were to be transformed in the twinkling of an eye.

To illustrate with a simpler example, we return to the young anthropologist who became convinced of the "need of first-hand observation of the interracial behavior of those upper-class whites who dominate southern living, apparently initiating or guiding all important developments." Here are the verdicts of this young anthropologist:

"It must be recognized that the South is a land of yesterday. That is the cause of her hostile and anachronistic behavior. Her institutions, her responses, her goals are outmoded, out of rhythm, irrelevant to the national trends. Her sectional feeling, so vehement as to all but differentiate her into another nation, her violent devices for social control, like her graceful hospitality, are survivals of an age long since left behind by the North. That is why the regions cannot understand each other. The habits of both frontier and plantation days are still real along the Mississippi, but the North has forgotten their compulsives. Mechanization and mass production, high standards of living without discrimination for all the millions of the giant cities, the extension of democratic privileges and responsibilities to every anonymous citizen—these northern ways are as yet impossible to the rural, isolated, pre-industrial South, inconceivable to her and repugnant. Of all the United States, the South is most trapped by poverty and disease, illiteracy, political corruption and a deep want of ambition. She holds no prevailing social convictions newer than those of the reconstruction years. She is unable to participate in modern American democracy. In conflict with our times, she is a demoralizing influence."

Yet this same student of cultures and the folk finds the solution simple:

"But this condition cannot last. Her very wartime conflicts with other regions bring her into closer contact with the nation than she has been for generations. Even now she is in transit to the twentieth century. War-contract factories have been springing up, and the countryside must become mechanized and urbanized. As economic and technological developments move ahead, and her ways and goals of living adjust in conformity, her thought and language must acquire meanings closer to those in more advanced parts of the country. The regal, dangerous personalness of southern living will become more like the egalitarian impersonalness of northern living. In an industrial civilization, sectional and racial differences necessarily become minimized, communications introduce people and issues to one another, universalize opinions and promote sympathy. When that development comes upon her, the South will grasp the wider orientations of the balance of the country. Through the changes in her own interests, her class and race and regional conflicts will resolve themselves. The South cannot and should not be eyed apart from the rest of the country. Her future is inseparable from that of the entire United States."

Needless to say, the last sentence and verdict of our anthropologist is the same as the recurring motif in our biography of the South; namely, the way of the South must be the way of America. Our complaint is about the naïve implication that the process is merely one of modern technology pushed along by intellectual and moral isolationism, of a sort of coercive totalitarianism. Cannot such a student, for instance, behold Britain and remember how short a time ago it was said that as soon as the English Channel was tunneled and communications of the everyday variety were set up—with standardized mechanisms of commerce and fashions and all that sort of thing—Britain and Europe would become a single great fellowship? Yet, now that airplanes and wireless, telegraph and television, radio, and all the developments in commerce and trusts have made a new world, with international relationships on all levels, the British folk are so much more British that it is often questioned even whether Britain is Europe at all.

A century ago Germany gave every indication, in science, invention, art, literature, and general culture, of leadership in a world of international fellowship. With the multiplication of technologies and with the tightening communications, Germany flowered into the most powerful national folk society in the history of human society.

In the United States the first years of the Second World War heightened southern attitudes and differences, southern loyalties and conflicts, so that the South drew much further apart from the rest of the nation than it was during the 1920's, in spite of all the improvements in technology and commerce and communications.

The South, admittedly sensitive, held the North responsible for blaming the South for everything. Admittedly ignorant, the South accused the North of ignorance of the South. It felt, too, that many of its critics were malcontents, maladjusted to life anywhere, who found in their assaults upon the South convenient means of gaining attention, while others were sincere but ignorant of history and of economic, social, or biological processes. If only the North would send its strong men and women leaders instead of the weak, pale, irritable ones or the professional agitators who had little standing at home! And all of its critics expected the impossible. The South felt that the North discriminated against it in intellectual ways and on many counts. No one, for instance, would think of holding Columbia University professors responsible for conditions on the East Side or in New York City politics, or University of Chicago professors responsible for the Thompson regime and gang rule; nevertheless the South was constantly reminded that there could be no liberal and progressive professors in southern universities—else, how could such conditions in race, industry, child labor, and religion exist? Again, a northern author wrote that the governor of North Carolina ought to try living in one of the mill houses, as if the governor were responsible for every condition in his state, although it would never have occurred to him to hold the governor of New York or Massachusetts or New Jersey responsible for the strikes that were so common there. Many southerners felt that the North made many ignorant, presumptuous, and impolite assumptions about the South, and took no pains to get the facts.

The South found fault with the North for its tendency to characterize everything "down there," "down South in Dixie," as peculiar to southern temperament or temper. If the South wanted normal geographical representation, like the rest of the country, it was accused of selfish desires. If it protested, it was accused of being temperamental. It objected to the playing up of isolated or sensational happenings or picturesque personalities. It was offended by the snap conclusions which distinguished editors, educators, and publicists drew from unverified newspaper reports or out-of-date facts and expounded at length. It was surprised by the emotional set of the intellectuals, so many of whom showed a dogmatism closely akin to that commonly attributed to southerners. It was tired of being solicited for funds to be added to the national surplus and used in remaking the South. It was sensitive to the constant call for "socially minded," "emancipated," "reconstructed" southerners.

The South thought the North was the more bitter of the two. There were evidences of an increasing invective and impatience in the North. The South had hoped to develop and strengthen liberal attitudes in race and industry as rapidly as possible. It regretted the efforts of a few outside extremists, which slowed down logical processes. The whole situation was mixed up and funny and tragic! The South, with the highest homicide rate in the world, was forever saying that something had to be done about crime-infested Chicago, and that the North should begin at home in reforming race relations. "They are trying to make us abandon our fundamental policy of race segregation," was a constant refrain, "when, if they would just let us alone we would work out our problem." Again: "There wouldn't be any trouble with the Negroes down here if you would just hush up and let us alone." While it was pointed out that a great deal of the tension and conflict would have occurred in the normal evolution of a quick-changing world, even without war and other outside pressures, it was clear that these were the chief immediate sources of tension and conflict.

One of the chief complaints of the South was that those who wrote about the South or libeled its personalities or sought to make it over were too often almost completely irresponsible. They were not acquainted with the facts. Another complaint was that the rest of the nation did not treat the Negro fairly. While this had little to do with the merits of the demand that the South widen its range of democratic opportunity and give the Negro a better chance, it had much to do with the South's reaction. The South felt that there should be an equally realistic picture of the total national attitude and an understanding of what ratio of the people at large constituted the basic power of the drive against the South.

The man who played Jeeter Lester in *Tobacco Road* so long that he looked the part tells the story of a young countryman whose "You tell 'em to leave us alone" seemed symbolic of what the South felt about the New Yorkers. "Look, Mr. Sam, when I heard you was goin' to be at Mis' Evelyn's for the barbecue today I thought maybe if I could git you to come over and see her and see how pretty she is and how much she means to me that you'd know how it was, and when you go back to New York you could just go right up to 'em and tell 'em to leave us alone." This youngster, Lon, and his wife had been sensational news for the newspapers for propaganda against child wives in the South.

"We didn't talk much on the way back to Cousin Evelyn's, but I could tell by the look on his face that he knew how I felt about things, and if you don't quite know, I'll tell you, as I promised I would: 'You leave Lon and his wife alone.'" The depth of Lon's feeling was reflected in what Lon had said: "By God, I love her so good that if these folks with their kodaks and their fun-making don't let us alone I'm goin' to take my gun and blow their guts out."

The Deep South, in the earnestness and emotional frankness of its tradition, has felt that the rest of the country does not respect that plank in the Atlantic Charter which emphasizes a belief in the right of a people to choose how it shall be governed. Most southerners who are frank have no inclination to deny many of the things that are said about the South. Contrariwise, the southern dilemma is nothing so simple as one of right and wrong. First of all, the South is forever asking: Can't you understand? Don't you see? Isn't it clear that all these problems have arisen as inevitable effects of some cause, and that the situation could not be otherwise? Don't you see the difficulties involved? Don't you see the tremendous progress which we have made? What would you do with 10,000,000 people to educate, and nothing to educate them with? Won't you help us to develop this situation instead of complicating it? Won't you give us responsible criticism and cooperation? How can we all, working together, best make adjustment to the balanced economy, to give landless men land and work-less people work? And isn't it true that the South has some-thing distinctive to offer, and that already in its new regional-ism it is rapidly balancing its people and resources, increasing its capacity to contribute to the richness of the nation's culture and economy, and rapidly reducing much of its violence of race conflict?

Now all of this is, of course, the white South. ("South" usually is taken as meaning the white South.) Alongside it, is the Negro South with all its excellence and extraordinary progress in culture and economy against difficulties and hazards. There is a new Negro South in the upper brackets of leadership and cultural development; in the middle-class group, of admirable proportions and achievements; in the Negro college youth. All these, like the white South, have the heritage of the best, and the hazards which have grown up in the biracial culture. Some of this is economic. All of it is magnificent in every sense of the word, including its part in the dramatic picture of the nation; including the sublimity and tragedy of rapidly growing racial culture; including the complex of the southern whites' aspirations and achievements. The South is afraid to face the situation and turn it over to the North for adjustment. "In our county," says one, "75 per cent of the people are Negroes. And other counties are like it. If we give them complete ballot and leadership, what will we do? Can't you see?"

The South wishes the rest of the nation to see how eloquent of the southern situation is the present South's ideological patriotism in military participation in the war. One of the most frequently asked questions was why the South was more militant in its support of the war than any other region. The South desires credit for this on the ground that it is truly national, conforming to the national creed except in the case of the Negro. Perhaps it wishes to make up for its limitations even here. The South seems to say:

We have been hammered and criticized so much for being outside the nation that here is a good opportunity to show that we are not only in the nation but all out for a greater participation than any other region. We have had so many problems of our own about which we differ that for once it seems good to tackle a problem about which we all agree, one that is far away from home. If we can fight for world democracy, it will give us time to come to a later reckoning with our own biracial civilization. Besides, the South with its homogeneity of people and with its traits of earlier America is a fighting South, subscribing to the doctrine that no foreign nation can insult us or hurt us and get away with it. The South, too, has always been close to Britain, and it knows what it is to be defeated and be overrun.

The South felt that a great war in which the utmost was demanded of all regions and folk was no time to split the nation wide open on issues upon which great progress was being made. And the South kept on saying in substance:

Don't you see what your inciting to riot will cost the Negro? Don't you see the tragedy and wounds that will be the heritage of a race war? And don't you know that all over the country there are those who are saying, "If the North and the Negroes do insist on a racial war, well, we don't want it, but that will be one solution of America's dilemma, because it will reduce the ratio of Negroes to the point where the problem can be handled."

The South pleads further for the rest of the nation to understand how quickly millions of whites from other regions will turn against the Negro when the situation is different and how the agitation for impossible action will also inflame the potential anti-Semitic tensions throughout the nation and especially in the South.

The South was begging the rest of the nation to remember that the Negro part of its culture and economy was not all of it. It was bad enough always to have these great obstacles and handicaps. Couldn't the South then be permitted to do its best in agriculture and industry and education and security without always receiving the verdict that, no matter what was done, it didn't make any difference because the South hadn't done right by the Negro? Already the Negro had been conditioned never to be happy about anything. No matter what came his way, he was to say it wasn't enough. If he smiled or sang he was traitor to his race; if he worked well he was being exploited. His wonderful personality was being warped from childhood up because, no matter how just the accusations against the whites might be, the Negro had no other environment in which to grow up, and all his children were being warped in a growing-up process that could result in nothing but tragedy. Many southerners thought that sometimes the agitators might secretly be the Negro's enemies, trying to see how much they could hurt him and retard his growth in a struggling folk culture which had always succeeded, and in which he was outdistancing many of his white neighbors.

All this and more was predicated on the admission by all thinking southerners who were fair in their attitudes that the South had made all the mistakes of which it was accused, and that steps must be taken and were being taken to remedy them. The South could look objectively at its past and could revise its judgment of itself and realize that, after all, there never had been a new South and now, with the new attacks upon the South, it looked as if there never would be. There was at one time, in the 1920's and 1930's, in the regional movement for interregional cooperation and national integration, real promise of a new South in a new nation, new deal, new freedom, new democracy; but that now was a long way off again. It was all very tragic and reminiscent of some of the European patricidal conflicts that destroyed their civilization.

There were other questions of reality which the South raised in all earnestness and honesty. With reference to the Negro's participation in equal opportunity, and with no reference whatever to any defense of the South, the question was asked: If Los Angeles, Seattle, Detroit, Chicago, Philadelphia, New York, Boston, after all the years of effort and after all the combined efforts of the militant workers, are unable to achieve even the semblance of equal opportunity, how could the South, with its powerful cultural conditioning, be expected to do the job? In this question there was no complaint against the North for not giving the Negro his place in university and college faculties, in social life in the universities, or equal opportunity in restaurants and hotels; and there was no inclination to defend the South. But the question was raised whether there was complete honesty in advocating coercion to make the South do what the North wouldn't and couldn't do, and, on the other hand, if there was honesty and sincerity, how realistic the minds were that would advocate the procedure. And there was yet another powerful element involved. What sort of sincerity, patriotism, or intelligence was reflected in advocating a cause that—it was admitted everywhere— *could not achieve* the desired ends and yet would result in the slaughter of millions of both white and Negro Americans and would throw back a long way the processes of progress which had been evolving?

These questions were asked not only by the white South of the Negro North, but by the Negro South of the white North —not that the Negro South did not want what the Negro North wanted and what all Negroes wanted. They were realistic questions, asked in desperation. One distinguished southern Negro leader wrote to the editor of a militant New York magazine:

"Resolved to the final analysis, the greatest difference between our position and yours is that you are interested chiefly in getting something said, and we are interested chiefly in getting something done. In your editorial note you said that segregation 'must go.' So say we all; but when and by what means? You imply that it will go from the mere repetition of catchwords and bristling popular phrases. These have been tried too long with lamentable results. We are trying to correct conditions that will be conducive to the destruction of prejudice, for then and not until then will segregation go. Some very able Negroes and some conscientious whites North and South have said before, 'Segregation must go'; but it has not gone, in spite of the laudable fight that has been made against it. If you have no overnight formula for the instantaneous elimination of race prejudice, then you are in the same boat with the sponsors of the Southern Regional Council. Moreover, should you come upon any magic formulae by which these great objectives can be attained without the painful processes of general and specific education, please let us have them at once; then and not until then shall we acknowledge your interracial omniscience, which, however great, cannot bring the desired consummation unless implemented by powers you do not seem to possess or at least are not bringing to bear on the problem. After all the major question is one of *modus operandi*, and you have not offered one better than the Southern Regional Council. If we fail we shall not have done worse than Democracy and Christianity and Humanity itself. 'Not failure but low aim is crime.' "

The situation, therefore, was again essentially and primarily an American problem, in which the nation was challenged to a major effort. The problem and the need were reflected again on two main levels. One was that there was real danger that America might fail in its major postwar obligation to achieve an adequate regional balance and work out its dilemmas of democracy. America had failed in the postwar period of the

1920's by reverting to a stolid normalcy which was not symbolic of the American Dream, and it had failed also to take advantage of its first great trends toward a regional integration of its diverse cultures. David Lilienthal has pointed out that, if sectional jealousies and economic rivalries prevent America from solving its own problems of regional balance and abundance, it cannot hope to attain these ends for the world. He points out the mutual interdependence of the different regions and the need of national liberalism in the search for what Vance calls interregional optima.

The second way in which the problem of regional balance and abundance is newly symbolized is found in the reverse side of the dilemma. Other nations and peoples have again and again emphasized the immeasurable value to the world, as example and procedure, of a successful solution by the United States of its problems of regional diversity and integration. This is of special significance in the newer concepts and far horizons of "the Americas," with all the diversified elements of the South American regionalism, and in relation to regional factors in postwar world planning.

In pointing up the organic and practical elements of the regional balance of America, we have no intention to shift the main emphasis and responsibility of the South from its own problems and responsibilities, but, on the contrary, to show that the South's role in the nation and its own forthright and vigorous leadership are matters not only of achievement but of the health and vitality of the nation. How this is true will be developed further in our picture of the maturing South in contemporary America.

PART III

Toward Regional and National Maturity

CHAPTER XVI

The Maturing South at Its Best

So CAME the South, at the end of World War II, to still another
epoch in its life and that of America. Clearly, it would be no
less rich in culture and in the dilemmas of the American way
of life. There were still the perennial questionings as to
whether there would be a new South and, if so, one of what
sort. Within the region the trend was to take stock, to make
inventory of resources and prospects. The outside trend was
still to take stock of the South's liabilities as well as its assets.
Yet both from the region and from the rest of the nation came
popular exhortations to convert the South from what had been
called the nation's Economic Problem No. 1 to its Economic
Opportunity No. 1. This conversion was to be perhaps more
cultural than economic. For the drama of the South was still
to be found primarily in the way of the folk and their heritage
of unequal levels of living and of biracial culture.

The South, in the reconstruction period after the Civil War,
had faced problems of sheer survival and of rebuilding a destroyed land and culture. In the subsequent period from
Henry Grady's New South through the 1920's—marked by a
gradual but steady rise in all phases of culture and economy—
the problems were of deficiency, waste, limitations, and an
uneven culture with the inherited handicaps we have already
pictured.

At the end of World War II the South, having reached its
greatest maturity both in material progress and in participation in the total national life, economic, cultural, and political,
faced new problems of two sorts. In the first group were the
application of scientific research to the development of resources, avoidance of waste, and improvement of agriculture

and industry; the training of leaders and workers; and the leveling up of an uneven culture and an unbalanced economy. In the second group were the unexpected revivifying of the North and South conflict pattern and the heightening of the South's interracial difficulties as they bore upon the whole southern economy and its participation in the national effort. The South again was faced with the problem of holding its share of the nation's prosperity and at the same time getting along with a critical and hostile North. It was as if time had turned backward and there was no new South, no new North, no new nation.

To say that there is and has been no new South, no new North, no new nation, is the same as to say that the way of the South, richly regional in character, has been and always will be the way of America. The same is true, of course, in different ways, of the other changing regions and of the nation. There had been great changes in all: in time, in technology, in the visible ends of material progress, in the sum total of achievements.

Yet the universals of folk culture and the regional essence of the nation still constituted the essential power and glory of a great nation whose strength must be in the diversity of its peoples and resources well developed and integrated in a national whole. The biography of the nation was still the biography of its regions and their people and culture, even as the biography of a man comprehends the story of his children and his children's children. And so the biography of the South or any other major region was increasingly important in the story of the nation, from which it could not be isolated. Whether in biography or in dilemmas and problems, there can be no separateness or partiality in the treatment of any region or of the whole nation apart from its regions.

In the total story of the South's growth toward maturity in the era following World War II, there were certain distinctive features. The first of these was the generous contribution the South made to the armed forces throughout the world, the participation of its youth on all battle fronts and on all levels of preparation and fighting. The second was the very active and dynamic part played by the national government in the direction of its activities during the depression years and the early war period.

Few more dramatic episodes in Amercan history can be found than the entry of southern youth into the armed forces of the United States in World War II, faithfully to exemplify the Marines' Hymn:

> From the halls of Montezuma
> To the shores of Tripoli,
> We fight our country's battles
> On the land as on the sea.

Here were thousands of southern youth who had never been beyond the confines of the next county or state, and whose life had been limited to farming or some local industry, participating in all the activities of a great war on a thousand fronts. A new world of adventure far transcending the old boundaries filled the lives of these youth. A new world of dread filled the waking hours and haunted the nights of their home folks, who prayed daily and hourly for their safe return and for surcease from loneliness. As the years went on, the whole South became part and parcel of the new world of war with its wide-flung horizons and, by the same token, of the heart and pulse of the nation. And hundreds of thousands of other youth from all the other regions were housed and trained in southern camps and cantonments, so that there was a concentration of military forces in the South such as had never been experienced before.

Among the recruits gathered into the vast American armed forces was a great host of Negro youth, to undergo experiences that would make the world over for them. Neither white youth nor Negro youth, returned to civilian life, would ever be the same. The South, meeting the needs and demands of all these youth, needed to be different in many ways from what it had ever been, for it was everywhere clear that the national and international contacts of the young men would contribute to their conservative regional loyalties and at the same time make them restless for wider opportunities and for justice in the new world to come. Such experiences always work both ways.

This new experience of the South with its own youth and youth from other regions, and its participation in the national effort to house the armed forces and to equip them through essential war industries, followed close in the wake of the vast New Deal experimentation of depression times in the 1930's. The South had been harder hit in many ways than the rest of the nation, and, to the rest of the nation, it had appeared at its worst. It followed naturally that the New Deal exerted great efforts to serve and, to some extent, reconstruct the southern economy and culture; and it is true that the South benefited tremendously from federal aid. The South joined the rest of the nation in appealing for all the help it could get. After that came the challenge to the South to overcome its deficiencies and achieve its optimum standards of culture and economy. Government support in research, public works, agricultural readjustment, public health, recreation, financing, and in all forms of conservation and wise use of resources had been large. The larger programs of land conservation, of diversified agriculture, and industries were close to the heart of southern culture and economy.

In many cases the South had naturally and logically been presented in its least favorable aspects. "The South at Its Worst" might well have been the title over much that was presented by both southern critics and national experts utilizing southern researches to point up their schemes for improving the regional economy. What was written in the South to stimulate and guide it toward a new regional development was utilized in the North to portray its deficiencies and limitations. There grew up a great body of writings in which the pathological was depicted as being representative of the whole culture, and of opinion and impression of the South from other regions the Tobacco Roads of literature and stage caricature gave general form to the opinion of the South held in other regions. In spite of *Gone with the Wind, So Red the Rose*, and other best sellers which reflected much of the realistic romance of the South, and the dynamic realism of Ellen Glasgow, the prevailing popular impression in other regions was that the South was a region of primitive folk who were scarcely civilized.

Manifestly if the drama of the South is to have a happy ending, its form and action must be in terms of the South at its best. Manifestly, too, they must be in terms that are flexible, comprehensive, enduring, and commensurate with the cultural, economic, and social framework of our American democracy. Attainable standards must be stated in terms of capacities for growth, of development of natural resources and people, of the devotion of the people and their wealth to institutional services through which we seek a balance and equilibrium between the people and wealth, between men and technology, between culture and civilization. We do not, therefore, say the South at its best is a wealthy South or an industrial South or an agrarian South, or that it is a Protestant South or a Catholic South, or that it is a democratic South or a republican South, or that it is a white South or a black South. What we do say is that the South at its best is a growing South, developing, conserving, and utilizing wisely all its resources in a balanced economy and culture of, for, and by the people and of, for, and by all its institutions. And it is an American South whose specific objectives and specific needs will then be fulfilled in relation to each diversified phase of life, each changing situation, and through the combined, cooperative effort of all.

This South at its best, a South actively developing its resources, enriching its culture, increasing its prosperity, and adding to the happiness and welfare of its people, has a new dynamic realism. It will reflect little of the traditional literary romance, or of the pathological caricature in "realistic" literature. There is plenty of the romance of epic struggle and new ventures, although it will not be visible to many of the onlookers of this new South. For the romance in the rebuilding of fortunes and the reconstruction of cultures is apparent only when the work is completed. In the doing of the work there is more strategy than drama, more sweat than romance. The romance of Nature and her endowment becomes the reality of resources to be used and conserved. The folk-beauty of the hills and the love of the land are transcended by schooling and planning for a better day. Things of beauty become also materials for use. The people of the mountains and the valleys, of the plains and the hills, by the rivers and by the sea, determine what sort of culture and economy they want and have the will to develop. Yet even in the modern world of science there will be millions of southern folk who will feel the thrill of new purpose and the excitement of new work.

This South at its best is still set in the framework of its resources and what the people do with Nature's endowment. A wealthy people in a lovely land, or a poor people on barren soil, is still the choice which the South at work will face; for romance and realism, high purpose and practical planning, are all bound up in the inventory of southern resources and their conservation, development, and wise use in this last of the new Souths.

Resources are of many sorts. It makes little difference how they are designated or classified if the catalogue is adequate to give a sense of their range and meaning and to make possible scientific and practical planning for the good society. One way in which this can be done is to classify all resources into five main divisions: natural resources, technological resources, money resources, human resources, and institutional or cultural resources.

Sometimes, when it is desired to make practical inventories, "wealth" is a more satisfactory term. The catalogue then reads natural wealth, technological wealth, capital wealth, human wealth, and institutional wealth.

Sometimes these five classes are reduced to three, as natural, human, and social or cultural. In this classification technological resources are ordinarily catalogued as social or cultural.

Sometimes these five groupings are reduced to two: namely, natural or material, and human. Under this classification, technological wealth belongs in both categories since science, invention, technology applied to natural resources yields capital wealth, but in discoveries, organization, and management services contributes largely to institutional and cultural wealth and to the satisfaction and welfare of the people.

Potential *natural resources* are so abundant that they have never yet been fully catalogued. Mountains and rivers, forests and plains, climate and situation are powerful forces not only because of the natural resources which they provide, but because of the tremendous influence which they exert upon the people and their culture.

Yet, land and water, minerals and lumber, animals and plants are no more resources than are science and technology when they utilize both the materials and the laws of Nature to produce continuing and immeasurable wealth and power.

Nor were the glory-vistas of nature's beauty made manifest as spiritual resources until the love of nature and the creative work of arts and crafts were articulate in human wealth.

Technological wealth not only translates natural wealth into capital wealth but transforms the face of nature and the lives of the people. Science, skills, invention, technology, machines multiply the quantity and quality of useful resources. Not only the basic five sciences—chemistry, physics, biology, mathematics, and astronomy—but a hundred applied sciences, in oceanography and aeronautics, in medicine and agriculture, in machines and in power, add limitless resources to the incredible catalogue.

Scientific research and technological laboratories, testing grounds and measuring technics, trained personnel and multiplied robots are new resources which make a new world.

Yet all these are not resources except as processes and products of human leadership and skills, education and training, organization and management. Nor can natural resources and scientific discoveries be utilized wisely and controlled well except as all our technological wealth is applied to institutional wealth, which in turn conserves, develops, and uses wisely again the basic human wealth.

The range and meaning of what we call *capital wealth* may be seen from an examination of the common synonyms which we use: riches, plenty, abundance, fortunes, wealth. The nature of such wealth may also be seen in the sources from which riches of individuals or nations have come.

Thus, in early America, millions were made from the fur trade, in which the natural resources of stream and field were translated into money or negotiable wealth, which in turn came to be invested capital. Other fortunes were made in minerals or from cotton or corn or from railroads and urban transportation or from merchandise and commerce.

Such wealth is measured in many ways: in money in banks, in invested capital, in per-capita wealth, in value or profits, in purchasing power, in standards of living, and expenditures; and in later years in corporate fortunes and new "billion-dollar industries." It is also measured in terms of evaluation or "worth" or inventories of natural resources and technological resources, as well as in terms of public works and institutional wealth.

But in whatever form money, exchange, capital wealth, finances—both the symbol and the reality of capital wealth are keys to utilization of all resources and become, therefore, the central measure of what the people have to do with and to live on in material wealth.

It must be clear, however, that the people represent the supreme wealth of any society: all other resources have meaning only in relation to the people and the society which they represent. "Only the people count," is a symbol of the evaluation of *human resources*. The people represent the universal human wealth which is the physical basis of society, even as natural resources and the earth itself are the tabernacle of all societies. The people are both creators and creatures of wealth. As creators, they have contributed the measurable wealth and institutions that go into the making of society. As creatures, they are susceptible to physical and technological forces.

Like other resources, the people are of many sorts. Millions strong, the people are of many groups and nationalities, many religions and political faiths, many occupational levels and many levels of achievement. Yet they cannot be catalogued merely as figures in a census or arbitrarily classified into blocks of resources. Elders and youths, men and women, children in a million homes and a thousand schools; white man, black man, red man, brown man, they represent the ever reproducing resources of human society. Of what sort and how many, working in how many ways and places, and what society does to them and for them—these are criteria of the sort of resources and wealth a region or a nation may have and hold.

The institutions of the people, however, as *institutional resources*, constitute the greatest wealth of all, the products of the people working with Nature and culture. The home and family, the state and government, industry and work, community and association—these represent the main catalogue of institutional wealth. Within these, thousands of schools, of churches, of helping institutions, of agencies of art and literature, of money and exchange, of capital and cooperation, of organization and management, reflect an almost unlimited catalogue of institutional resources that go into the making of a rich culture and economy.

To catalogue all these resources of a region or a people is necessary before its culture and economy can be understood. To sense the meaning and power of the aggregate wealth of all kinds is to give momentum and concreteness to planning and direction. The first step in translating potentiality into power, and in bridging the distance between deficiency and abundance, is to apply the yardstick of this fivefold framework of natural, technological, capital, human, and institutional wealth. It is in translating natural wealth into capital wealth, and in using this for the creation and development of institutions through which the lives and culture of the people are enriched, that a society proves it is the good society.

When we come to apply these criteria in pointing to the South at its best, the task is not only a practical one but one in which the resources of the region may be inventoried and compared with those of other regions to the end that there may be approximated a better balance and quality among all the regions. Such an inventory of the South is especially important in understanding what the region is, how it came to be what it is, what its promise and prospect may be, and also how to go about attaining the desired ends.

In the portraiture of the South at its best, set in the framework of its resources and their interrelationships one with another, there is no assumption of merely material culture or technological development. For the romance of the South is inseparably tied in with the realism of resources and what they mean to the people and their institutions. Nor is such a picture one of generalities, since the whole concept and strategy of balancing men and resources must be in terms of concrete measures and practical planning.

We begin our appraisal and planning by asking and answering, in order, a half-dozen questions:

What is it that the South has?

What is it that the South wants?

What is the difference between what it has and what it wants?

What will it take to bridge the distance between what it has and what it wants?

How can the South get what it takes to bridge this distance?

What is the best way to get what it takes?

The first question is: *What is it that the South now has—* particularly in terms of resources?

The South excels in two of the major resources and lags in three. It has a superabundance of natural resources, but is deficient in technological resources—namely, research, skills, technology, management, leadership—which would translate them into money and capital wealth—the third type of resources.

The South, therefore, is deficient in money and capital wealth.

On the other hand, with its superabundance of people, the South excels in human resources.

Because, however, of its deficiency in capital wealth, it has not developed its institutional resources to anything like the point of making the most of its human wealth, the people.

Therefore, what the South now has is a superabundance of natural wealth and human wealth; but it lags in the other three types—namely, technological, capital, and institutional wealth.

These resources, the South has not properly conserved.

There has been an unhealthy waste of natural and human resources—in many instances a larger waste than in other regions of the United States.

In line with its deficiency in skills and science, the South has failed to educate and train its youth for the fullest employment, and for the wisest development of its great resources.

As a result, the economy has not been balanced so as to contribute to a rich regional culture.

In addition to the resources, deficiencies, and waste listed, what does the South have?

It still has an abundance of handicaps and special difficulties which reflect the old epic of struggle and bitterness of defeat; and it has a rich cultural heritage of excellence in living and great achievement in national leadership, which have strengthened it in the tendency to substitute the memory of the past for achievements in the present or future.

Now for the second question: *What is it that the South wants?* The answer is relatively easy to state in technical terms of achievement.

The South at its best would very clearly be a South excelling, not in two, but in all five resources:

It would be a South conserving its resources and eliminating its waste.

It would be a South achieving a well balanced economy and culture.

It would be a South overcoming its hazards.

It would be a South realizing the assets of southern culture, looking to the future, and developing a leadership adequate for new tasks.

The third question to be answered is: *What is the difference between what the South has and what it wants?*

The southern states generally rank in the lowest fourth of the states of the Union in standard measurements of income, wealth, levels of living, education, and public health and welfare facilities.

Now, if we take the level to be attained as that of the highest states, the difference to be made up will be that between the fourth and the first quartile—practically 100 per cent increase as the minimum.

Or, if more specific comparisons are wanted, it would be possible to select the southern state which is lowest in, let us say, educational achievement and compare it with the highest state in the nation. Such a comparison might show a multiple difference; for instance, the southern state with three times as many children to educate, and a dual system of schools for Negroes and whites involving extra costs, might have one-third of the wealth of the other state. If that southern state should expend 100 per cent of its public funds for education alone, neglecting highways, health, agriculture, security, it would still fall short of the educational achievement of the highest state.

Yet, these figures have been given in season and out, in the South and out, until the story needs more of orientation than of negative narration. This distance between the states and its bridging must figure prominently in the continuing story of the South finding its true place in the regional balance of America which is surely the heart of the new realism of the South and the nation.

The difference between what the South has and what it wants, then, has been displayed in many arrays of statistics of potentiality and deficiencies. We come next to the fourth question:

What will it take to bridge the distance between what the South has and what it wants?

If the South would excel in skills, education, organization, leadership—in other words, in *technological wealth*—it could translate its natural wealth into capital wealth, which in turn could be devoted to human institutions and, therefore, to the development of human wealth. Immediately, therefore, *the South would have attained excellence in all types of resources, which is what is wanted.*

First, however, we must face the more specific question: *What will it take to attain excellence in technological wealth* – applying skill to natural resources and translating them to technological wealth? Several measures are necessary to bring this about:

Into the younger generations must be instilled a new appreciation of natural wealth and its relation to the people and their welfare.

The youth must be trained to have a new sense of the value of work and of high standards of achievement.

The range of occupational opportunity must be widened through new developments so that the superabundance of southern youth may find work of their own choice, which they are trained to do.

Such training must be provided for these youth, so that they may function adequately in competition with workers everywhere.

There are, however, still other essentials. To begin with, manifestly, capital wealth is necessary for the undertaking of these measures through which the ultimate goal of resource use may be attained. This wealth may come from several sources:

There is already a reservoir in the South's extraordinary economic gains in the last few years.

There is a powerful cumulative reserve in the savings of southerners who have joined in pushing back the frontiers of southern development. It is estimated that the South now has enough actual savings to duplicate its present industrial plants.

There is an increasing reserve of wealth owned by persons outside the region who see in the new industrial South an opportunity for regional and national development.

There is also a considerable reserve available in contributions for research and experimentation of national foundations which give leverage to regional support.

Finally, there are increasingly large reserves from the federal government in equalization programs—agriculture, roads, health, education, public safety, and the like.

There are still other answers to the question as to what it will take to bridge the distance between what the South has and what it wants. They are in terms of the elimination of waste, the attainment of a balanced culture and economy, the wise utilization of the cultural heritage, and a closer approach to regional equality and balance in America. The things to do, however, enter more largely into the answer to our fifth question—*How can the South get what it takes to bridge the distance between what it has and what it wants?*—which will be given at length in our final chapters, devoted to a planning South at work and to the search for regional equality and balance in America.

Yet the very concept of the South at its best offers certain other general challenges.

Such a challenge was the friendly appraisal of Walter Lippmann, whose vigorous admonition just before the great depression of the 1930's intensified the new trends toward regional-national development appears peculiarly timely again. In *Social Forces* in 1927 he wrote:

"There are many observers in this country who believe that nothing, since the opening of the West, has so great a meaning to the future of America as the profound transformation which is now taking place in the economic structure and with that in the political and intellectual outlook of the southern states. For nearly seventy-five years the South has lived in the shadows of a great controversy, of a great war, and of the awful consequences of that war. Within my own lifetime the proposal has been seriously considered in Congress to govern it by military force. During that time the South has not been able to play an adult role in the management of American affairs. But now the period of the eclipse is over. There is no longer any doubt about it. From now on the South will be part of this epoch-making change."

But this is not all. The spirit and genius of the South have been agrarian. The specifications of the new era will change

this. "The South will be called upon to guide a radical altera-
tion in agricultural life. She will be confronted with the rise
of great industries. She will have to solve the problems which
industrial progress brings in its train, the problems of the
great city, of congestion, of health, of education, of relations
between employer and employee, of the relations between
town and countryside. She will have to ask whether her political system, her peculiar party system, is adequate to these
new times. The South, along with all other sections and regions, will have to decide what she will do about the imperial
destiny of this nation, and of how it is to adjust itself to the
needs and ambitions of the other great nations of the earth."

Here is involved again one of the South's essential traits;
namely the high esteem which it has always placed upon its
cultural heritage. Here is opportunity to realize on this asset.
Mr. Lippmann continues:

"Nevertheless, those who build a new civilization should be
reminded that they must not shrink from contemplating a
great future for themselves. Those nations which have left
the deepest mark upon history have always been greatly conscious of their destiny. The Greeks, the Romans, the Jews in
ancient times, the English and the French in modern times,
have had no doubt that they were a great people. The South,
if my observation is correct, is still doubtful of its own possibilities. It need not be. Everything that was ever possible for
civilized men is possible here. If the South fails she will have
only herself to blame, and if she succeeds she will have only
herself to thank."

There are finally certain other considerations which, however, are part and parcel of the continuing major premise of
the South at its best and the oft emphasized recurring motif
of this story; namely, that the South at its best will be a part
of America at its best. The South's superlative achievement
can no longer be measured by the old standard of "good—
that is, good for the South." The verdict will be "Good" in

comparison with any standard and with any region of the nation, no longer assuming a differential in measures of excellence. This applies just as much to northern appraisals of southern achievement as to the South's own self-satisfied verdict of relative values. There is no longer any reason for the South to praise itself for its great progress unless that progress be in terms of the best that the nation can produce. There is no longer justification for the nation's verdict that it is presumptuous for the South to aim at the best in universities, in agriculture, in industry, and in cultural attainments.

All our institutions are needed more and more in a technological civilization, and must constantly be strengthened; and a chief end of the new technology must be to balance men and machines. Just as the South at its best means the nation at its best, so both imply the democratic society at its best anywhere, of, for, and by all the institutions and all the people, to which, however, it is assumed the South will be expected to contribute its superlative part even as the rest of the nation. This is the way of the South and the way of America.

We turn next then to the answer to the question, *What is the best way to get what it takes?* and we continue within the framework of resources and planning, in which we picture further requirements for the development and leadership of the people for the appraisal and elimination of waste and for realistic planning. Such planning is no more nor less than definite workable ways in which the people may succeed best within the framework of their regional situation and their inherent endowments.

CHAPTER XVII

A Planning South at Work

FROM THE western hills and the eastern shores of Virginia and the Carolinas, and from the deep South and the Gulf coast, came men saying they would welcome guidance in the ways of a more abundant economy than that of their fathers and of their fathers before them. What they said, in substance, was that for generations now the South had tried certain ways, and that these ways had netted scarcity and deficiencies instead of the abundance which they wanted and believed themselves capable of attaining. Instead of prosperity and plenty they had experienced want and waste. Instead of health and happiness they had seen sickness and sorrow. Their romance and their religion, in the role of living reality, were like the waste of their barren lands. Now, if they could be shown more of the actual workable ways of doing the job, they were willing to try new ways and new work and to substitute something of planning for the listless drift of a losing economy.

There were two or three things they wanted in addition to action and improvement. They wanted to substitute the reality of doing something for the habit of being told of their mistakes and failures. They wanted to become a part of this thing they heard so much about—a New South at its best which they were willing to concede was a South at work; but they wanted that work to be planned and done in their communities, by their state legislatures and educational institutions, and they wanted to do more and more of the job themselves. They still believed in the South, and they wanted to translate their faith into living reality.

In so far as a complaint went with this assurance of cooperation and new release of energies and purpose, it was a protest against several things. In the first place, the complainers felt that the professors, the planners, the experts, were often too theoretical and too far away from reality to be effective in their talking and their teaching—too often, they did not have all the facts and did not relate their facts to realities. Furthermore, recommendations and writings were in such general terms and in such technical language that, no matter how good they might be, not many of the people could use them. Moreover, just calling attention to faults and scolding the people seemed like a poor substitute for providing ways and means whereby the people and leaders, experts and common men, could work together. Finally, the people were not only afraid of planning which was too far away from the reality of their resources and their needs, but afraid of coercion by a too centralized government and a standardized cultural planning superimposed upon the South by intellectuals and moralists who neither knew the facts nor understood the realities of the region.

The story of the South and the understanding of the people make it clear that the objectives of planning and the projection of basic factors of excellence must surely comprehend whatever potential distinctiveness of regional culture the future may have in store. Comparisons of the South with the nation are to be motivated not for imitation, equalization, or standardization alone, but often for differentiation. There must surely be room enough in the regional cultures of America for experimentation, for exploration, for a genuine liberalism that seeks a quality civilization in a quantity world. The mechanized perfections of light and heat, of moving pictures, of airplanes and automobiles, of the new industrial economy may not rank higher than the vigorous satisfaction of the mountain folk, deep in the living experience of their music and liberty. Folk beauty in the hills may transcend technological pathology. Lyric heritage of the people may be superior to new reaches in technology. Yet progress and capacity in a technological age must somehow be inventoried by means of certain objective measures which neither permit pathological lag nor become mere propaganda standardization. Inherent in a new cultural equilibrium to be planned is the promise of regional excellence.

Here then is a key measure of the reality that is the South; and implied in the objective stated is a fair, functional definition of planning. In the simplest terms, planning is clearly a way of helping the people get what they want and need within the framework of their resources and the high standards of cultural and economic living. Yet it takes facts, skills, specifications. The very heart of the planning concept as set forth so brilliantly by Patrick Geddes was, on the one hand, the bridging of the distance between science, research, and theory, and, on the other, the solution of problems. Thus, planning becomes the process of providing the tools and technological facilities, the specific, practical, workable ways of bridging the distance between what we have and what is wanted. Nevertheless, always there is the folk element in the problem, such that neither goals of achievement nor timbers of bridging are ever to be found exclusively in terms of mechanics. On the other hand, a careful examination of total framework of cultural development and of desired trends emphasizes minimum considerations as including attainable standards of life and culture as measured by the whole range of social and cultural indices. They will be measured partly by economic indices, partly by the tests of the physical and geographical heritage, partly by a congruous set of values, which, within the bounds of inside and outside influences, fix the conditions and capacities of human life. All of these, inventories with due regard to equilibrium and balance, are measures of the difficulties and prospects of planning.

For the purposes of planning and for illustrating the promise and prospect of regional planning, we recall the special importance of the regional balance of the South, not only within its own culture and economy, but also in relation to other regions and the total nation. Separation and isolationism in America, as well as in world affairs, have been obstacles to regional-national planning. Among our objectives, therefore, is to present a picture of the South that will indicate its place in the nation and explain something of the dramatic struggle of a large and powerful segment of the American people for mastery over an environment capable of producing a superior culture, yet so conditioned by complex, cumulative handicaps as to make the nature of future development problematical. Repeat and repeat, over and above any conventional social inventory, it is important to point toward greater realization of the inherent capacities of the South; and to indicate ways and means of developing the full potentialities of the superabundant physical and human resources, and of overcoming technical deficiencies and waste. It is equally important to point toward a continuously more effective reintegration of the South into the national picture and thereby toward a larger regional contribution to national culture and unity.

That was the goal long set in our regional studies, and that is the goal in what we may call the newest American problem —of social planning. In addition to bridging the distance between what we have and what we want, and seeking balance and equilibrium, another practical meaning of planning is expressed in its major objective of providing ways and means whereby American society can develop itself through the orderly processes of growth and interrelationship.

On the functional side it means that we must provide for conservation and development of all resources, physical and human, and the utilization of our science, skill, and technology toward an equilibrium between the people and their resources, between the culture of the people and the civilization of the state, and between the people and their institutions on the one hand, and social change on the other.

On the administrative level, it means that there must be such arrangements as will provide, first of all, for the integration of the total American society into a strong and dynamic culture, attained, however, through such decentralization as will give representation and opportunity to all peoples in all the regions in conformity with their culture and resources.

Social planning, as it follows from the story of the South, naturally assumes a knowledge of how societies, bottomed in Nature and in simple primitive groups, have developed under pressure of environment and neighboring cultures, into complex, urban, industrial civilization, still more powerfully conditioned by physical factors and technology than by general culture. To understand the relation between men and resources, between culture and geographic environment, between races and groups, and the impact of change and technology upon the individual, upon culture—to understand all these is essential before we can understand what problems are to be solved and what needs are to be planned in terms of social achievements and social values. So, too, to understand the essential elements of modern civilization in terms of urbanism and the megalopolitan culture, of industry and technology, of scientific humanism and intellectualism, of centralization and power, and of the totalitarian State, and the resulting rise of modern *techniways* is necessary before we can understand what planning means and what sort of planning may be assumed for modern contemporary society. Here is contradiction in that these are basic considerations for the specialists although their genesis and nature are in the common man.

Yet, we must not expect too much of planning. It is so easy, with the new popularity of the planning concept both in public affairs and in private business and industry, to expect the impossible. It is also easy to assume that planning, with the usual good "paper program" of words and with numerous reports, will automatically be successful. We know, of course, that the success of a plan will be a relative matter, flexible not only in each state and region, but in each level of planning undertaken.

On the other hand, too little should not be expected of planning. Planning now is well-nigh universal, both as a concept to talk about and as a framework for state, local, and national action groups. There are thousands of individual community and city planning agencies, in addition to the state planning boards, and perhaps as many thousand planning committees in the fields of education, religion, industry, and business. Whether we will it or not, planning is here, and it is important to have the best arrangement for planning that it is possible for us to have.

Now we may focus upon two main levels of planning: *functional* and *administrative*. These follow closely the framework of the South at its best as measured by the attainment of excellence in the fivefold classification of wealth already catalogued. That is, the general objectives of planning have primarily to do with the two major types of wealth, *natural* and *human,* while the technical ways of planning center upon the other three types, *technological, economic,* and *institutional.* From these in turn arise three levels or main types of planning on the functional level; namely, *physical* planning, *economic* planning, and *cultural* planning.

It is logical that the first level should be *physical planning.* This seeks the best possible equilibrium between people and the places where they live, the resources which they use, and the natural environment by which they are conditioned. Sometimes it is concerned with the land and man's relation to and use of it. Sometimes it is concerned with rivers and waters, forests and minerals, and what they can mean to the people. Sometimes it has to do with wild-life sanctuaries, parks, and scenic places. Sometimes it has to do with the beauty of nature and the aesthetic aspects of towns, cities, and highways. Sometimes it has to do with national domains and publicly owned lands, and sometimes with private properties and national communication lines. Sometimes it has to do with states, sometimes with counties, sometimes with cities, and sometimes with villages and rural communities. But always planning for the physical foundations has to do with the great organic, natural bases upon which happiness, culture, prosperity, and human welfare rest.

Important in the field of physical planning is land planning. In its general aspects this includes planning for the best use of land and its adaptation to the largest number of purposes and needs. In towns and cities it includes planning for the best use for businesses, institutions, residences, highways, industries, parks, playgrounds. In the state and national domain it includes planning for the conservation and use of great forest areas, parks, forestry and mineral conservation, recreation. In rural life and agriculture it includes planning for balanced agriculture, forest crops, increasing production capacity and value and conservation of agricultural lands.

Water planning will necessarily vary in different areas and at different altitudes. In such planning high-rainfall areas will contrast with desert areas. Rivers and drainage in their general aspects will include planning for river valley development in relation to the nation or the state at large, with irrigation in some areas and drainage in others. Flood control and power will include planning reservoirs for power and for the prevention of floods. Navigation and transportation will include planning for the best use of rivers for commerce and recreation as a part of the transportation system. Other aspects of water planning will include sanitation and recreation or purification for health and recreation. Wild-life conservation and use will include planning for the conservation and enlargement of resources of fish and game, including the development of small streams, lakes, and ponds. Ocean, Gulf, lake water fronts will include planning for the utilization of fish and oyster resources, for transportation and recreation, and for harbors and shipping.

There are other items of physical planning. Minerals in their general aspects will include planning for the conservation, development, and wiser use of mineral resources. Discovery and development of new mineral resources implies research and planning for new uses of minor minerals. Climate in its regional variations assumes planning for the best possible use of climate in relation to culture and economy. Finally, transportation and situation comprehend planning for the wisest utilization of situation through highways, railways, airways, and other communication and transportation arrangements. To all of these, then, must be added the inventory of total natural resources, involving research and planning to insure an adequate knowledge of all resources with a view to their wider and more effective use on behalf of the people.

The second functional level of planning is *economic planning*. This involves the relation between government and economics, and is required by trends.

First of all was the essential universal demand for postwar planning, looking to the transition from war economy to peace economy. The two major areas here were conversion of war industries and activities to normal peacetime work and provision to forestall unemployment. There was, then, the special provision for the millions of returning servicemen of occupations or occupational insurance and training in the period of transition.

Economic planning is special in the sense that the relation between government and politics on the one hand, and business and industry on the other, becomes a technical problem of adjustment, critical in modern life.

There are many divisions in this field. Widening the range of occupational opportunity, which we have already found essential to southern development, includes local planning in each community, industry, and state of jobs for returning servicemen as well as for all youth growing up. In this, individual businesses and industries do their own planning for expansion, development, new markets, labor.

Economic planning in the South should give special and increasing attention to rural industries, part-time industries, arts and crafts, and development of industries for processing fibers, farm products, etc. Even more important, agricultural development provides especially for the small farmer and for diversified farming, including livestock and dairying. Certain industries peculiarly appropriate to a state, region, or locality, such as housing and air cooling, require special planning. In the South a new era in farm fencing, with the need for wiring, for posts, and for concrete and forest products, can mean the development in steel of an almost major industry overnight.

Finally, banking and finance will include planning to finance industry and cooperative arrangements between bankers and individuals and corporations, and between private banks and federal government. And always alongside the general private business planning are public works, including planning for special public works programs in support of needed industry and institutional buildings and for the demobilization of business.

The third level is *social and cultural planning*. Although all plans look to the development of the people and their welfare, certain types are often neglected in the overemphasis on physical and economic planning. Such planning emphasizes the social institutions and agencies and looks toward population policies with reference to the people themselves. In this field planning seeks to bridge the distance between research, resources, and the like on the one hand, and the solving of problems and the adjustment of difficulties of the people on the other. In this field, too, are many of the major services of government to the people—local, state, regional, federal.

Among the selected divisions on this level, governmental public works programs will represent planning through the cooperation of local, state, and federal governments for constructing buildings needed by institutions of learning, public service agencies, or housing facilities. Again, there are special programs for agriculture and rural life which include planning for agricultural development and for cooperative efforts to strengthen country life and diversified farming. So, too, programs of recreation include planning community, state, and federal programs of leisure-time activities and recreation, while public welfare programs include planning more adequate and better balanced services for the handicapped and the deficient, and preventive measures. Closely related to these are the public health programs, with planning by local, state, and federal authorities for more adequate health services, including health education. Public education programs include planning not only for educational buildings and administration but for channeling research and theory into more practical educational curricula and work, with special reference to elementary and high schools.

Finally, on the level of social and cultural planning, there are other, more composite problems: population policies or planning for wise distribution and optimum population; and strategy for race and minority groups—planning local and regional adjustments, and opportunity for races and minorities. And always there is the problem of a balanced economy and culture, which means planning for well balanced communities, industry, and agriculture in relation to high standards of cultural development.

To such goals there are several concrete, practical approaches: through research and analysis, providing the necessary facts and the essential perspective; through administrative planning, which we shall presently outline in functional organizations; and through the essential regional balancing of America, as indicated in our final chapter.

First, we may illustrate research and analysis of problems. To this end we have already indicated at length the nature and range of functional planning on three general levels, so that the needs of the South for realistic planning to bridge the distance between actualities and possibilities may be the more clearly seen. Yet planning manifestly demands much more than general outlines. We next analyze, therefore, the major fields of tension and deficiency in the South, in order to focus upon a large number of elements and attack them in a succession and on a scale commensurate with planning facilities. For the sake of concreteness, we may look at four major fields: that of *rural life, agriculture, and conservation;* that of *labor, industrial development, and security;* that of *race development and race relations;* and that of *political development and public administration.* Each of these great fields recapitulates the way of the South as it has developed and has already been described.

Now let us picture the key problems in *rural life, agricultural development, and conservation.* Farm tenancy is a key problem, menacing the country's foundations. Two-thirds of the nation's farm tenants are in the South, and three-fifths of all southern farmers are tenants. Their living conditions are critical. Many houses are unfit for human habitation, unpainted, have windows without glass, leaking roofs, flimsy walls, and no plumbing at all. Frequent moves inhibit interest in soil conservation, in farm improvements, in community affairs, in education of children. Perpetual debt and disappointment kill hope and ambition.

Increasing mechanization aggravates the tenants' insecurity, bringing the tragedy of farmers without land, families without homes, children without a chance (sons with less opportunity than their fathers had, always in debt at high interest charges). A meager, unbalanced diet and low vitality encourage pellagra. Patent medicine is often the only family doctor, and babies are born without medical care.

Soil erosion is a problem closely connected with tenancy. More than three-fifths of the nation's eroded land is in the South—a national loss of staggering proportions. It is the result of "money crop" farming, absentee ownership, the tenant system, unscientific methods, carelessness in the past, thoughtlessness of the future, ignorance of a better way. If past losses in erosion are to be redeemed and further losses are to be prevented, the public must be taught the seriousness of the problem, its stewardship of the soil for future generations, scientific methods of conservation—a vast educational task.

Another key problem is the cotton economy, with its drain of land and men, loss of world markets. New crops and a new system are needed; a balanced agriculture, and the development of a farm chemurgic possibilities.

A problem that must be faced is consumption and marketing. The South must consume more, with farm production for use and the encouragement of small industries. Dietetic and hygiene standards must be raised.

Rural housing, universally neglected, offers an extraordinary opportunity for the raising of standards of hygiene and sanitation, which will provide employment and a market for producers' goods.

There is a crucial need for trained leaders, for scientific research, for experimentation, and here lies opportunity for rural youth.

We will look next at the major field of *labor, industrial development, and security,* in which the way of the South still conforms to regional patterns that need reexamination. This is essentially a problem of the people and work.

The South is the nation's seedbed of population, replacing this faster than any other section and contributing millions to other regions. Suppose this excess population is unemployed, undereducated, undernourished, physically unfit.

What will happen to the South if it does not migrate? What will happen to the nation if it does? Development of the South is more than a regional problem.

Natural resources are a key problem. The South is a region naturally rich, with a rare combination of climate, land, timber, minerals, water power, river system, coast line, yet for lack of development its per-capita income is less than half that of the nation. Potentially the South is the nation's garden spot; yet its people are the poorest fed, and are impoverished by their waste.

The natural resources of the South are adequate; but a balanced development of agriculture and industry is necessary. Without this the region cannot educate or employ its people; a hopeless rural population will be added to the urban unemployed, and relief needs will swell. The nation will pay the bill.

The national and regional objectives in general are development of the South to the end that its resources may be utilized, its wastes eliminated, its deficiencies overcome, unfavorable conditions ameliorated; and its present high motives implemented. More specific objectives are to make the South conscious of its needs, its opportunities, its obligations, national cooperation; to make vivid and articulate the meaning of natural resources, work, and wealth—lands, forests, grasses, minerals, standards of work, standards of living; to seek wider range of occupational opportunity for whites and Negroes; to train for skill and efficiency.

Increasing the South's income, capital for investment, is a vital measure in order that the South may produce more and retain more.

These great fields of need and tension, together with the third and fourth fields catalogued, constitute the basis upon which the Southern Regional Council was formed in 1943. In the *third* field of tensions and problems the primary emphasis is upon democracy, *through race development and race relations,* as organic parts of the southern way. Again, the way is through resources and planning.

Race is an essential part of human resources and problems: the dilemma of white and black; consequent problems of adjustment, justice, opportunity, cooperation, Negroes going North in great numbers (Pennsylvania, New York, and Illinois, all have more Negroes than Kentucky, and the biggest five Negro centers are all north of the Potomac). What will be the effect upon the South if the Negro is left underprivileged, undereducated, untrained in citizenship? What will be the effect upon the nation?

Basic elements in the problem are consciousness of kind, which tends toward racial grouping; consciousness of difference, which tends to widen the breach; group consciousness and competition along racial lines; assumption of superiority for one's own kind and group; assumption of the right to dominate the assumed inferior; assumption of the right to exploit the assumed inferior.

Complicating factors are the backgrounds of slavery, Civil War, reconstruction: persistence of the master-slave psychology; bitterness born of the civil strife; fear born of reconstruction blunders; fear of economic and social competition.

Emergent aspects of the problem are discrimination in the expenditure of public funds for education at the rate of four dollars per white child to every dollar for a Negro child; inadequate public health service for Negroes, especially in rural sections; high incidence of preventable disease. These conditions menace the entire community, because disease germs recognize no color line. Contagion in the alley finds many paths to the avenue.

Economic handicaps of Negroes are lower wages for equal work, resulting from discrimination regardless of skill, and meager opportunities for business training.

The theory of white supremacy requires unquestioning subservience in the Negro and acceptance of his "place." It is commonly enforced by social pressure, sometimes by direct intimidation, with personal or mob violence the ultimate weapon. Lynchers are still immune to punishment, and no Negro is safe from the mob. Negroes often are arrested on groundless suspicion, and the "fee system" is a contributing factor. Courts tend to assume a Negro's guilt, and money is often lacking for adequate defense.

The ballot is commonly denied to the Negro, by social pressure, intimidation, or legal pretexts. Jury service by Negroes is almost unknown.

The addition of administrative planning to the functional levels of planning may be anticipated by analyzing our *fourth* major field of problem and tension—*political development and public administration.*

The South is the testing ground of American democracy: the country has become more conscious of national unity through strengthening of each of its regions. The South, challenged to translate its earlier sectional bias into regional participation, needs to attain social security through economic and administrative measures; and it confronts the supreme test of democracy in its treatment of ten million Negroes. Can democracy be made to work?

The South's inherited problems of finance and administration include the destruction of wealth in the Civil War, with an overturn of the economic system, the after effects of reconstruction, the educating of 4,000,000 freedmen, administrative chaos and untrained leaders, provision for landless and propertyless men. Where were the taxes to come from, for solving these and bringing to reality the new dream of public education?

Since 1900 the new South has struggled toward national integration. In this cause there have been leadership and fellowship North and South, with cooperation from philanthropic boards. Industries have multiplied and grown. Farm tenancy and cotton-mill labor have increased. There has been a development and strengthening of public health and public welfare departments. A larger and larger share of the total public moneys has been expended for public administration. Economic and social problems have developed faster than the ability to cope with them.

Among the inequalities and deficiencies, the one-party system has been fatal to democracy, causing the lowest voting percentage in the nation. Millions of Negroes have been disfranchised by legal means, by force, by fraud, while millions of whites, for lack of interest, have disfranchised themselves to avoid taxation. Public services have been substandard; schools, poorly equipped; health services, inadequate—counties without health units, without hospitals. Preventable illness has taken heavy toll, and the mortality has been the highest in the nation. Social legislation is still far behind. The labor standard is low, and social security is not yet "secure." The penal system is in many aspects outmoded, indecent, inhuman, hardening criminals instead of reclaiming them; it needs careful study and reform. The administrative units are too many and too small.

Regional administration and planning is a key problem. There is need for less state rivalry, for more cooperation among states, for national-regional cooperation, for politics of issues rather than persons, for education in public administration, for an educated public.

The provision of trained leadership is a vital matter, requiring research in personnel, the recruiting of new leaders, and an administration clearing house.

The second major level of planning—namely, *administrative planning*—is of paramount importance because governmental participation presents the essentially new aspect of planning in the modern world, and because the South's American way of individualism and free enterprise makes planning by the government somewhat more difficult than it is in the urban, industrial regions. Both considerations are basic to any planning for the South. For, in the first place, when "planning" has come to mean almost anything and when its popularity makes its effectiveness quite problematical, it is important to recognize the specific attribute of all planning that can be called authentic. That is, planning as it increases in maturity and effectiveness must always be projected in relation to government participation. Planning in this sense, then, can be defined only in relation to government, through which the people may determine the range and the ways and means through which its specifications and ideals may be made effective. Hence, the administrative level of planning.

Within this major administrative level there are five or six major sublevels corresponding to the levels of American government: the *federal* or *national,* the *regional,* the *state,* the *county,* the *district,* and the town or city or other *local level.* In any complete, American program, therefore, there would be an organic relationship between and among the different planning agencies—national, regional, state, county, and city —since these represent the basic units of American government.

These are not, however, merely mechanical or routine levels; they exemplify the organic relationship existing between local communities and the state government, between the state and the regional body or the federal government, and between the regional body and the federal government. We have already pointed out that there can be no planning "American style" except through direct representation of the states; the counties and communities are organic parts of the states. Thus, these administrative levels of social planning agencies in the United States have as their objective the continuation of the democratic process through national, regional, and local planning agencies as organic units of total American planning. All of this is not merely a formal, ambitious arrangement to indicate completeness of concept, but is the minimum requirement to insure both the grass-roots participation of the people and the service of trained leaders. *The federal and the local are mutually essential,* for without a strong central-ized and duly constituted federal agency there can be no en-during and strong decentralization.

And there can be no *strong central government* except as it is the *product of strong regional groups effectively integrated* into the national whole. This is of special importance in seek-ing the regional balance of America described in our next chapter.

In the planning arrangement through which the South can hope to achieve permanent development the mutual inter-dependence of the several levels is of great importance. That is, in the assumptions of a national planning agency, state and regional planning are inherent, just as provisions for state planning automatically include arrangements for cooperating with regional and national agencies. In this way there is in-surance that all states shall have equal opportunity, and that grouped together in regional arrangements they shall cooper-ate with one another and with the federal planning agency, thus approximating interregional balance and equilibrium. This is of special importance in the South, assuring on the one hand that *the region participates equally* in essential American planning, and on the other that it *overcomes its cumulative sectional handicaps and discrimination.*

The two levels of planning on the general basis of *function* and *administration* are predicated on sound theory and prac-tical application for the nation as a whole; but they appear peculiarly appropriate and practical for the South, with its special needs for bridging the distance between possibilities and actualities, for a better balanced economy, for eliminating its waste, for overcoming its hazards, and for a more rapid and complete integration into the total national picture. Yet, also, the facts strongly suggest that the South may be nearly ready for such comprehensive programs, and that this may be the only way it can attain the desired ends.

Naturally, many questions must be asked about so comprehensive an arrangement, and many criticisms will be offered. Two requirements must constantly be kept in mind: *specific, definite, workable ways of doing things* in the South which *will transcend its heritage of neglect, generalities, and negative objectives;* and maintenance of *the regional balance of America.* So far from being abstract and theoretical, the very nature of the total planning program has been determined by the specific, concrete, practical needs of every region, with due regard for all the other regions and the nation; and it is assumed that the people shall participate, where they live, in both the planning and the work, with whatever assistance may be available from other sources. The assumptions are therefore for the American way of continuing voluntary community agencies alongside the government agencies, in an enduring philosophy as well as in action programs.

The criticism of engineering or landscape planners, that the arrangement for all levels of planning, cultural as well as physical, is overambitious and utopian, is not justified. Such planning does not neglect the skill and artistry of the city planner or the landscape planner, and their criticism goes far toward illuminating the need for all levels of planning in our technological age. The whole arrangement is of the essence of simplicity, cataloguing specific problems and conforming exactly to the structure of American life. It does, however, negate the ancient doctrine that all planning is physical and local, and is essentially for cities at the cost of their great hinterlands and for mechanical and technological ends rather than for the benefit of the people.

It is not enough, therefore, for the engineer and the technical professional planner to join the politician in fear of a planning procedure in which all the people, and the social sciences as well as the natural sciences and engineering, are adequately represented. It is not enough to object that the people will stand for planning only in natural resources. On the contrary, the people need leadership on all levels of planning; and, since planning is already well-nigh universal, they need and desire the safeguards of a constitutional and realistic planning arrangement.

It is not enough for the critic from other regions to imply that such a comprehensive concept of planning is a flight from the reality of the South's own problems of agriculture, industry, race, and limitations in nearly all aspects of life. The exact contrary is true: only through standard, enduring arrangements sponsored by the regular levels of governmental and voluntary civic effort can there be permanent and effective achievement. The South's long history of voluntary organizations and the North's long catalogue of national voluntary reform organizations are eloquent evidence of the need for stability and effectiveness in planning that is actually planning. Even in such organic and unsolvable problems as race, planning on the regional-national level is the only way in which desired ends may be approximated.

It is not enough for the South to be afraid of comprehensive planning because it is socialistic, or because it gives the federal government too much power. On the contrary, it is essentially the most organic type of democracy that can be set up. No more appropriate is the criticism that comprehensive planning is academic and slow-moving. On the contrary, it is based upon the essential premise that enduring practical results can be attained only through sound, responsible theory. That is what the South needs above all else.

National planning, however, could fail to contribute effectively to an abundance economy for the South or to the regional balance of America. In the depression 1930's, when America's consumer purchasing power was scarcely more than sixty billion dollars, a report was prepared by a national planning agency looking toward full employment. In the program it recommended under the title "Resource Utilization," it was pointed out that when the total purchasing power of the nation reached seventy or eighty billion dollars the nation could give full employment to all employable persons, yet even if the purchasing power should rise to ninety or ninety-five or even one hundred billion dollars scarcely any increase in agricultural workers would be needed. Thus, when industry was reaching its peak of prosperity, the farming folk would still be in depression with too little employment and the necessity of paying high prices for commodities made on the basis of high prosperity. The original program not only failed to plan for agricultural regions and their populations, but on the contrary assumed that the logical thing would be for the rural folk to migrate to industrial centers, where already people were congested; failing to do so, they would constitute a drain on public funds.

A second type of planning takes the youth from one region to another, trains them, and concentrates them in the urban industrial centers, to the inevitable impoverishment of the region from which they are drained. This is not a sound policy for the nation or the region. Failure of any region to provide training and work opportunity for its youth inevitably results in deficiency areas. It assumes an uneven distribution of "have" and "have-not" regions, with the corollary that the latter can best be helped through federal aid and should be expected only to come as near self-support as possible.

It has often been pointed out that the South affords the best testing ground for regional planning in the United States. This is true for several reasons that keep recurring in the story of the South. In the first place, regional imbalance is more marked in the South than in any other region. This imbalance is found in many aspects of life: in educational opportunity on all levels; in the field of research, where science and invention as applied to resources and regional development have made a smaller contribution and played a smaller role than in other regions. The South lacks balance between agriculture and industry, as well as in agriculture. The population needs new balance both within the region and without, and further distribution throughout the nation. Particularly, the South is out of balance in its ratio of Negro to white and in its power to give equal opportunity to both. Therefore planning for a better balanced culture and economy is needed, so that it may offer a wider range of occupational opportunity and institutional service.

In all these aspects of regional imbalance, planning is a national problem as well as a southern one. It also is two-way, since achievement of regional equality and balance is the Number One postwar domestic problem of planning, and since much of the South's imbalance is due to national procedures and national economies since the Civil War.

The achievement of regional equality and balance in America is of the greatest importance not only to the South and to America but to the international order also. For, in tariff, exports, good-neighbor policy, and the like, the South will have increasingly large possibilities, and in proportion as the United States of America solves its problems of regional balance in the total culture and economy, the rest of the world will be both reassured and will profit by the technique which America uses. The ultimate goal, therefore, of a planning South at work will comprehend total planning for the regional equality and balance of America, which we will now discuss in our final chapter.

CHAPTER XVIII

The Regional Quality and Balance
of America

WE RETURN now to our starting points in this story of the way of the South. The first was the assumption of regional excellence in resources and natural endowment which, conserved, developed, and wisely used, would make a wealthy people in a lovely land but, exploited and wasted, would make a poor people in a barren land. Realistically enough, the South is constantly characterized both as a lovely land, and as the tragic South.

The second starting point was the assumption of regional quality and balance within the framework of American life. A part of the American dream of equal opportunity has always been soundly bottomed in the great range and variety of that part of the North American continent which came to be known as the United States of America. There the first plantings and the later fruits of American democracy set the incidence of the American way of life, distinctive from that which had gone before or was European. The regional nature of America was both physical and cultural and set the stage for a nation strong because of its successful integration of great diversities, whose supreme task was to be the achieving of a realistic and adequate regional balance of America.

It follows, therefore, that the way of the South, and the way of any region, is the way of America. By the same token, the way of America is the way of its regions, explored, developed, conserved, and integrated into the fabric of the whole nation. Whatever America might have been under different conditions, this is the way it grew; this is the way it is; this is the way of America forward. Just as the strength of America is in its diversity of well developed and well balanced regions,

292

resources, peoples, and cultures, so the heart of American democracy is in the freedom of opportunity, the wealth of resources, the development of public welfare within the framework of this diversity and the increasingly effective national government of federated states and regions.

Yet that diversity frames not only the historical pattern of national development and strength but also national weaknesses and undeveloped potentialities, tragedies of sectionalism, and unhealed wounds from the Civil War of three generations ago. Hidden in the waste and weakness of the regions, in the discord among them, and in regional imbalance and pathology, are still dangers and troubles capable of swelling to floodtide conflicts that threaten the modern world.

It must be clear, therefore, that even in normal periods of American development regional quality and balance existed as a key problem. It was so from the beginning of the great frontier expansion in uneven and unplanned development and exploitation. It was true in colonial days, before North and South took clearly defined form. It was true after the Civil War, when fortunes multiplied and wealth became concentrated into fewer hands. It was true in the heyday of the 1920's when the nation reached its crest of quantitative achievement in peacetime civilization. Since then the depression of the 1930's, World War II, and the early postwar years have strongly accentuated the importance of planning anew for the regional balance of America. And the global situation has finally made clear the organic significance of this regional quality and balance of people the world over.

Several aspects of the global situation reemphasize the importance of the regional quality and balance of men. One is, of course, the affect of scientific achievements on international relations in the modern world. Isolation, separatism, exploitation, wealth and abundance in one place and poverty and scarcity in others can no longer be defended.

On the other hand, there has never been a time when the individual was so important, when the spiritual values inherent in humanity were so articulate, and when the distinctive folk cultures and personalities of the world clamored so for recognition and appreciation.

It must be very clear that any attempt to mold all the diversified individuals and personalities and cultures of the world into one pattern runs contrary both to democracy and freedom and to the laws of growth and progress.

Yet it must be clear, also, that the one undebatable strategy that is needed now it to equalize opportunity and to redistribute resources and the good things of life so that there may be a genuine regional equality and balance of men, instead of economic and military conflict of peoples. The way out of current dilemmas will be in some major strategy which enables the people of each region to produce wealth and use it wisely and at the same time facilitates the interchange of both people and resources between regions, with opportunity for achievement outside as well as inside a region.

Many, perhaps most, of the tragic maladjustments, disorganizations, and pathological situations, the world over, are due to regional inequalities and imbalances, natural or industrial.

Therefore the main strategy of planning will be to balance and equalize regions, not only in economic opportunity but in cultural development and justice in world organization, now so much stressed. Yet justice, admittedly basic to adequate and enduring arrangements, is not a moralistic abstraction, but an essential equalizing of regions and balancing of opportunity in the places where people live, in the frame of world standards and interrelationships.

The assumptions of balance comprehend a great deal more than balanced economy as technically defined, with its factors of balanced agriculture and industry and the other factors so well defined by the economists. The heart of regional balance is found in the provision of equal opportunity for all the people through the conservation, development, and use of their resources in the places where they live, adequately adjusted to the cultures and economies of the other regions of the world and of the nation. The goal is, therefore, clearly one of balanced culture as well as economy, with equality of opportunity in education, in public health and welfare, in the range of occupational outlook, and in the elimination of handicapping differentials between and among different groups of people and levels of culture.

With reference to the functional definitions of regionalism, it is necessary to reemphasize the fact that the primary objectives of regionalism are found in the integration of regions more than in the mere study and development of regions themselves. The regions are studied and planned to the end that they may be more adequate in all aspects of resources and culture; yet regionalism itself is primarily interested in the total integration and balance of these regions. In the case of American society it is not so much a question of centralization of authority in conflict with state rights as it is of developing an adequate federalized control authority capable of achieving realistic decentralization.

The way of the South, therefore, is first of all American and then southern. The South is American, or it is nothing of enduring culture. Yet the situation is always one of double responsibility on the part of both the nation and the South. That is, the nation's obligation is clearly twofold: so to cooperate with the South in administering the American democracy and economy as to help develop the region; and to enrich the nation in so doing. The nation owes the fullest possible development of the South not only to that region, but to the other regions and the nation at large. No matter of regional development and planning can be a simple one-way problem.

The South on its side has a twofold task in planning its part in the regional balance of America: to develop itself, and to get along with the rest of the country and become increasingly integrated into the nation. This is a recurring motif in the southern symphony. There is pathos in the fact that the South's chief deficiencies and tragedies have resulted from its failure in these tasks: for its waste of resources, its failure to develop and conserve them for the enrichment of the people, has resulted in vast handicaps. Yet the greater tragedy of war and continued sectional conflict has multiplied basic problems and has continued the old economic handicaps. In the search, therefore, for a better regional balance of America it is difficult to estimate which side of the task is primal or more fundamental—the development of the region, or its integration into the national picture. They are, of course, in reality inseparable.

Clearly, however, the task is first of all a national one; and a first essential is the recognition of this fact by the nation and by the South and all the other regions. To understand the essential regional quality of America and of world problems and translate the old sectionalism and separatism into the newer regionalism and unity, clearly emerges as a *must* in the new era.

Something of the epic story of this earlier regional America may be recaptured through the symbolism of America's Walt Whitman in "The shapes arise" or in some gigantic "broad-axe" set to the building of a frontier nation. To sense anew the range of the incredible and swift-moving cavalcade of America as "the shapes arise" is to recapture the epic of the nation's powerful heritage of resources set in the midst of every region, and of every folk at work at every occupation, in which the "main shapes" of democracy were made enduring because of the diversity of people, place, work, and wealth.

In the new regional balance of America, "as the shapes arise"

there is recaptured the powerful and colorful multiple meaning of the old "welcome" to new frontiers. "Welcome are all
earth's lands, each for its kind." Welcome, welcome, welcome.

> Lands of pine and oak
> Lands of the lemon and fig
> Lands of gold
> Lands of wheat and maize
> Lands of sugar and rice

and all the other lands, of the grape, and cotton, and the white
potato and sweet potato, the measureless grazing-lands, the
teeming soil of orchards, flax, honey, hemp. And "welcome
just as much the other more hard-faced lands," of mines, of
the manly and rugged ores, of coal, copper, lead, tin, zinc,
iron. And equally again,

> Welcome are mountains, flats, sands, forests, prairies,
> Welcome the rich borders of rivers, table-lands, openings,

Yet more, for "the shapes arise" as of the folk, too, as of
those who sought, and seek again, New England and found
it or Virginia and the Carolinas or the Deep South and on
westward. Or those who found the waters of the Mississippi
or of the Red River or deeper South on the Rio Grande; or
north again by the Colorado or up beyond by the Northwest's Snake River valleys or the widening thousand-miled
Columbia or by Willamette; or down by Death Valley and
the desert lands and to the California redwoods; and then eastward again to mountain plateau and Great Plains and Great
Lakes; and on to great eastern woodlands and mountaintops;
and in the way places across a continent by springs and rivers
and valleys and back to Appalachia that looks down to the
sea. But always the folk and always "Welcome" and ever "the
shapes arise." Yet of many shapes, one; of all shapes, America,

> The main shapes arise!
> Shapes of Democracy total, result of centuries.

First of all, it must be recalled that realistic Americanism
was grounded in the physiographic measures of the continent

and in the adaptation of the people to the places where they lived. This was true not only because of the extraordinary wide range and kinds of natural phenomena but because of the sheer size of an America in whose mountain fastnesses or river valleys or Great Plains all Western Europe, so to speak, could be lost. In this happy convergence of superabundant natural wealth and human wealth was to be found the measure of the nation's extraordinary strength and power as well as her growing pains and sectional conflict.

For a full understanding of this physiographic America and her people the observer might well begin by approaching the continent at a reasonably low altitude from the Atlantic Ocean. He would see an extraordinary rugged eastern coast line, and would fly across it and over the seaboard with its small rivers and valleys. He would then see the great Appalachian Mountain region extending all the way from New England down into Georgia and Alabama. Then he would continue across broad flat plains, a thousand miles of the middle America, drained by great rivers, stretching from the Great Lakes to the Gulf of Mexico. Next he would fly over the great Rocky Mountains and high plateaus, looking down on valleys and snowcapped ranges and then his plane might drop abruptly toward the California coast line, here smooth and there rugged, and the Pacific Ocean. In the midst of these larger parallel regions of mountains, of river valleys, of plateau, each of which became a frontier in American expansion, he would glimpse hundreds of smaller valley regions and no fewer than seventeen major river valleys symbolic of the richness of all resources and power, of flora and fauna of the great American domain. This would be the physiographic regional picture of America along north and south lines. Then, flying north to south over the same regions he would encounter the great climatic regions and many of those environmental factors which conditioned people of the United States, dividing them into North and South.

If, then, the observer would return for a closer regional inspection of a great nation and study of the combination of physical and cultural factors, he might well start in the Northeast. Here he would see the great coast line and fisheries, ships and shipbuilding, industries and technological equipment, centers of urban culture and commerce, an abundance of colleges, universities, art and recreation, philanthropy and wealth, and the concentration of the melting-pot population. As he flew south beyond Washington he would see a different sort of American culture, yet strangely uniform in the fabric of its highways and communications. In spite of growing cities and the changing balance of agriculture and industry, the culture would appear mainly rural and agricultural. Here would be lands of cotton and tobacco and millions of black folk growing up and apart. Still farther south he would see a great Gulf Coast line, with resorts and new reaches in agriculture balanced with livestock, and with prospects of new developments in South American commerce and perhaps in oil and chemical industries to take effect on the southern and northern balance of America.

On across the Mississippi to Texas and Oklahoma, the observer would be amazed at the broad plains and their cotton farming, cattle raising, turkey ranches, tropical vegetables, and empire of oil and at the rapid increase of cities and industries transforming a frontier culture again into a youthful civilization of growing pains and immaturity of years. On then across the continuing fringe of Southwest through New Mexico and Arizona, and moving into San Diego and up the Pacific coast he would find the most exotic "American" and "un-American" culture, in which the East and West of America and the East and West of the world meet. Extending from southern California up to Oregon and Washington and into the first reaches of Canada he would find a culture and economy of the Pacific Far West, reputed to have the highest standard of living of any region in the world. Thence he would complete the exploration, starting east again over the great mountains and plains. Here he would see examples of the most remarkable power and irrigation dams in existence, as well as the most notable national parks and forests, mines of copper and of gold, great expanses of winter wheat lands, and grazing lands again with sparse population. Continuing eastward, the observer would slip into the great industrial urban middle states vying with the East in the concentration of wealth and manufacturing and people but also holding steadfast to the agricultural and rural tradition of America. And in the upper reaches of the Ohio River valley with its cities and industries, he would come to the Pennsylvania and West Virginia coal fields.

If, then, the observer wished a still more detailed view of his America, he could obtain a more intimate picture from a three-level travel and exploration review of all the great regions. He might begin with the Pacific Northwest and move eastward, by railway and automobile as well as by plane. By plane he could circle over the Columbia River country from the Canadian border through Washington and Oregon seeing the almost incredibly powerful Grand Coulee dam and other seemingly superhuman achievements of the world's greatest engineers in which new waters may make over lands for a million folk.

Yet no air view could be adequate for noting the wealth of detail. Another level of travel, therefore, is needed; namely, by train. More still is needed, and a third level of travel is by automobile, with any desirable stopovers. Such a threefold survey could give a knowledge of realistic regional potentialities adding up the totals of what regional resources and development may mean to the strength and unity of America if adequately integrated into the national culture. And so for the other regions. For instance, such a three-level view of the Great Plains and of the old area of the Dust Bowl, under the planning and decentralization of a war period, would give a

dramatic impression of what can go into the regional balance
of America. Or again, preview to a new Missouri River Valley
development would be an intensive review of the South with
its Tennessee Valley, its Appalachian and Piedmont regions
of industry and cotton and tobacco, its Black Belt or its Gulf
and Atlantic coasts. Such a three-level observation of all the
American regions would bring out both the facts necessary
for understanding and the assumptions for planning a better
balance among all the parts of America and all the levels of
life.

There are still other ways in which we can sense the regional
quality of America and the need and opportunity to harness
its power and integrate the component parts into a stronger
and better balanced nation. One way is through an understanding of its rivers and river valleys, and that can be ob-
tained through the biography of the rivers of America. The
rivers formed the people as they won their way in the New
America and as they developed in character and fixed their
loyalties. This is true of the little valley of a Sweetwater, just
as it is of the composite Tennessee River Valley with all its
tributaries bringing in the waters and the folk alike to the
powerfully vibrant total. It is true of the tiny creeks with their
mountain folk and their highways and creek bottoms and
their names and community spirit coinciding in the patterns
of folk culture and identification. It is true in the big and
powerful rivers, the Missouri and the Ohio, the Columbia
and the Mississippi. It is true in the rivers selected for
the Rivers of America Series in a notable literary contribution to the understanding and enrichment of America. As
Constance Lindsay Skinner wrote, "It is as the story of
American rivers that the folk sagas will be told." And in this
effort to "make a whole interpretation of a few American folk"
as symbolized in river localities, there is the "greater adventure, namely a composite study of the American Folk as a
Nation." There could be multiplied many times the saga of

the twenty-four rivers symbolized by *Kennebec—Cradle of the Americans; Upper Mississippi—A Wilderness Saga; Suwannee River—Strange Green Land; Powder River—Let 'Er Buck*. "History warmed by love of spacious country."

Another way in which it is possible to understand this America through its rivers is to measure the length and breadth and power of its great river valleys as integral regions of this nation of regions and folk. There is the picture of the Tennessee Valley with its TVA as "Democracy on the March"; or the winding Columbia, upper valley in Canada and Washington, lower reaching through Washington and Oregon to the Pacific and taking in the Willamette and its lesser tributaries. There is the wide expanse and the long turning of the Missouri and its prospective MVA, to match Tennessee's TVA.

In these river valley regions are measurable units of culture and economy, susceptible of scientific study and planning, contributing to the diversity and unity of the American scene. A great Ohio River valley, encompassing so much from Dayton, Ohio, to Dayton, Tennessee, must surely represent the need and symbol of unity because of the very diversity of its culture and people. Yet it must somehow be symbol of the regional distinctive quality and variety of the folk themselves because of the many states whose tributary it is. Such a valley, therefore, is not only measure of economy and problem, symbol of folk and nation, but also problem for central administration of government balanced with state and regional priorities.

So are the other major river valleys, each and every one designated by the National Resources Planning Board as a basic area for water planning and river drainage problems. There were seventeen of these American river valley regions estimated to approximate one measure of the regional quality and balance of America. These regions were designated as the major river valleys of New England, the North Atlantic, the Middle Atlantic, the Southeast, the Tennessee, the Ohio, the lower Mississippi, the western Gulf, the southwest Mississippi basin, the upper Mississippi and Red River, the Great Lakes and St. Lawrence, the Missouri basin, the Colorado, the Great Basin, California, the upper Rio Grande, and the Pacific Northwest.

The regional diversity of America may also be understood through a knowledge of the metropolitan regions of America, in contrast with its rural regions. In the urban picture may be found prevailing trends of population and industry, measures of unevenness and imbalance, and areas of conflict between labor and agriculture, the consumer and agricultural producer, and evidence of the need for both economic and cultural balance. For in many ways urban centers drain the hinterlands and exploit the folk and resources of the rural regions and set the incidence for inequalities of culture and opportunity. The total urban quality of the nation may perhaps be observed best in two ways. One way is to examine the nearly one hundred metropolitan districts as classified by the Census into areas of more than 100,000 population. The other is to analyze the two great industrial-urban regions of concentrated population and wealth in the Northeast and in the middle states, in both of which the dominant power of urban and organized America finds its greatest expression.

Still another approach to the understanding of the regional quality of America may be found in the historical aspects of regionalism. For, in order to understand the premises and need for regional balance of America, and the South's role in its attainment, we have to go a considerable way back into America's experiences. Our main assumptions are that the promise and prospect of the nation, and specifically the South, are to be found in the substitution of a genuinely realistic regionalism for the historical sectionalism featuring separatism, isolationism, competitive states and economy, and political pressures and conflict. Yet the very need makes it all the more important to understand the nature and power of the earlier American conditioning.

First, of course, was the American frontier on the several regional levels, and its influence upon the character of American culture. Both fundamental aspects of this conformed in part to the Frederick Jackson Turner concepts of American history, but with variations. The first of Turner's concepts was that in a new geographical environment, the economic, social, and psychological demands made upon the pioneers resulted in the creation of new culture patterns which progressively became more American than European. But, unfortunately, this frontier culture set the incidence for something that was also reminiscent of European conflict: American sectionalism, the significance of which "in American history is that it is the faint image of a European nation and that we need to reexamine our history in the light of this fact. Our politics and our society have been shaped by sectional complexity and interplay not unlike what goes on between European nations. The greater sections are the result of the joint influence of the geologists' physiographic provinces and the colonizing stocks which entered them. 'We must shape our national action to the fact of a vast and varied Union of unlike sections.'" The types of American sectionalism which have grown out of these premises include: the conflict between the North and the South, which James Truslow Adams called "America's Tragedy"; the conflict between New England and the West; a conflict between the urban and the rural, and subsequently a continuous secondary conflict between different geographic areas and between states.

The essential framework through which sectionalism was evolved, and upon which the new regionalism must be built, had its genesis in the overexpanding series of frontier regions commonly designated as "wests" in American expansion. The first wests consisted of the approaches to the Appalachians prior to the breaking over to the real wests. This took place in movements from eastern New York and Pennsylvania toward the western parts of these states, and the great southwest trek to the state of Franklin and western North Carolina and Tennessee, and the exploration of Kentucky. A next western frontier was formed by movements into Ohio, preliminaries to the settlement of the whole Northwest Territory, reaching to the Great Lakes and the Mississippi River.

Still another series of frontiers marked the westward movement across Alabama, Mississippi, Louisiana, and all the Louisiana Purchase area, including the great migration of the Mormons. Then came the great Oregon Trail and the California gold rush, followed by a rebound from the Far West and a revival of the movement northwest into the northern Great Plains. Following these, then, were the great southwestern movements into Texas, New Mexico, and Oklahoma.

Then, too, the historical development of the concept of regionalism helps to interpret the total picture. Perhaps the first of these in the order of historical priority was what was generally called a cultural and literary regionalism, in which differing groups of people, their cultures, folk-ways, and institutions were described as definitive indices of homogeneity. Such a regionalism has been richly documented and has a distinguished background.

Next perhaps was metropolitan regionalism, which was a logical outgrowth of the rise of urbanism and the subsequent extension of the cities into suburban areas, and, with the multiplication of cities and the concentration of population, gave rise to two trends; namely, decentralization of residential and industrial activities, and the comprehensive planning and widening inclusion of metropolitan districts. Such a regionalism, like literary regionalism, was primarily local and was focused upon the improving of a situation within given areal concentrations.

The more recent developments included what might be called the regionalism of convenience and organization, in which business concerns, industrial corporations, banking organizations, chain stores, educational and religious associations all found it convenient to break the Great Country down into divisions for practical purposes of distance, size, decentralization, organization.

This regionalism of convenience and organization naturally was a forerunner of a main type of American regionalism; namely, administrative regionalism. As a major division and movement this was primarily in the field of governmental administration, in which the nation has been variously divided into areas, corps, districts, regions, zones and so on until more than a hundred and thirty such divisions have been designated by various governmental agencies for administrative purposes. A few examples are the earlier army area corps, the federal reserve banking system, FSA, WPA, and other New Deal administrative subdivisions.

Finally, a very specialized combination of physiographic, economic, cultural, and administrative regionalism is that in which the Tennessee Valley Authority explores the possibilities of regional planning within specific geographic areas for both cultural and economic development and as strategy for river valley regional planning in harmony with the states and regions and the nation.

One of the best testing grounds for understanding this regional quality of America is the exploration of what the people of the several regions know about and think about each of the other regions.

> Everyone knows this land of ours:
> Sing, "My Country, 'Tis of Thee"
> or
>   "God Bless America"
> Everyone knows this land of ours,
> And no one knows it.

This is peculiarly true of the younger generation, whose knowledge and experience leave a wide gap between general political history and modern ideological principles and philosophy set in the midst of a busy world of specialisms. This was vividly explained in one way by Constance Lindsay Skinner in the statement: "If the average American is less informed about his country than any other national, knows and cares less about its past and about its present in all sections but the one where he resides and does business, it is because . . . few writers have displayed to him the colors and textures of the original stuff of American life; or made him comrade of the folk." Out of this ignorance, one region of another, grow conflict and misunderstandings and failure to realize on the powerful factors of union in diversity.

Yet, after all, the greatest evidence of the regional quality of America is found in the cultural quality and loyalties within each great region. How the people love their own regions and criticize others! "Where I come from" is still the perennial proverb for excellence. From a multitude of southerners: "I hope I shall never have to live outside of the South long. I have enjoyed California and the Middle West and I love New York, but I don't want to live there." And of the windy plains of the Northwest one writes: "I loved the fabulous sunsets, lakes of gold and the dreamy purple mountains." Among the multitudes who love California, some would be found to be seekers of health, sunshine, change, beauty, rest, shunners of toil, care, routine, and tumult, haters of closed walls, and lovers of the open air; and others, just Americans demonstrating that East and West do meet—East and West of America, East and West of war.

Soldier boys from New England, temporarily in the South: "I want to go back where one can really live. I don't see why anybody would want to live in the South." And soldier boys from the South: "I don't see why anybody would live up here in this God-forsaken Michigan winter—I want to go home."

Or "Deep in the Heart of Texas" may be symbol of all the regional romance of America. One writes, "It is easy to see why Lee loved Virginia so much." Another calls attention to the fact that New England assumed her culture was most American because she defined American culture in terms of what New England had.

In his *Upper Mississippi: A Wilderness Saga*, Walter Havighurst has featured the regional quality of the folk. What he says of that region applies equally to the South and to any other region.

"There is," he writes, "a stamp that a country puts upon men's faces and upon their speech, and, more mystically, upon their minds. Not by coincidence did Stefansson and Lindbergh, Garland and Turner and Veblen, come from the same great prairies above the Mississippi. Their work has an affinity which makes it a single contribution, repeated in their separate fields of adventure, in earth and air, in vision and in thought. Imagination and will were required of pioneers in that wilderness. It is no accident that the Middle Border produced men resolute and original whose minds have started rivers of new thought that are enlarging still.

"Prairie men, these all saw space in their youth and lived amid tasks bounded only by the horizon. They walked toward the sky. Later, they had no fear of space—not of blank miles of ice, not of blue oceans and blue air, not of spacious ideas that swing arcs of power over the slow thought-world of tradition. Like the homestead seekers, they feared confinement more than hazard. There is a nostalgia that America knows for tasks that come only to a first generation and are not now recoverable. But the wind still blows over the prairie where the grass bent under the wagon wheel and then sprang up again. And the prairie mind still holds the instincts of horizon-land, impatient of boundaries, questing, impelled by an old need and led by purposes forever new."

All this means simply that the way of each region is the way of its culture, and that each culture is inseparably identified with its regional character. This not only is nothing new but has always been recognized as a definitive part of understanding peoples and their institutions. It has always been recognized by the common people in their loyalties and devotion to their own customs and institutions and in their criticism of others. It has always been recognized by anthropologists and sociologists in their study of cultures. Regional attitudes and mores are so definite and powerful that they constitute rights and wrongs; they determine the nature of behavior and institutions. Intolerance, therefore, of the mores of a people reflects narrowness and provincialism of outlook.

In the United States there has recently been an increasing tendency among urban intellectuals to belittle and to characterize as bad many of the mores of rural America and nearly all the ways of the South. This would be inevitable since the types of culture differ so radically. Manifestly, however, here is one source of conflict and imbalance in the nation, the conflicting part being unnecessary. And there is an increasing tendency in the North and the South, each to evaluate its own attitudes and behavior highly and to discount those of the other, without understanding them. This reflects a strange backwardness in an age of communication and intellectual liberalism. The depth and width of the growing chasm and the reasons for it are unbelievable but true.

Regionalism in culture, behavior, and institutions exists, of course, in all parts of the world. The recognition of this, of the imbalance between regions, and of the need for regional arrangements in world organization and peace, while relatively new, is rapidly becoming basic in nearly all plans for stabilizing world organization. Symbolic of the swelling tide of regionalism is the conviction of Sumner Wells that "an effective international organization can be constituted only through the creation of regional systems of nations . . . under an overall international body representative . . . of all regions." But the point of emphasis is that it is through co-operative arrangement, and the integration of diversified cultures, that strength and stability are to be found.

Now, all of this is of the utmost importance if we are to sense the urgency of the problem of the regional quality and balance of America and the role of the South in the future development of the nation. For, assuming that the South is the chief testing ground for American regionalism and American democracy, we have assumed also that its problems are more difficult and varied, and that it has inherited a larger number of handicaps than other regions. This explains why the South must devote itself more earnestly to its regional development than other regions, and why, by the same token, the South seeks reasonable national cooperation. There is no other way. The South is as it is. It is the only South we have. The nation is as it is. It is the only nation we have. There must surely be some way of attaining this better balance and equilibrium.

This means, again, that the oft recurring basis upon which we seek to understand and develop the new way of the South in the nation must be bottomed in the new American regionalism in contradistinction to the old American sectionalism. It assumes that the balancing of men and resources in the major regions of the United States is no longer a matter of generalities or of ideology alone. It assumes a science of the region in which there is agreement upon the delineation of a reasonable number of major composite groups-of-states, through which actual planning may be done where men live and work. This means that planning is not just a matter of words and items; it is action close to reality, and in priority schedules of time, place, and relationship that have to do with each job to be done.

Repeat and repeat, regionalism and regional planning are set forth as tools to provide definite, specific, workable ways of attaining concretely what is generally advised in contradistinction to mere ideology and education or again in contradistinction to sectional rivalries and conflict.

Such a regionalism affords uniform measures through which balance and equilibrium between people and resources, men and machines, the state and the folk may be attained. It is a tool of the democratic process in that it provides for the redistribution of the good things of life and of the opportunity to work within the framework of every people's geography and inherent cultural equipment. It is a tool for democratic reconstruction of the postwar world, because it is through cooperative regionalism rather than economic nationalism that the society of tomorrow will be organized for human welfare instead of for military achievements. It is a tool for social planning, because it takes into consideration the rights, privileges, resources of people and areas, and stresses self-government and self-development as opposed to coercive centralized power. It is a tool for social planning, also because it offers specific technical workable ways of developing and conserving resources for human-use ends.

Since regionalism, as the opposite pole of sectionalism, isolation, and separatism, exists in every nation, it wants no self-sufficiency in economy. It wants no isolationism and separatism. There can be no region except as it is a part of the total nation or of world society, each region being a constituent unit in the whole, and the wealth and welfare of the total measured through the integration of the wealth and welfare of each. By the same token each region can be enriched and developed only through the principle of cooperation and representation set in the framework of both governmental and voluntaristic effort.

Such a regionalism is insurance against any economy which allows for the "haves" and the "have-nots" in areas of American democracy. This is exactly what exists in the South today and what a surprising number of "scholars" have assumed must continue. There could be no justification in a well integrated American democracy for a public administration and philosophy which would perpetuate weakness, deficiency, and poverty in one region alongside strength, efficiency, and abundance in another. The whole situation is especially tragic when pathology and deficiency are assumed as permanent traits of a region with great potential resources. It would be unbelievable if it were not true that such a framework of American democracy should come so near to realization. Regionalism therefore, on the one hand, strengthens the economic total of the nation and avoids conflict, and, on the other, prevents the necessity for special relief, special differentials, and privileges. And, of course, it features the American credo of self-adequacy and mastery over environment.

Regionalism provides the only way to an enduring and effective redistribution of wealth and opportunity by creating in each region the capacity to produce and use wisely wealth from the development and utilization of resources and men within the framework of the region and the equipment of the people. This is the key to the regional balance of man everywhere in which the goal is a better equilibrium between men and full resources and between men and situation, communication, and transportation. This is the way to utilize science and technology in the mastery of man's problems.

The enrichment of each region, the development and use of its resources, training of its people, and balance of its industry, contribute powerfully to the wealth of the nation, and this may be used by the nation in cooperative and equalizing funds for leadership, research, training, and planning essential to the democratic processes of state and regional representation. The way to train youth, for instance, and to guarantee security and reality for the new generation, to raise standards of living and insure equal opportunity and security, is to develop regional capacities and programs and to work out interregional optima rather than drain some regions to the benefit of others or concentrate abnormal situations subversive to the development of a great unified nation.

The strength of a nation in war or peace, is the sum of the strengths of all its regions, each providing its part in the nation's total and in particular guaranteeing the national reserves essential for permanent defense and permanent prosperity. Such a power of regional decentralization, yet of national order, was brilliantly demonstrated by Russia against Germany. The way to effect a wholesome decentralization of wealth, of power, of people is explored through the regional balance of men and resources, but always with the national integration and unity of a strong people as the first concern.

On the other hand, the surest way to prevent totalitarian overcentralization of power is to provide safeguards and guarantees in a sound regionalism bottomed in the American principle of geographic representation and the balance of power of the people. Furthermore, the surest safeguard to the American ideals of democracy of the folk and the rule of laws and constitution rather than persons is through a continuing equilibration by way of the regional balance of wealth, control, population, of land and resources developed within the framework of balanced communications, transportation, and exchange which makes possible the best adjustment between the people and their total heritage and environment.

This problem of balance and equilibrium is not entirely a matter of balanced economy and culture within the region. It is also a matter of adjustment and balance with other regions. A large part of the imbalance has been due to deficiencies of national strategy in holding the South back from full participation in the life of the nation. Thus, the South has the double handicap of its self-adopted sectionalism and the cultural separatism which the rest of the country almost universally assumes to be the true South.

Furthermore, in so far as the lack of balance in the nation is one of culture as well as economics, it reflects not only vast inequalities of education and welfare but lack of balance between urban and rural America, between majority and minority groups. Imbalance includes also conflict between the East and the West, as well as the North and the South, between white and Negro, between capital and labor, between opposing groups of organized labor, between classes in cities and between industries. The cultural imbalance includes overconcentration of population, and pathology in the cities as well as in isolated population areas. And it includes a vast ignorance among the people of the facts of cultural and historical America and in one region of another.

In the United States, therefore, there is need to understand not only the romance and pathology, the political history and geography of America, but its regional economic reality and cultures. There is need to realize that the South and America are not alone in having problems of racial and minority groups and an unsatisfactory regional balance of culture and economy. Our problems are minor in comparison with those of many of the suffering and conflicting folk of war-torn countries, except as they enter into a new global situation.

It must not be overlooked that the path of the South, and of all America, lies athwart the great sweep of time, technology, and change. Revolution and restlessness among the folk, science and technology in the material world, are part of the South's heritage. Youth, race, labor, and all the folk, in their tendencies to revolt, are in constant conflict with tradition and the resistance of other folk. There is conflict between the urban intellectual and labor-consumer folk and the rural work folk of the farm. This conflict is not "southern," even though much of it is in the South. There is conflict between races and regions, nation and nation the world over, such that many of the stirrings in the South reflect universal culture and human nature in the resistless tides of folk sweeping toward a deeper and wider expression than the stream beds of their culture can contain. And still other parts reflect another world problem framed in the resistance to a sweeping societal pressure that seeks to integrate all peoples and all areas into a common culture, which manifestly is a problem of great complexity, conflicting forces, and of the time quality as well.

Yet, on the other hand, the particular problems of race and regional conflict approximate a crisis and emergency in America more ominous than anything within the last century. And it must be clear that the drama of the South appears increasingly in the stage setting of an America in which a powerful imbalance of Negro people in the South creates a realistic, distinctive problem. It must be clear, too, it is drama equally for the black man and the white man, both of whom need the normal help and understanding of all regions of the nation.

This brings us face to face with the extraordinary dilemma of planned voluntary migration through which the Negro people may be more evenly distributed throughout all the regions of the nation. This requires a master strategy capable of bearing the burden of a many-sided dilemma. There is not only the difficult task of balanced distribution of the people, but also that of providing ways and means of educating and training the Negro in his new environment and planning work for him to do before he is relocated for his training and education.

The assumptions of such planned migration are many. First is the consent and cooperation of the other regions. Second is the consent and cooperation of the Negro people. Last is the consent and good will of the South. There are other assumptions on other levels of approach. One is that the increasing demand for the elimination of discrimination and segregation for the Negro in American life carries with it both the willingness and the capacity of the nation to provide facilities when there is adequate wealth and will to make satisfactory arrangements, and when legal restrictions are not present. This means,

in practice, ascertaining how many Negroes, in what classifications of age, training, family equipment, can be wisely used
in what regions of the nation, and in what capacities and
through what procedures.

There are other complicated assumptions, four of which are
perhaps fundamental to any such planned migration. The first
is that it is not possible to approximate the balanced culture necessary to guarantee the Negro equal opportunity in
America in any other way than through the migration from
the South to all other regions of perhaps one-half its total
Negro population. The second is that the rest of the nation
is sincere in its militant advocacy of equal opportunity and is
willing to do its part toward the desired ends. The third is that
increased provisions for training Negroes and for setting up
additional industrial opportunities can be made through
national, regional, and state planning agencies much more
economically for the nation than any attempt at coercive en-
forcement by the nation of a non-segregation economy advocated by many agitators. And the fourth assumption is that
the South, in the face of losing a large part of its Negro
population and in the light of reduced numbers, would provide equal opportunity for those who remain, would eliminate
all unnecessary differentials between the races, and would
modify its policy of segregation in many respects.

Now manifestly, because of the unreality in nearly all of
the assumptions stated, so far as any immediate results may
be anticipated, such a program of planned migration can be
little more than a vivid presentation of the complexity of the
situation and the urgency of the need. Yet such a program
must be faced frankly and something of its equivalent must
be planned if there is to be anything like balance and equilibrium in this area of Negro-white relationships in the United
States, and if stark tragedy is to be avoided in the present
trends. It will be objected that the great mass of Negroes will
not agree, although many Negro leaders think that the Negro

cannot attain democracy until he leaves the South. It will be objected that the various regions will protest that they are not prepared, and that the South itself will not cooperate. This again, however, is another way of indicating the difficulties and hazards of the South in its search for equality and balance in the nation.

In the drama of this way of the South in the nation there is no hiding the fact that the supreme task of region and nation in their search for a better regional balance of America is a better adjustment of race relations and opportunities, with all the implied obligations of both races and all regions. There is no overlooking the fact that the South's attitudes and behavior on most levels are wrong, judged from any general, abstract principle of democracy or Americanism. If it be offered in defense that New England or any other region would in all probability have behaved exactly as the South did, New England or any other region would then have been equally wrong. If it be said that no other peoples have been successful in a compound biracial civilization, and that race prejudice is as old as civilization, and that all the other regions of the United States discriminate against the Negro in high places and low, it has no effect on the obligation of the South and the nation to work together for the amelioration of conditions. If it be said that the other regions should study and plan for the improvement of their own situations and unfair practices, the answer is that they are doing just that, which adds to the South's obligation to do its part. Or if it be said that race discrimination is increasing in other regions, this is indication of the supreme need for better regional quality and balance everywhere.

On the other hand, since the job is one for all the nation as well as for the South, it must be apparent that the nation's part is also a two-way task. If, as is clear, the nation is assuming greater responsibility toward the southern part of the problem, there are two sides to this. The nation is troubled

over the vast injustices in the South and realizes that it must
do something about them. And the nation has the duty to
understand the total situation, to participate in working it
out on the levels of American democratic government, and to
plan with the South in terms of attainable reality. The nation
must surely know the nature of the problem and understand
that the way of the South is the way of Nature with all her
powerful conditioning forces; the way of the frontier and the
folk with their loyalties and enthusiasm for causes for which
they, both white and Negro, are willing to die; the way of
religion and race, more powerful than all abstract moralities;
and the way of culture and of America and of history through
which the way of the South has been interwoven in the total
fabric of the nation and the way of the nation in the fabric
of the South.

There is another sense in which the nation's part is a double
approach. If it is said that the nation cannot face the world
of nations and the search for global democracy unless it can
forthwith reshape its own undemocratic procedures, it must
be said also that America cannot lead the world toward
abiding peace and fellowship through organization unless it
can prevent violent revolution and civil war within its own
limits. The fact that there are wrongs to be righted is no license
to right them through fighting and war, especially since these
wrongs are of the same sort as the wrongs and tragedies of
the rest of the world, if less complicated and often less ex-
tensive. Some of the movements, attitudes, and activities, both
North and South, within these areas, have come close to
treason in time of war; they can bring on new war when peace
has come. America can adopt the procedures of planning and
interregional and interracial organization and cooperation,
and be ready to join the world in international organization
and cooperation for peace. Or America can join the conflicting
nations and races in perpetual warfare and violence and lose
its leadership in international organization for peace. This

problem is no more a one-way obligation in the United States, with its opportunity for interregional and interracial balance, than is the obligation of nations and races and folk in tragedy and travail the world over.

That is how important the problem is. That is how near America comes to crisis. That is why the supreme task, for the way of the South and for the way of the nation, is found in the regional quality and balance of America. That is why there is no other way to achieve the desired and attainable standards than through complete cooperative state, regional, and national planning under the auspices of governmental and voluntary programs, adopted and enacted through the consent of the people and through new reaches in the effectiveness of education. The nation has had no greater responsibility than this. The South has had no greater opportunity.

Yet to planning there must be added something more. There must be understanding and knowledge. To these must be added purpose and the will to do. And to these must somehow be added a guarantee of the South's spiritual and intellectual integrity in the new day. It is as if there were a new renaissance of the South's high motivation and singleness of purpose. It is as if there were a genuine rededication to the spirit and objectives of a Southern Regional Council that means what it says.

In the name and spirit of America's science and education the South will seek to find and to tell the truth. In the name and spirit of America's democracy it will seek the way of equal opportunity. In the name of America's patriotism, it will strive for loyalty to the American dream, and for statesmanship adequate to carry the burden of the new America. In the name and spirit of America's Christianity, it will search for the new faith of fellowship. In the name of humanity, can the South substitute the measures of the good society for the old biological struggle for physical survival?

To this end the South seeks a new declaration of American principles and a new dedication to the task of covenanting with all regions and all races for the continued better ordering of our society. In the present crisis this covenant is as important as the compacts of the forefathers, and the framework must comprehend a concept and a charter which guarantees equality of opportunity for all peoples. This means specifically that the Negro in the United States and in every region is entitled to, and should have, every guarantee of equal opportunity that every other citizen of the United States has within the framework of the American democratic system of government.

Here is needed also an unswerving dedication to the achievement of this task. Since in the order of all nature and in the growth and development of the people and society there are always certain features peculiar to each society; since in the order of democracy there are certain elemental principles of self-government that are inherent in each folk and regional society; and since in both the physical and the cultural heritage of the South there are certain cumulative and tragic handicaps that represent powerful factors in the situation, the South appeals to the nation to join forces with it for the working out of methods, procedures, and rates of change in the spirit of, and in conformity with, the principles of our American democracy.

So comes the South to a new era in the annals of America. We return to our starting points in which a new region grew up in the tutelage of Nature and of the folk seeking the promised land through the mastering of a distinctive environment. We recapture something of the heroic story of the region with all its tragedies and hazards and the perennial problems that are close to the soul of a people. We recall the sayings of the historian that to learn the life and times of an individual we have to know a lot about his background and experiences;

and that to learn the life and times of a region we have to know a lot about that region's experiences and backgrounds. Now, we have learned a lot about this South of the United States but we have also learned a lot about the way of Nature and culture in a magnificent reality that knows no turning back and gives no special privilege to any culture and no special priorities to any region or race. "The shapes arise" anew, challenging a new youth and maturity of the South and the nation to be strong, as America is strong to meet all tasks.

> She receives them as the laws of Nature receive them, she is strong,
> She too is a law of Nature—there is no law stronger than she is.

In the knowledge about the way of America and the way of emergency and crisis, there is warning as well as promise:

> And whether I come to my own today or in ten thousand or ten million years,
> I can cheerfully take it now, or with equal cheerfulness I can wait.

In the way of the South as in the way of America, its literary story is inseparable from its sociological portraiture. The history of the South is in its total biography, and the biography of the South is still the biography of Americans.

> With firm and regular step they wend, they never stop,
> Successions of men, Americanos, a hundred millions,
> One generation playing its part and passing on,
> Another generation playing its part and passing on in its turn.

And never America in general shall diminish one whit the specific part which the South shall play in its own epic; nor the concrete task of the South diminish the nation's part in the new southern epoch. Always northerner the same as southerner and always southerner the same as northerner; easterner the same as westerner and westerner the same as easterner; Negro the same as white and white the same as Negro. Again, the American Poet of Democracy: "Take my leaves America, take them South and take them North, Make welcome for them everywhere . . . Surround them East and West . . . In the name of these states . . ."

PART IV

Postscript and Preface

CHAPTER XIX

Looking Both Ways

As LATE as the fall of 1946, when in the fiftieth anniversary issue of the *New York Times Book Review* a number of south-ern writers of biography, history, and fiction were given top rating, and others were reflected on the screen of best sellers and Pulitzer Awards, a distinguished New York book review editor wrote a startling comment upon the attitude of the rest of the nation toward the South. What this author of several biographies, himself a southerner, wrote in confidence was: "My belief is that people in other sections are beginning to regard the South with cold distaste that is worse than hatred. They regard the South not so much as wicked but merely as brainless, ridden by demagoguery and an extraordinarily bigoted priestcraft, avaricious, ignorant and insolent. This low opinion has spread terribly within the last ten years."

This estimate of low opinion was made at a time when southern participation and influence was greater at Washing-ton than at any previous time since the early days of the Re-public. At Washington were a Chief Justice and Associate Justice of the Supreme Court; the Secretary and an Under-secretary of State; the Secretary and an Undersecretary of the Treasury; an Undersecretary of War; the Director of the Budget; the Director of the Reconstruction Finance Corpora-tion; the Director of the Office of War Mobilization and Reconversion; the administrator of the National Housing Agency, and a host of minor officials in many of the major departments of the Federal Government at home and diplo-matic and postwar work abroad. In addition to these ap-pointive positions, there were the leaders of both Houses of

Congress and, by seniority, the chairmen of many of the ranking committees of the House and Senate.

This verdict was ventured also at a time when the leading
southern colleges and universities had enrolled a larger ratio
of students from without their region than any other region
of the nation, including the Northeast, if Harvard, Yale,
Princeton, and Columbia are excluded as primarily national
universities. These same southern institutions had turned
away, because of limited facilities and priorities to veterans
and constituencies, many other thousands, reflecting a cumulative popularity for undergraduate enrollment and college
life in the South.

There were at the same time other thousands of college
and university students in other regions, particularly the
Northeast, who assumed, apparently almost uniformly, that
the other states and regions should combine together to make
the South alter its segregation patterns of culture, and that
something must be done about this South which increasingly
was reflected to them in the folkways of attack and satire,
symbolized by Bilboism and *Tobacco Road* as a southern way
of life. And there was, in the upper brackets of the moral and
intellectual leaders called liberal, an uncompromising deter-
mination to force the South to change its laws of segregation
and its ruthless discrimination against the Negro, at the same
time that the great national conferences could find no major
city in the United States whose hotels would sign agreements
of nondiscrimination. Here was dilemma for which again and
again conferees found no way out; but little was said about
it in the way of popular appraisal.

Although criticisms were usually pointed to the biracial situation, on the other side of the picture there was considerable
discussion of what was called "the revolt of the South and
West," particularly against the financial domination and economic discrimination of the North and East. There were the
first fruits also of western protest against what was sensed
as the political domination and irresponsible government of

the East. There were the beginnings of a decentralization trend, and also many southern industries were being bought up by eastern capital.

Early in 1946, as one way of looking both ways, we sent a personal letter, together with a little catalogue of questions, to nearly two thousand individuals listed in *Who's Who in America*, born in the South but residing outside the South. In this inquiry-prospectus we asked a lot of questions about the South and the rest of the nation, and we gave opportunity for a wide and free range of fact, opinion, and discussion. The response to these inquiries was nothing short of extraordinary, resulting in both a very high ratio of returns and a fine spirit of cooperation, reflecting many long hours of work. And yet there were the same conflicting opinions and contradictory evidences offered as are reflected in these other situations we have mentioned in this Postscript and in the text of the book. The South was good, and it was bad; it was not unlike the rest of the nation, and it was different; it must be let alone, and it must have help; the Negro was a great fellow, but he must earn his equality as an individual; there were two ways for the South, diametrically opposed, the one to eliminate segregation and the other to continue a biracial culture. Most of the writers were worried about the increasing race tension, and about growing antagonisms between the South and the "North." Most of them thought that regional adjustment was one of the nation's main jobs, but they frankly felt too far away to offer many suggestions. Most of them wanted change; few would go all the way.

Then we asked a lot of college students the same questions. And among these students were G.I. veterans who were stepping up both the tempo and the quality of American college work. Our inquiries were primarily from the upper college classes and graduate students and still need to be repeated and checked with a much larger number. Yet the mode of attitude and the dynamics of their replies were such as to leave no doubt about the positive trend and the sweeping

change that was going on, in contrast to the larger bodies of
high-school students and the non-college youth who worked
on farm and in factory, or in public and private services. Here,
again, there were of course differences of opinion and approach; but in general the verdict was as if college youth were
saying: "We know'this is a big job; it is a *must*, and the South
has no license to ignore the task any longer. The South has
no claim, in the language of Jimmy Byrnes, 'to ignore or veto
the aggregate sentiments of mankind.' We know the job cannot be done, but while we are contemplating that it can't be
done we will do something about it." This refers to the white
college youth. For Negro youth it was all one way, and they
aimed to do something about it. The two groups working together might prove to be the object lesson the nation needed,
provided the unavoidable tensions could be resolved, and immaturity and frustration might be bridged by time and wisdom.

Now we have reviewed these factors as rather simple evidence of the conflict and complexity of the situation. For
here, as in many points of world tension, and as in some
Sholem Asch's story of the universal human system, of the
living, everlasting materials of man and his society, there
abound fundamental differences of systems and beliefs. But,
as a recent Federal Council of Churches report has emphasized, these do not have to lead to war. Here are differences,
not in the same category but in the same intensity, comparable to the differences between the philosophy of the
United States and that of Russia. A part of the attack upon
the South demonstrably stems from communistic sources; a
part reflects the same urban pattern which led the New York
City Council to vote 17 to 2 to demand that the President of
the United States "seize" all cattle and meat in the great western regions. The South ought to be ashamed of itself for its
immaturity and sensitiveness, and the rest of the nation surely
ought, by this time, to understand that here is a dilemma of
universal cultures and conflict. And culture is what men live

and die for. The heart of this problem has been stated well by F. S. C. Northrop in his *The Meeting of East and West*. "It is literally true," he points out, ". . . that what one people or culture regards as sound economic and political principles the other views as erroneous, and what the one envisages as good and divine the other condemns as evil or illusory. . . . The time has come," he continues, "when these ideological conflicts must be faced and if possible resolved. Otherwise, the social policies, moral ideals and religious aspirations of men, because of their incompatibility with one another, will continue to generate misunderstanding and war instead of mutual understanding and peace."

We have reviewed these samplings of current relationships also to indicate how lively the present era is; how stirrings among the people reflect wholesome symbols; and how many actions, reactions, and verdicts must inevitably be temporary stages in cyclical developments. These samplings also illustrate how some of the observations in our Postcript and Preface may appear to contradict conclusions in the text which has preceded it; for instance, in the diagnosis of the South's lack of leadership in contrast with its dynamic representation in all parts of the nation's life. In so far as that is true, it reflects simply the paradoxical situation in which the South and the nation, alongside much of the total world society, reflect an unusual degree of confusions and dilemma, with consequent contradictory evidences of progress and regress. But especially, these contradictions are important from the viewpoint of this book because they emphasize the cultural and sociological approach so important as a key to understanding and directing further development. That is, we are interested not only in "what is true" but in "what else is true"; not only in facts but in other facts and the relations of one set of facts to another. We want to know not only what is bad but what else is bad; not only what is good but what else is good; and withal what else is worse and what else is better. In these settings of relationships will be found responsible science and responsible action.

Contradictory elements are especially apparent in attempts to appraise progress or to judge the reliability of our conclusions, not only here in *The Way of the South* but in many other places during the last forty years of empirical study and generalizations. We have complained that the South not only has not made the progress which we expected of it but seems to have gone backward in many matters of ideology and interracial and interregional culture. This, of course, is relative in several ways. Not only the South but many parts of world culture reflect regressions. Moreover, this refers to only one part of the South's culture. And here the South has made extraordinary progress in many details of its culture and economy; in race relations and education, progress in the measurable aspects of a biracial culture has exceeded expectations in a period of time. And there is a freedom for discussion and experiment unknown in earlier periods. But when the demand has been made that the South retreat entirely from its major cultural ideologies and practices, and that it grant "all or none" and adopt an "or else" policy, there has been a solidifying of ranks and a militant and stubborn taking of sides on the level of the past. Something similar has been true in northern and western cities with reference to hotel discrimination and the problems of race prejudice. That is, although there has been extraordinary progress in both ideology and practice, the demand that hotels and other public establishments sign contracts for nondiscrimination and ignore the existence of race prejudice has resulted in a dilemma symbolic of regression. So, too, the impression so often conveyed that race prejudice is increasing in the North and West is buttressed, not necessarily by measurable facts, but by the procedures of cataloguing, publicizing, and interpreting situations both real and imaginary. The base of measurement of race prejudice has been widened, and the count has multiplied. This is a part of the cultural and democratic process; and progress will be measured in the future somewhere in the framework of equal opportunity for all peoples in interregional and interracial balance and equality.

It is important, therefore, that our story of the South be presented in the most realistic perspective possible, in relation both to the long time "looking both ways" and to all the factors involved. It is for this reason that we have presented in Part III what is often irritating to the public and the literary reader; namely, something of the technical meaning and procedures of planning and something of a social analysis of problems and processes. We do not know how to write sensationally about "firsts," "seconds," and "thirds," about resolving what the South must do to be saved; and, if we could do it, we should insist stubbornly that this is not what is needed, and that the rest of the nation has already had too much of the easy, one-way road to salvation. It is for this reason, also, that we must look at the setting in which our story has been written and must point to the array of sources and acknowledgments that would have to be made if detailed credit could be given.

The Way of the South is presented in the setting of forty years of uneven study and empirical research, set in the framework of the South's relation to, and conflict with, other regions of the nation, and interpreted in the light of the processes of universal cultural development and historical writing. The range and span of our study and observations have the advantage of logical, step-by-step unfolding, through exploration and experiment, in different time and area levels of experience. For in the first-hand work in all parts of the South and in all the other regions there has been opportunity for comparative studies, not only from decade to decade but of all parts of the nation.

Our observations and inquiries have, in general, covered three levels and periods. The first began in 1906 with a concrete study of the Negroes of a Mississippi town, followed by a similar concrete study of the Negroes in a Georgia town.

Following these were comparative studies of something like fifty towns in the different southern states. The first fruits of these studies were attempts to characterize the folk culture of the Negro in the South. These studies were basic to a period of exploration and survey, preparatory to further study. The actual results were published as dissertations for Ph.D. degrees. One was at Clark University in Psychology and Anthropology, under the direction of G. Stanley Hall and Alexander Chamberlain, published under the title of *Religious Folk Songs of the Southern Negro,* in 1909. The other was in Sociology at Columbia University with Franklin H. Giddings, under the title of *Social and Mental Traits of the Negro,* in 1910. With Franz Boas, other studies, under the subtitle of "A Study in Folk Thought and Folkways," were published in the *Journal of American Folklore,* in 1911. These were followed by a comparative study of the Negroes of Philadelphia, partial results of which were published in the *Annals* of the American Academy of Political and Social Science in September 1913. The Negro studies in Philadelphia were pointed toward the problem of education and environment and afforded some opportunity for comparison with W. E. B. Du Bois' previous study of the Philadelphia Negro. Out of these studies grew the maturing conclusions that assumptions of inherent superiority and inferiority are false premises, but that on the contrary race traits are group products of differentials due to the cumulative power of the physical and folk-regional cultural environment. This was a long cry from *Social and Mental Traits of the Negro;* yet the thirty years of subsequent inquiry have tended to support these preliminary conclusions and have important bearings upon what has been written in the present work.

The later and more immediate inquiries basic to *The Way of the South* began during the 1920's, constituting the framework for the research program of the Institute for Research in Social Science at the University of North Carolina which was set up as a sort of living social science laboratory for regional study. From this vantage point were published many books and articles covering the wide range of regional economy and culture and constituting the basic materials for scientific conclusions and subsequent follow-ups. The complete list of manuscripts, with titles, pages, authors, and dates, including both published and unpublished, may be examined by reference to *In Search of the Regional Balance of America* (University of North Carolina Press, 1910). Of published books and monographs by members of the Institute staff, there were nearly a hundred; of articles and chapter contributions to other works, more than two hundred; and of unpublished manuscripts more than two hundred.

The third period of basic inquiry which is most recently reflected in *The Way of the South* begins roughly with the publication of *Southern Regions* in 1936 and *American Regionalism* in 1938. From this point there was more of the attempt to systematize findings into sound theory and practice which would fit into the framework of regional planning and Southern development. From this has come the emphasis upon the regional equality and balance of America as the key problem, not only to southern development, but to the strengthening of the nation through the integration of its diverse regions. In this period, too, we have tried to check and test the results of our studies and assumptions, and to make application of findings to practical problems of southern economy. From these findings President Roosevelt characterized the South as the nation's Number 1 problem which later changed to the nation's Number 1 opportunity. In the meantime, it need scarcely be emphasized that there was a great body of literature to be examined, inside and outside the South, and that many conferences and councils looking toward southern regional development contributed their part in experiment, exploration, and survey, and in promotion work.

One of the limitations of the present volume, inherent in the purpose and length of the work, is our failure to review the extraordinary body of literature about the South and American regionalism. The streamflow of both books and periodical literature continues almost at flood tide, if we include the large tributaries of fiction. Even as *The Way of the South* came from the press, many titles had just appeared and still others were on the way—the manuscripts of some of which, we had read. It must be clear that a review of these, however much we may want to add "the last word," would almost assume the proportions of a supplement to Parrington's *Main Currents in American Thought*. As the matter must stand, this will be a part of the annotated bibliography of southern and regional writing to which reference is made subsequently.

Of current criticisms of the manuscript of *The Way of the South* one is that we placed too much emphasis upon the biracial aspects of its culture. The main answer to this is that, whatever else may be true, it must be clear that this is what makes the South distinctive from other regions, and is elemental to all other aspects of the southern culture. Another criticism was that we did not place enough emphasis upon certain special economic factors, such as freight-rate discriminations, financial handicaps due to the Civil War heritage, and the continued colonial, debtor policy of the region. The main answer to this is that, while they are important, they are superficial in comparison with the main streams of southern economy and culture. There are deeply rooted handicaps in the South's negative policies of defense attitudes, its neglect of science and invention, its refusal to use its labor force of both races, and its lack of forthright aggressive planning, preceded by adequate preparation. What can be done is indicated by the fact that since the 1930's the South has made such remarkable progress in widening the base of its industry and increasing its income and wealth, as to mark increases in many instances of from 25 to 50 per cent. In per-capita income, for instance, it is estimated by the Bureau of Labor Statistics that the increase was from 55 to 69 per cent of the national average. Likewise considerable progress has been

made on the freight-rate equalization problem, and the move
toward decentralization of industry has already resulted in the
transfer of many millions of invested dollars to southern industry. If, therefore, it be true that we have not stressed gains
and virtues enough, the answer is that these are for the present
relative in comparison to what is ahead, and that they are
logical assumptions of "the South at its best."

Nor do we feature as a major situation the one-party system
which is essentially inherent in the traditional, separatist,
and sectional attitudes which strangely enough appear to increase the differences and distances between South and North.
Nor do we ascribe to the Scottish or Protestant religious heritage of the people or any other single factor more than their
share in the total influence upon the present South.

In the first plans for *The Way of the South*, we had given
it the subtitle "A Biography of the Southern United States."
Manifestly this was too large an undertaking for the time.
Yet it is on this level that we have been trying to tell the
story of the South as a living regional culture in the nation;
it is "Of these years . . . how they pass and have pass'd
through convuls'd pains, . . . the vehement struggle so fierce
for unity. . . ." We have tried, therefore, to recapitulate
something of what we wrote in *Southern Regions of the
United States, An American Epoch, American Regionalism,
Race and Rumors of Race, In Search of the Regional Balance
of America, Understanding Society*, and in many other places
where we have tried systematically to see "Southern portraiture in the national picture." If we have mixed the swing
and rhythm of *Rainbow Round My Shoulder, Wings on My
Feet*, and *Cold Blue Moon* with the hard reality of regional
development and social theory, this still reflects the mixtures
of "the fruits of society . . . the wrestle of evil with good
. . . the models departed, caste, myth . . . the sounding
and resounding," of "what all sights, North, South, East, and
West, are," to recall again the universalism of Walt Whitman.

In all these usages, complete permission has been given, by the publishers cited, for the author to use freely both form and substance from previous writings as essential parts of his story of the South. From *Southern Regions*, published by the University of North Carolina Press in 1936, we have tried to continue the spirit, methods, and purposes of the Southern Regional Study, the objective of which was

to present an adequate picture, partial but representative, of the Southern regions of the United States in fair perspective to time-quality, to geographic factors, and to the cultural equipment and behavior of the people.

It was desired further to present this picture in such ways as to indicate the place of these regions in the nation and to explain something of the dramatic struggle of a large and powerful segment of the American people for mastery over an environment capable of producing a superior civilization, yet so conditioned by complexity of culture and cumulative handicaps as to make the nature of future development problematical.

Over and above any conventional social inventory, it was important to point toward greater realization of the inherent capacities of the Southern regions; and to indicate ways and means of bridging the chasm between the superabundance of physical and human resources as potentialities and the actualities of technical deficiencies in their development and waste in their use.

It was equally important to point toward a continuously more effective reintegration of the Southern regions into the national picture and thereby toward a larger regional contribution to national culture and unity. To this end, it was important to make available and to reinterpret to special groups and to the public in general, within and without the regions, and in as many ways as possible, the facts basic to the understanding of the situation and to the planning of next steps.

From *Southern Regions* we have also continued the frame of reference for a fivefold classification of resources and their utilization for "the South at its best." More specific references may be found on pages 219, 221, 224–226, 266, 273.

From *An American Epoch,* published by Henry Holt and Company in 1930, with reprint permission also from Peter Smith, we have tried to conserve and continue the spirit of the portraiture "of Southern Americans whose changing cultures have provided the most dramatic episodes in our national history, whose backgrounds and experiences comprehend all of the basic elements in the architecture of modern civilization." And because we have wanted to conserve both form and substance of this story, and because we have been able to produce no satisfactory substitute, we have adapted freely and integrated much of that story into *The Way of the South.* More specific reference is to Chapter II, pages 24–28 and Chapters VI–X with a reweaving of the elements of Chapters XI, XII, XIII, XVI. Chapter VII, "The Grandfathers to the Grandchildren," is the almost unretouched story of the Uncle John and Major Leaven of *An American Epoch.*

From *American Regionalism,* published by Henry Holt and Company in 1938, we have tried to continue the framework of the theory and practice of regionalism as "A Cultural-Historical Approach to National Integration." We have also attempted to retest and restate our assumptions of regional-national planning and have insisted upon the increasing validity of our premises that the new regionalism must be substituted for the old isolationism and sectionalism. More specific references are to pages 305, 310, 311 of *The Way of the South.*

From *Race and Rumors of Race,* published by the University of North Carolina Press in 1943, we have tried to portray, in retested perspective, the "Challenge to American Crisis," in "the story of two great regional folk cultures caught up in the midst of transition between the powerful heritage of the past and the mighty pull of the future . . . the two, white South and black South . . . part and parcel of a national culture whose dynamics, scarcely less than the two regional cultures, needed the sense of time and wisdom, of organic regional perspective, and of the essence of cosmopolitan, global culture." And we have tried to point out that while the South's problem of race relations is its most difficult one, and is still symbolic of national and world problems, too, still that "hidden in crisis of folk and race are elements of the spiritual world that transcend the ways and means of ordinary routine." Specific references in *The Way of the South* are to pages 37–39, 45–50, 66–67, 314–315.

From *In Search of the Regional Balance of America,* reprinted by the University of North Carolina in 1945, from a special issue of *Social Forces,* as one of the University of North Carolina Sesquicentennial publications, there are samplings and basic bibliographical references, as already cited. In this volume, the second article is in the way of a summary and symposium of Part I, and the third article comprises the substance of the final chapter of *The Way of the South.*

From *Understanding Society,* published by The Macmillan Company in 1947, we have adapted the systematic framework for the sociological study of culture to *The Way of the South* as reflected in the chapters on Nature and Resources, The Folk, Race, Culture, Frontier, in Part I, and the general framework of social planning and the regional basis of society in Part III. Specific references are to pages 4–14, 62, 65–66, 69–70, 280–288, 297–305.

There are also page references where longer passages are quoted from other authors and bibliographical references given in *Southern Regions* and in *An American Epoch.*

In Chapter II, pages 11 and 12, and in Chapter XVIII, pages 297 and 321, the credit is to "Song of Myself," from *Leaves of Grass* by Walt Whitman, copyright 1924 by Doubleday, Page & Company.

In Chapter IV the reference to Ben Robertson is to his *Red Hills and Cotton,* published by Alfred Knopf in 1942. The samplings of folkways are typical of others so vividly illustrated on pages 3–13, 20–30, 98–100, 101–102, 294–295 of his book.

In Chapter III, the lines quoted on pages 41–44 are from *John Brown's Body* by Stephen Vincent Benét, copyright 1928 by Doubleday, Doran & Co.

References in Chapter III to the planter class and to the "poor whites" are to "The Planter Class: Symbol of the Old South Aristocracy" by Melville Corbett Ivey; and "The Southern Poor White" by Mildred Mell, in the *Saturday Review of Literature*, January 23, 1943.

In support of the general description in Chapter V ("The Way of Culture and History"), special references, not quoted, in addition to those cited in *An American Epoch*, may be found in the following: Paul H. Buck's *The Road to Reunion*, pp. 62–63, 74–75, 150–153, 235, 299–300; James Truslow Adams' *The Epic of America*, pp. 257, 258, 259, 275–276, 283, 284; Charles A. and Mary Beard's *The American Spirit*, pp. 279, 281, 301; T. J. Wertenbaker's *The Old South*, pp. 97, 117, 219, 351.

Specific references for Chapters VIII, IX, X, XII, and XIII are cited in the bibliographical references under Chapters III, IV, V, XII, and XIII of *An American Epoch*.

Omitted in *The Way of the South* are personal references and tributes to contemporary leaders. The reasons are self-evident. I do not know of any way in which acknowledgment and tribute can be paid to some while others are ignored, without doing great injustice to the regional culture to which they are contributing so much. Such reference and catalogue also would appear to be unfair both to those who would be omitted and to those who would be superficially praised. And who is to be cited first and last? How and in what areas of work? In politics, in religion, in education, in public welfare, in public health? In race relationships and race leadership? Or in agriculture or in industry or in journalism or in the new achievements of science and technology? Or catalogue of men and women, Negro and white, southern and "northern"? Such reference would be in the nature of either superficial journalistic reporting or careful measures of biographical study, neither of which is the nature of the present work.

We referred to the inquiry made of southern leaders who have achieved outside the South. This is a part of a larger study of leadership in which the total catalogue of leaders will be examined. Edna Cooper is doing the special study of southern leaders outside the south. Then, too, there is a major section on southern biography in Anna Greene Smith's forthcoming bibliography of southern writing which, it is hoped, will be the first annotated bibliography arranged in such topical order as to recapitulate the story of the South itself. Then there is the mature work of Rupert Vance both in his *Spellbinders of the Old South* and in his notable book, *All These People: The Nation's Human Resources in the South*. This book is also a sort of double source for checking and rechecking *Southern Regions* and *The Way of the South*.

This brings us to one *must* in the matter of personal acknowledgment and tributes. There is one group that is inseparably a part of *The Way of the South;* and that is the body of students and research workers who were catalogued in *Southern Regions* and who, in many parts of the South and nation, have continued to do both creative and planning work. But in particular it is a rare privilege to pay top tribute to that small group who began early with us in the Institute and still *remain* at Chapel Hill to continue their work and to excel in their own fields what we began in the 1920's. These are: Katharine Jocher, Rupert Vance, Harriet Herring, Roy Brown, Guy Johnson, Lee Brooks. Finally all of us are inseparably indebted to those Foundation grants, listed in chronological order, as made by the Spelman Fund through Beardsley Ruml and Sydnor Walker, the Rockefeller Foundation through Edmund E. Day and Sydnor Walker, the General Education Board through A. R. Mann and Jackson Davis, Fred McCuistion and Flora Rhind, as well as later ones by the Rosenwald Fund through Edwin Embree and Will W. Alexander and the Car-

negie Foundation through the late President Jessup. All of
these have had a part in this portraiture that tries to make all
states and regions the same as all others, and set in the framework of the University of North Carolina program in which
there has invariably been given powerful support and complete freedom for work and writing. But it is to the still
younger group that is now giving promise of greater things
that we dedicate *The Way of the South*.

Included in this group-dedication would naturally be that
great body of dynamic youth in the centers and hinterlands of
all the regions of America. For it will be their understanding
and their work, more than that of any other group, that will
bring to pass this thing we call the regional equality and balance of America. Matured and freed from the enslavement of
traditional politics and prejudices, freed from the drives of
frustration—whether American southern rural or northern
urban or of the European vintage—this is the generation of
free men and women, South, North, East, West, in whose
hands the destiny of America again rests. Never has a generation been more capably endowed in science and social
science and in the framework of abundant opportunity. Never
was a generation more in need of the double portion of the
mantles of America's two greatest prophets of understanding
and cooperation, Walt Whitman and Abraham Lincoln. What
they saw and what they said still stand as both symbol and
reality in the American Dream, set in the new framework of
myriads of conflicting folk cultures in an all world society.

Index